YiJing (I Ching)
Chinese/English Dictionary
with Concordance
and Translation

YiJing (I Ching)
Chinese/English Dictionary
with Concordance
and Translation

Daniel Bernardo

http://yijingdao.org

Fourth Edition: October 2013

The cover image shows the arrangement of the trigrams in the *HouTian* (Later Heaven) order, traditionally attributed to the King Wen. The South is at the top, following the traditional Chinese style. The two characters in the middle read *ZhouYi*.

Contents

Preface

The *YiJing* (or *I Ching*, when using the Wade-Giles romanization system) is a book from the Chinese Bronze Age (about 1000 BC) and as many other ancient texts, it was written by a process of aggregation of material from different periods and authors.

By the time of the Han dynasty (206 BC to 220 AD) it became something similar to the text we know today as the "Classic of Changes" or "Book of Changes" (易经). Of course, the interpretation of the text has changed over time, but the ordering of the material has remained unchanged since the Han Dynasty to the present.

The Classic of Changes is composed of 64 short chapters, composed of several elements and 10 appendixes, known as "The Ten Wings".

The parts of each chapter (commonly called hexagrams) are:

- A graphic symbol (卦 *Gua*), which is a drawing composed of six parallel lines, some filled and other broken. Example: ☷.
- A text that explains the meaning of the hexagram and whose first one or two characters give it its name (卦辞 *GuaCi*), commonly called "The Judgment".
- Short texts attached to each of the six lines (爻辞 *YaoCi*), except for the hexagrams 1 and 2 that have seven texts.
- Several texts, from the Ten Wings: The Image (*DaXiang*), the *Tuan* Commentary, etc.

Composition of the text according to Chinese tradition

Legend has it that *FuXi* (伏羲) designed the 64 hexagrams (hypothetically about 3000 BC) and King *Wen* (周文王) wrote the texts that accompany each hexagram, *GuaCi*, "The Judgment".

7

His son, the Duke *Dan* of *Zhou* (周公旦) added explanatory texts for each line of the hexagrams.

The texts due to King *Wen* and his son were know in his time (the Bronze Age in China) as *ZhouYi* (周易), "The Changes of the Zhou" being *Zhou* the name of the dynasty started by King *Wen*.

Several hundred years later, the Confucian school added comments to the text, which are known as the Ten Wings (十翼 *ShiYi*), and are divided into ten parts.

These comments can be placed at the end of the text, as appendixes, or inserted into each hexagram, as is usually done with the commentary called "The Image", which comprises part of the Wings 3rd and 4th.

Modern hypothesis about the origin of the text

On the origin of the hexagrams symbols and the texts that accompany them there is no certainty, but it might be possible that the traditional story about the composition of the text (The Judgment and the lines) is correct and that King *Wen* —which was a real historical figure— was the compiler of texts from the oracular tradition (circa 1000 BC), and that his son did something similar for the lines of the hexagrams.

The Ten Wings come from various sources, some of them certainly are of the Confucian school, but it is not currently believed that they are a direct work from the hand of Confucius. Probably the Ten Wings were composed between 200 BC and 200 A.D., during the *Han* dynasty

European translations

The first translations from Chinese to Western languages were done by Jesuits, who translated the text into Latin and French. Much later, during the nineteenth century English and French translations began to appear.

The most prestigious of the English translations of the nineteenth century was that of James Legge; the following translation of importance (in German) was the one from Richard Wilhelm, which was published in 1924. Later, this same translation was translated into English by Cary Baynes, and published in 1950. It remains the most popular English translation until today.

Throughout the XX century many other translations appeared, but most of them were only recombinations of previous versions but not true translations.

In the last decades of the twentieth century several new English translations tried to shed light on the original meaning of the *YiJing*, going as far back to its origins as a document from the Bronze Age, trying to separate the layers of the original text to understand the original meaning of the earlier parts of the text. Some of them are the translations from Kunst, Rutt, Shaughnessy and Whincup; all of them attempt to elucidate the original meaning of the Chinese characters in the earlier layers of the *YiJing*.

Limitations of translations to Western languages

Most Chinese characters have a wide range of meanings, and its symbolic richness makes them particularly suitable for oracular use. When translated into another language it is impossible to preserve the multiple meanings in the original text, because the translator is forced to choose words that cannot cover the full range of meanings of the Chinese characters.

As an example, a common character (repeated 34 times) in the *YiJing* is 悔, *hui*, commonly translated as "repentance." That translation is not incorrect, but the word originally meant "problems." Considering both meanings, the word refers to an objective situation and the internal reaction to it, but there is not an English word that covers the two meanings.

Another common word is 亨, *heng*, which appears 47 times, and means "success, achievement, satisfaction, growth, penetration, offering, sacrifice." Any translation into a Western language will exclude some of those meanings. It is usually translated as "success" but that word does not cover the rich array of meanings of the original word.

Introduction to the Translation

This translation attempts to facilitate an approach to the *YiJing* original text*. It includes The Judgment (*GuaCi*) and the comments for the lines. From the Ten Wings it only includes The Image (*DaXiang*).

For each Chinese character it shows its pronunciation and its assigned number, to allow finding it in the dictionary.

The characters shown on a gray background at the start of each hexagram are the ones used as tag for each hexagram, which are the hexagram's "title". Most of the hexagrams use a single character as tag, although some use two.

This translation attempts to maintain balance between two extremes:

- A literal translation, which would be very difficult to understand, and;

- A translation of high literary level that for the sake of style would distort the meaning of the text.

Since Chinese characters have gained new meanings but also lost some archaic meanings, along the millennia, when possible, we choose words that cover both the original and the newer meanings**, always inside the time frame from

---

* The original text used for this translation is 周易折中 *Zhouyi Zhezhong*, "Balanced Comments on Zhouyi", published in 1715 under the patronage of *Qing* Dynasty, is the same text used by Wilhelm and many other sinologists as the basis of their translations.

** A good example is the term in *JunZi*, 君子, which appears 73 times in the text. In many translations it is translated as "noble," which captures well the range of meanings of *JunZi*, but in some versions it is translated as "superior man", a term used by the Confucian school. It is not wrong to use the term "superior man", but it restricts arbitrarily the range of meanings and leaves out the original meaning used by the author of the *ZhouYi*. Using "noble" is preferable because it covers both the original (son of a lord) and and the newer (superior man) meanings.

1000 BC to 200 AD, which was the approximate time when the Ten Wings were ended.

The graphic layout of the Chinese characters was designed to reduce the space occupied on the page, so that each hexagram can fit in two pages. Line breaks are not significant.

The Chinese characters indicating the numbering of the lines were omitted, because they do not add anything to the text's meaning.

Introduction to the Dictionary

The dictionaries of Chinese characters can be divided into two different types: dictionaries of single characters and dictionaries of words (composed of multiple characters).

Currently, most Chinese language words are composed of several characters, but in antiquity that was not the case.

This dictionary is primarily a dictionary of characters, although it also explains many multi-character words.

Unfortunately the Chinese characters do not have a single pronunciation; multiple characters may share the same sound. For example 悔 pronunciation is *hui3*, but also other 16 characters have the same pronunciation, and there are 127 different characters that are pronounced *hui*, regardless of the accent (which is indicated by the number).

For most of the twentieth century the Wade-Giles system was used to indicate how to pronounce Chinese characters. Wade-Giles is a romanization system, which shows the pronunciation with western letters. But in the last decades of the 20th century, the *Pinyin* pronunciation system (meaning "sound-spelling") was adopted by China and since then it prevailed almost universally.

Pinyin uses four tones to indicate the pronunciation of each syllable, indicating the tone either with different accents (e.g., *huī, huí, huǐ* and *huì*) or with numbers (e.g. *hui1, hui2, hui3* and *hui4*).

In this dictionary, the pronunciation of each character is indicated using Pinyin. The numbers shown in Pinyin syllables indicate the accent. The appendix on PinYin pronunciation has more information about this topic.

The numbers assigned to the characters are the same used by the Mathew's Chinese-English dictionary. Notice that characters with numeration over 7773 are not included in Mathew's dictionary. Also the numbers used by Karlgren's *Grammata Serica Recensa* dictionary are show for each character.

The radical number and stroke count for each character are indicated as well. This is useful when looking for the definition of a character in others dictionaries than Mathew's or Karlgren's, since locating characters by radical number and stroke count is very common in Chinese dictionaries.

The meaning of some Chinese characters has been maintained throughout the ages, but in many cases new meanings have been added and/or old meanings have changed.

In general, we have attempted to provide both the archaic and the modern meanings. To avoid confusion anachronisms and modern meanings, not in use in the past, are omitted.

To indicate where characters are located in the text, the placement of the characters is shown by adding a point and a letter or number after the number of the hexagram.

0   indicates The Judgment;

1 to 6 indicate a Line number;

7   indicates the comment for the cases when all lines change, in hexagramas 1 or 2;

X   indicates The Image.

Characters included in this dictionary

This dictionary includes all the characters found in The Judgment, The Image and the lines. Although the image is of much later origin than the Judgment and lines (the texts known as *ZhouYi*), it has become common to include the image next to the oldest texts and we follow that custom. In total the dictionary includes more than 900 characters, plus dozens of words composed of multiple characters.

Since 1956 simplified characters are in use China, but this work shows only the traditional characters used for the last two millennia.

Archaic characters are found in inscriptions on oracle bones (mostly from the *Shang* Dynasty). Other ancient characters can be found in archaic bronzes of the *Shang* and *Zhou* dynasties. In many cases these archaic character are shown in the dictionary, below the normal ones, when they clarify the character's original meaning.

YIJING TRANSLATION

1. The Creative / Activity / Dynamic Force

☰

Judgment

qian2	yuan2	heng1	li4	zhen1
3233	7707	2099	3867	0346
乾	元	亨	利	貞

The Creative. Outstanding success. The determination is favorable.

Image

tian1	xing2	jian4
6361	2754	0854
天	行	健

jun1	zi3	yi3	zi4	qiang2	bu4	xi1
1715	6939	2932	6960	0668	5379	2495
君	子	以	自	彊	不	息

Heaven action is strong and dynamic.
Thus the noble never ceases to strengthen himself.

First Nine

qian2	long2	wu4	yong4
0918	4258	7208	7567
潛	龍	勿	用

Submerged dragon. Do not act.

Second Nine

jian4	long2	zai4	tian2	li4	jian4	da4	ren2
0860	4258	6657	6362	3867	0860	5943	3097
見	龍	在	田	利	見	大	人

Dragon in the field. It is favorable to see the great man.

Third Nine

jun1	zi3	zhong1	ri4	qian2	qian2
1715	6939	1500	3124	3233	3233
君	子	終	日	乾	乾

xi4	ti4	ruo4	li4	wu2	jiu4
2485	6263	3126	3906	7173	1192
夕	惕	若	厲	无	咎

The noble is active throughout the day.
At night he is cautious, as if in danger. No defect.

Fourth Nine

huo4	yue4	zai4	yuan1	wu2	jiu4
2402	7504	6657	7723	7173	1192
或	躍	在	淵	无	咎

Hesitates before jumping over the chasm. No defect.

Fifth Nine

fei1	long2	zai4	tian1	li4	jian4	da4	ren2
1850	4258	6657	6361	3867	0860	5943	3097
飛	龍	在	天	利	見	大	人

Dragon flying in the sky. It is favorable to see the great man.

Top Nine

kang4	long2	you3	hui3
3273	4258	7533	2336
亢	龍	有	悔

Arrogant dragon. There will be occasion for repentance.

All lines are Nine

jian4	qun2	long2	wu2	shou3	ji2
0860	1737	4258	7173	5839	0476
見	羣	龍	无	首	吉

A group of dragons without heads. Auspicious.

2. The Receptive

☷ (hexagram image)

Judgment

kun1	yuan2	heng1	li4	pin4	ma3
3684	7707	2099	3867	5280	4310
坤	元	亨	利	牝	馬

zhi1	zhen1	jun1	zi3	you3	you1
0935	0346	1715	6939	7533	7519
之	貞	君	子	有	攸

wang3	xian1	mi2	hou4	de2	zhu3
7050	2702	4450	2143	6161	1336
往	先	迷	後	得	主

li4	xi1	nan2	de2	peng2	dong1
3867	2460	4620	6161	5054	6605
利	西	南	得	朋	東

bei3	sang4	peng2	an1	zhen1	ji2
4974	5429	5054	0026	0346	0476
北	喪	朋	安	貞	吉

The Receptive. Outstanding success favorable for the determination of a mare.
If the noble takes the lead he goes astray, but if he follows, he finds a master.
It is favorable to find friends in the west and south;
avoid friends in the east and north. A quiet determination is auspicious.

Image

di4	shi4	kun1
6198	5799	3684
地	勢	坤

jun1	zi3	yi3	hou4	de2	zai4	wu4
1715	6939	2932	2147	6162	6653	7209
君	子	以	厚	德	載	物

The earth condition is receptive obedience.
Thus the noble, who has a munificent character, sustains all living creatures.

First Six

lu3	shuang1	jian1	bing1	zhi4
3893	5919	0825	5283	0982
履	霜	堅	冰	至

Walking on hoarfrost one reaches hard ice.

Second Six

zhi2	fang1	da4	bu4	xi2	wu2	bu4	li4
1006	1802	5943	5379	2499	7173	5379	3867
直	方	大	不	習	无	不	利

Right, square and large, inexperienced.
But nothing will be not favorable.

Third Six

han2	zhang1	ke3	zhen1	huo4	cong2
2017	0182	3381	0346	2402	6919
含	章	可	貞	或	從

wang2	shi4	wu2	cheng2	you3	zhong1
7037	5787	7173	0379	7533	1500
王	事	无	成	有	終

Hidden brilliance; can be determined.
If you're still in the service of a king you will not have achievements,
but will carry to conclusion.

Fourth Six

kuo4	nang2	wu2	jiu4	wu2	yu4
3519	4627	7173	1192	7173	7617
括	囊	无	咎	无	譽

A tied up bag. No defect, no praise.

Fifth Six

huang2	chang2	yuan2	ji2
2297	5671	7707	0476
黃	裳	元	吉

Yellow lower garment.
There will be outstanding happiness.

Top Six

long2	zhan4	yu2	ye3
4258	0147	7592	7314
龍	戰	于	野

qi2	xue4	xuan2	huang2
0525	2901	2881	2297
其	血	玄	黃

Dragons fight in the open country.
Their blood is black and yellow.

All lines are Six

li4	yong3	zhen1
3867	7589	0346
利	永	貞

Long term determination is favorable.

3. Initial Difficulty

Judgment

zhun1	yuan2	heng1	li4	zhen1	wu4	yong4
6592	7707	2099	3867	0346	7208	7567
屯	元	亨	利	貞	勿	用

you3	you1	wang3	li4	jian4	hou2
7533	7519	7050	3867	0853	2135
有	攸	往	利	建	侯

The Initial Difficulty. Outstanding success. Favorable determination.
It should not be pursued any goal.
It is favorable to appoint officials.

Image

yun2	lei2	zhun1	jun1	zi3	yi3	jing1	lun2
7750	4236	6592	1715	6939	2932	1123	4252
雲	雷	屯	君	子	以	經	綸

Clouds and thunder: The image of the Initial Difficulty.
Thus the noble sorts the threads of warp and woof.

First Nine

pan2	huan2	li4	ju1	zhen1	li4	jian4	hou2
4904	2236	3867	1535	0346	3867	0853	2135
磐	桓	利	居	貞	利	建	侯

Looking to overcome an obstacle.
It is favorable to maintain the determination.
It is favorable to appoint assistants.

Second Six

zhun1	ru2	zhan1	ru2	cheng2	ma3	ban1
6592	3137	8010	3137	0398	4310	4889
屯	如	邅	如	乘	馬	班

ru2	fei3	kou4	hun1	gou4	nu3	zi3
3137	1820	3444	2360	3426	4776	6939
如	匪	寇	婚	媾	女	子

zhen1	bu4	zi4	shi2	nian2	nai3	zi4
0346	5379	6942	5807	4711	4612	6942
貞	不	字	十	年	乃	字

Difficulties impeding progress.
Horse and cart separate.
It's not a villain, but a pretender.
The girl has determination and does not plight her troth.
After ten years she will pledge herself.

Third Six

ji2	lu4	wu2	yu2	wei2	ru4	yu2
0495	4203	7173	7648	7066	3152	7592
即	鹿	无	虞	惟	入	于

lin2	zhong1	jun1	zi3	ji1	bu4	ru2
4022	1504	1715	6939	0409	5379	3137
林	中	君	子	幾	不	如

she3	wang3	lin4
5699	7050	4040
舍	往	吝

Chasing the deer without forester, entering in the depths of the forest.
The noble sees the signs and desists.
If he went forward, he would regret it.

Fourth Six

cheng2	ma3	ban1	ru2	qiu2	hun1	gou4
0398	4310	4889	3137	1217	2360	3426
乘	馬	班	如	求	婚	媾

wang3	ji2	wu2	bu4	li4
7050	0476	7173	5379	3867
往	吉	无	不	利

Horse and cart separate.
Look for the union. Advance brings happiness.
Everything will be auspicious and without blemish.

Fifth Nine

zhun1	qi2	gao1	xiao3	zhen1	ji2
6592	0525	3296	2605	0346	0476
屯	其	膏	小	貞	吉

da4	zhen1	xiong1
5943	0346	2808
大	貞	凶

Difficulties with their wealth.
Determination in small matters is auspicious.
Determination in major ways brings misfortune.

Top Nine

cheng2	ma3	ban1	ru2	qi4	xue4	lian2	ru2
0398	4310	4889	3137	0563	2901	4012	3137
乘	馬	班	如	泣	血	漣	如

Horse and cart separate.
Tears of blood are spilled.

4. Youthful Folly

Judgment

meng2	heng1	fei3	wo3	qiu2	tong2	meng2
4437	2099	1820	4778	1217	6626	4437
蒙	亨	匪	我	求	童	蒙

tong2	meng2	qiu2	wo3	chu1	shi4	gao4
6626	4437	1217	4778	1390	5763	3287
童	蒙	求	我	初	筮	告

zai4	san1	du2	du2	ze2	bu4	gao4
6658	5415	6515	6515	6746	5379	3287
再	三	瀆	瀆	則	不	告

li4	zhen1
3867	0346
利	貞

The Youthful Folly is successful.
It is not I who seek the young fool, the young fool seeks me.
At the first oracle I inform, but a second or third time is troublesome;
and I do not instruct the annoying.
The determination is favorable.

Image

shan1	xia4	chu1	quan2	meng2	jun1	zi3
5630	2520	1409	1674	4437	1715	6939
山	下	出	泉	蒙	君	子

yi3	guo3	xing2	yu4	de2
2932	3732	2754	7687	6162
以	果	行	育	德

Under the mountain flows a spring: The image of the Youthful Folly.
Thus the noble makes his actions resolute and nourishes his virtue.

First Six

fa1	meng2	li4	yong4	xing2	ren2	yong4
1768	4437	3867	7567	2755	3097	7567
發	蒙	利	用	刑	人	用

tuo1	zhi4	gu4	yi3	wang3	lin4
5939	0993	3484	2932	7050	4040
說	桎	梏	以	往	吝

To develop the foolish man it will be favorable to discipline him.
The fetters must be removed, otherwise there will be regret.

Second Nine

bao1	meng2	ji2	na4	fu4	ji2
4937	4437	0476	4607	1963	0476
包	蒙	吉	納	婦	吉

zi3	ke4	jia1
6939	3320	0594
子	克	家

Supporting the Youthful Folly is auspicious.
To take a wife is auspicious.
A son can take care of the family.

Third Six

wu4	yong4	qu3	nu3	jian4	jin1	fu1
7208	7567	1615	4776	0860	1057	1908
勿	用	取	女	見	金	夫

bu4	you3	gong1	wu2	you1	li4
5379	7533	3704	7173	7519	3867
不	有	躬	无	攸	利

Do not marry a girl who, on seeing a man of metal,
loses her self-possession.
No place is favorable.

Fourth Six

kun4	meng2	lin4
3688	4437	4040
困	蒙	吝

Trapped by his folly he will suffer shame.

Fifth Six

tong2	meng2	ji2
6626	4437	0476
童	蒙	吉

Children's folly is auspicious.

Top Nine

ji1	meng2	bu4	li4	wei2	kou4	li4	yu4	kou4
0481	4437	5379	3867	7059	3444	3867	7665	3444
擊	蒙	不	利	爲	寇	利	禦	寇

Punishing Youthful Folly.
It is not favorable to commit transgressions,
but it is favorable to defend [yourself] against transgressors.

5. Waiting

Judgment

xu1	you3	fu2	guang1	heng1
2844	7533	1936	3583	2099
需	有	孚	光	亨

zhen1	ji2	li4	she4	da4	chuan1
0346	0476	3867	5707	5943	1439
貞	吉	利	涉	大	川

Waiting. With brilliance and sincerity you will succeed.
The determination is favorable.
It is favorable to cross the great river.

Image

yun2	shang4	yu2	tian1	xu1
7750	5669	7643	6361	2844
雲	上	於	天	需

jun1	zi3	yi3	yin3	shi2	yan4	le4
1715	6939	2932	7454	5810	7364	4129
君	子	以	飲	食	宴	樂

Clouds ascend to heaven: The image of Waiting.
Thus the noble drinks, eats and parties.

First Nine

xu1	yu2	jiao1	li4	yong4	heng2
2844	7592	0714	3867	7567	2107
需	于	郊	利	用	恆

wu2	jiu4
7173	1192
无	咎

Waiting in the suburbs.
It is favorable to have perseverance.
No defect.

Second Nine

xu1	yu2	sha1	xiao3	you3	yan2	zhong1	ji2
2844	7592	5606	2605	7533	7334	1500	0476
需	于	沙	小	有	言	終	吉

Waiting in the sand.
They say little things.
Finally there will be good fortune.

Third Nine

xu1	yu2	ni2	zhi4	kou4	zhi4
2844	7592	4660	0984	3444	0982
需	于	泥	致	寇	至

Waiting in the mud attracts bandits.

Fourth Six

xu1	yu2	xue4	chu1	zi4	xue2
2844	7592	2901	1409	6960	2899
需	于	血	出	自	穴

Waiting in blood.
Outside the pit!

Fifth Nine

xu1	yu2	jiu3	shi2	zhen1	ji2
2844	7592	1208	5810	0346	0476
需	于	酒	食	貞	吉

Waiting with wine and food.
The determination is favorable.

Top Six

ru4	yu2	xue2	you3	bu4	su4	zhi1	
3152	7592	2899	7533	5379	5505	0935	
入	于	穴	有	不	速	之	

ke4	san1	ren2	lai2	jing4	zhi1	zhong1	ji2
3324	5415	3097	3768	1138	0935	1500	0476
客	三	人	來	敬	之	終	吉

One falls into the cave.
Three uninvited guests arrive.
Treat them with respect and in the end there will be good fortune.

6. Conflict / The Lawsuit

▤

Judgment

song4	you3	fu2	zhi4	ti4	zhong1	ji2	zhong1	xiong1
5558	7533	1936	0994	6263	1504	0476	1500	2808
訟	有	孚	窒	惕	中	吉	終	凶
li4	jian4	da4	ren2	bu4	li4	she4	da4	chuan1
3867	0860	5943	3097	5379	3867	5707	5943	1439
利	見	大	人	不	利	涉	大	川

The Conflict. You are sincere but you are hold back.
Cautiously stopped halfway brings good fortune.
Going to the end is ominous.
It is advantageous to see the great man.
It is not favorable to cross the great river.

Image

tian1	yu3	shui3	wei2	xing2	song4
6361	7615	5922	7093	2754	5558
天	與	水	違	行	訟
jun1	zi3	yi3	zuo4	shi4	mou2	shi3
1715	6939	2932	6780	5787	4578	5772
君	子	以	作	事	謀	始

Sky and water move in opposite directions: The image of the Conflict.
Thus the noble, in all his tasks, plans well before starting.

First Six

bu4	yong3	suo3	shi4	xiao3	you3	yan2	zhong1	ji2
5379	7589	5465	5787	2605	7533	7334	1500	0476
不	永	所	事	小	有	言	終	吉

If one does not perpetuate the affair, there will be some gossip,
but eventually it will be auspicious.

Second Nine

bu4	ke4	song4	gui1	er2	bu1	qi2
5379	3320	5558	3617	1756	5373	0525
不	克	訟	歸	而	逋	其
yi4	ren2	san1	bai3	hu4	wu2	sheng3
3037	3097	5415	4976	2180	7173	5741
邑	人	三	百	戶	无	眚

One cannot succeed in the suit and escapes back to his home.
The inhabitants of his city, three hundred families will not suffer misfortune.

Third Six

shi2	jiu4	de2	zhen1	li4	zhong1	ji2
5810	1205	6162	0346	3906	1500	0476
食	舊	德	貞	厲	終	吉

huo4	cong2	wang2	shi4	wu2	cheng2
2402	6919	7037	5787	7173	0379
或	從	王	事	无	成

Subsisting on old virtue.
Determination in front of danger.
There will be good fortune in the end.
If you are in the service of a king you will not be able to complete your work.

Fourth Nine

bu4	ke4	song4	fu4	ji2	ming4
5379	3320	5558	1992	0495	4537
不	克	訟	復	卽	命

yu2	an1	zhen1	ji2
7635	0026	0346	0476
渝	安	貞	吉

One cannot win the fight.
Turns back and accepts fate.
Changes his attitude and finds peace.
The determination is auspicious.

Fifth Nine

song4	yuan2	ji2
5558	7707	0476
訟	元	吉

Litigating.
Outstanding fortune.

Top Nine

huo4	xi1	zhi1	pan2	dai4
2402	2505	0935	8005	6005
或	錫	之	鞶	帶

zhong1	zhao1	san1	chi3	zhi1
1500	0233	5415	1028	0935
終	朝	三	褫	之

If you get rewarded with a leather belt,
by late morning it will have been snatched away three times.

7. The Army

Judgment

shi1	zhen1	zhang4	ren2
5760	0346	0200	3097
師	貞	丈	人

ji2	wu2	jiu4
0476	7173	1192
吉	无	咎

The Army.
The determination brings good fortune for a strong man. No defect.

Image

di4	zhong1	you3	shui3	shi1
6198	1504	7533	5922	5760
地	中	有	水	師

jun1	zi3	yi3	rong2	min2	chu4	zhong4
1715	6939	2932	7560	4508	1412	1517
君	子	以	容	民	畜	眾

The earth contains water inside it: The image of The Army.
Thus the noble takes care of and increases the crowd.

First Six

shi1	chu1	yi3	lu4	pi3	zang1	xiong1
5760	1409	2932	4297	1902	6704	2808
師	出	以	律	否	臧	凶

The Army should set forward in orderly rows.
If discipline is bad there will be misfortune.

Second Nine

zai4	shi1	zhong1	ji2	wu2	jiu4
6657	5760	1504	0476	7173	1192
在	師	中	吉	无	咎

wang2	san1	xi1	ming4
7037	5415	2505	4537
王	三	錫	命

In the midst of The Army. Good fortune. No defect.
The king gives rewards and promotions thrice.

Third Six

shi1	huo4	yu2	shi1	xiong1
5760	2402	7618	5756	2808
師	或	輿	尸	凶

Perhaps The Army carries corpses in the carriage. Ominous.

Fourth Six

shi1	zuo3	ci4	wu2	jiu4
5760	6774	6980	7173	1192
師	左	次	无	咎

The Army camps on the left. No defect.

Fifth Six

tian2	you3	qin2	li4	zhi2	yan2
6362	7533	1100	3867	0996	7334
田	有	禽	利	執	言

wu2	jiu4	zhang3	zi3	shuai4	shi1
7173	1192	0213	6939	5909	5760
无	咎	長	子	帥	師

di4	zi3	yu2	shi1	zhen1	xiong1
6201	6939	7618	5756	0346	2808
弟	子	輿	尸	貞	凶

There is game in the field.
It is favorable to capture them for questioning.
No defect.
The eldest son should lead The Army, if the younger brother leads the carriages
will be used to carry corpses.
The determination is ominous.

Top Six

da4	jun1	you3	ming4	kai1	guo2
5943	1715	7533	4537	3204	3738
大	君	有	命	開	國

cheng2	jia1	xiao3	ren2	wu4	yong4
0386	0594	2605	3097	7208	7567
承	家	小	人	勿	用

The great king has the mandate to found a state and inherit the house.
Small men should not be used.

8. Union

Judgment

bi3	ji2	yuan2	shi4	yuan2	yong3	zhen1
5077	0476	7725	5763	7707	7589	0346
比	吉	原	筮	元	永	貞

wu2	jiu4	bu4	ning2	fang1	lai2
7173	1192	5379	4725	1802	3768
无	咎	不	寧	方	來

hou4	fu1	xiong1
2143	1908	2808
後	夫	凶

Union brings happiness.
Look deep and divine to see if you have great long-term determination;
if so there will be no defect.
They will come from the lands without peace.
Those who arrive late will have misfortune.

Image

di4	shang4	you3	shui3	bi3	xian1	wang2
6198	5669	7533	5922	5077	2702	7037
地	上	有	水	比	先	王

yi3	jian4	wan4	guo2	qin1	zhu1	hou2
2932	0853	7030	3738	1107	1362	2135
以	建	萬	國	親	諸	侯

On earth there is water: The image of Union.
So the kings of old established ten thousand different states and kept close
relations with all the feudal lords.

First Six

you3	fu2	bi3	zhi1	wu2	jiu4
7533	1936	5077	0935	7173	1192
有	孚	比	之	无	咎

you3	fu2	ying2	fou3
7533	1936	7474	1905
有	孚	盈	缶

zhong1	lai2	you3	tuo1	ji2
1500	3768	7533	6439	0476
終	來	有	它	吉

If there is sincerity, the Union will be without defect.
Full of sincerity as an overflowing earthenware vessel.
Finally, through others, happiness will come.

Second Six

bi3	zhi1	zi4	nei4	zhen1	ji2
5077	0935	6960	4766	0346	0476
比	之	自	內	貞	吉

Union from the inside.
The determination is fortunate.

Third Six

bi3	zhi1	fei3	ren2
5077	0935	1820	3097
比	之	匪	人

Union with worthless people.

Fourth Six

wai4	bi3	zhi1	zhen1	ji2
7001	5077	0935	0346	0476
外	比	之	貞	吉

Solidarity with people outside.
Determination brings good fortune.

Fifth Nine

xian3	bi3	wang2	yong4	san1	qu1	shi1
2692	5077	7037	7567	5415	1602	5806
顯	比	王	用	三	驅	失

qian2	qin2	yi4	ren2	bu4	jie4	ji2
0919	1100	3037	3097	5379	0628	0476
前	禽	邑	人	不	誡	吉

Noticeable Union.
The king uses beaters for hunting prey on three sides,
but lets the animals in front of him go.
The villagers are not wary.
Good fortune.

Top Six

bi3	zhi1	wu2	shou3	xiong1
5077	0935	7173	5839	2808
比	之	无	首	凶

Union without a leader.
Misfortune.

9. Little Domestication

Judgment

xiao3	chu4	heng1	mi4	yun2	bu4	yu3
2605	1412	2099	4464	7750	5379	7662
小	畜	亨	密	雲	不	雨

zi4	wo3	xi1	jiao1
6960	4778	2460	0714
自	我	西	郊

Little Domestication is successful.

Dense clouds, no rain from our western borders.

Image

feng1	xing2	tian1	shang4	xiao3	chu4
1890	2754	6361	5669	2605	1412
風	行	天	上	小	畜

jun1	zi3	yi3	yi4	wen2	de2
1715	6939	2932	2999	7129	6162
君	子	以	懿	文	德

The wind crosses the sky: The image of Little Domestication.

Thus the noble refines the outward manifestation of his virtue.

First Nine

fu4	zi4	dao4	he2	qi2	jiu4	ji2
1992	6960	6136	2109	0525	1192	0476
復	自	道	何	其	咎	吉

Returns to the own road.

How could it be wrong?

Good fortune.

Second Nine

qian1	fu4	ji2
0881	1992	0476
牽	復	吉

Led to return. Good fortune.

Third Nine

yu2	tuo1	fu2	fu1	qi1	fan3	mu4
7618	5939	1980	1908	0555	1781	4596
輿	說	輻	夫	妻	反	目

Rays are removed from the carriage wheels.

Man and wife avert their eyes from each other.

Fourth Six

you3	fu2	xue4	qu4	ti4	chu1
7533	1936	2901	1594	6263	1409
有	孚	血	去	惕	出

wu2	jiu4
7173	1192
无	咎

If you are sincere, the blood disappears and concerns are cast aside.
No defect.

Fifth Nine

you3	fu2	luan2	ru2	fu4	yi3	qi2	lin2
7533	1936	4300	3137	1952	2932	0525	4033
有	孚	攣	如	富	以	其	鄰

If you are sincere with your neighbors the alliance will bring prosperity for all.

Top Nine

ji4	yu3	ji4	chu3	shang4	de2	zai4
0453	7662	0453	1407	5670	6162	6653
既	雨	既	處	尚	德	載

fu4	zhen1	li4	yue4	ji1	wang4
1963	0346	3906	7696	0409	7043
婦	貞	厲	月	幾	望

jun1	zi3	zheng1	xiong1
1715	6939	0352	2808
君	子	征	凶

The rain fell and he could rest.
His spiritual power brings him recognition.
The determination is dangerous for a wife.
The moon is almost full.
Enterprises are unfortunate.

10. Treading

≡≡

Judgment

lu3	hu3	wei3	bu4	die2	ren2	heng1
3893	2161	7109	5379	2456	3097	2099
履	虎	尾	不	咥	人	亨

Treading the Tiger's Tail.
The man is not bitten. Success.

Image

shang4	tian1	xia4	ze2	lu3	jun1	zi3
5669	6361	2520	0277	3893	1715	6939
上	天	下	澤	履	君	子
yi3	bian4	shang4	xia4	ding4	min2	zhi4
2932	5240	5669	2520	6393	4508	0971
以	辨	上	下	定	民	志

Above the sky, down the lake: The image of Treading.
Thus the noble distinguishes between high and low
and makes certain the will of the people.

First Nine

su4	lu3	wang3	wu2	jiu4
5490	3893	7050	7173	1192
素	履	往	无	咎

Simple Treading. Go forward without defect.

Second Nine

lu3	dao4	tan3	tan3
3893	6136	6057	6057
履	道	坦	坦
you1	ren2	zhen1	ji2
7505	3097	0346	0476
幽	人	貞	吉

Treading a smooth and easy way.
The determination of a lonely man brings good fortune.

Third Six

miao3	neng2	shi4	bo3	neng2	lu3
4476	4648	5789	5317	4648	3893
眇	能	視	跛	能	履

lu3	hu3	wei3	die2	ren2	xiong1
3893	2161	7109	2456	3097	2808
履	虎	尾	咥	人	凶

wu3	ren2	wei2	yu2	da4	jun1
7195	3097	7059	7592	5943	1715
武	人	爲	于	大	君

A one-eyed man can see, a lame can tread.
The tiger bites such a one who treads on his tail. Misfortune.
A warrior acts as if he were a great lord.

Fourth Nine

lu3	hu3	wei3	su4	su4	zhong1	ji2
3893	2161	7109	5494	5494	1500	0476
履	虎	尾	愬	愬	終	吉

Steps on the Tiger's Tail with great caution.
At the end there will be good fortune.

Fifth Nine

guai4	lu3	zhen1	li4
3535	3893	0346	3906
夬	履	貞	厲

Resolute Treading.
The determination is dangerous.

Top Nine

shi4	lu3	kao3	xiang2
5789	3893	3299	2577
視	履	考	祥

qi2	xuan2	yuan2	ji2
0525	2894	7707	0476
其	旋	元	吉

Watch the trodden path and examine the omens.
The cycle starts back. Great good fortune.

11. Harmony / Great

Judgment

tai4	xiao3	wang3	da4	lai2	ji2	heng1
6023	2605	7050	5943	3768	0476	2099
泰	小	往	大	來	吉	亨

Harmony. The petty depart and the great are coming.
Good fortune and success.

Image

tian1	di4	jiao1	tai4	hou4	yi3	cai2
6361	6198	0702	6023	2144	2932	6664
天	地	交	泰	后	以	裁

cheng2	tian1	di4	zhi1	dao4	fu3	xiang1
0379	6361	6198	0935	6136	1945	2562
成	天	地	之	道	輔	相

tian1	di4	zhi1	yi2	yi3	zuo3	you4	min2
6361	6198	0935	2993	2932	6774	7541	4508
天	地	之	宜	以	左	右	民

Heaven and earth are closely related: The image of Harmony.
Thus the sovereign regulates and completes the course of Heaven and Earth,
and assists Heaven and Earth in the right way; thereby helping the people.

First Nine

ba2	mao2	ru2	yi3	qi2	hui4	zheng1	ji2
4848	4364	3139	2932	0525	2349	0352	0476
拔	茅	茹	以	其	彙	征	吉

When reeds are pulled,
they pull up others of the same kind together with them.
Enterprises bring good fortune.

Second Nine

bao1	huang1	yong4	ping2	he2	bu4	xia2	yi2
4937	2271	7567	1895	2111	5379	2517	2995
包	荒	用	馮	河	不	遐	遺

peng2	wang2	de2	shang4	yu2	zhong1	xing2
5054	7034	6161	5670	7592	1504	2754
朋	亡	得	尚	于	中	行

Bear with the uneducated, wade the river, do not neglect the distant.
Thus factions disappear.
One get honors if stays in the middle path.

Third Nine

wu2	ping2	bu4	pi2	wu2	wang3	bu4
7173	5303	5379	5345	7173	7050	5379
无	平	不	陂	无	往	不

fu4	jian1	zhen1	wu2	wu4	xu4
1992	0834	0346	7173	7208	2862
復	艱	貞	无	勿	恤

qi2	fu2	yu2	shi2	you3	fu2
0525	1936	7592	5810	7533	1978
其	孚	于	食	有	福

There are no plains without slopes.
There is no going forth without a return.
Fortitude under trying conditions. No defect.
Do not regret this truth.
Enjoy the happiness you still possess.

Fourth Six

pian1	pian1	bu4	fu4	yi3	qi2	lin2
5249	5249	5379	1952	2932	0525	4033
翩	翩	不	富	以	其	鄰

bu4	jie4	yi3	fu2
5379	0627	2932	1936
不	戒	以	孚

Flapping, fluttering. Not using his own rich resources to deal with his neighbors.
Without having to ask gets confidence.

Fifth Six

di4	yi3	gui1	mei4	yi3	zhi3	yuan2	ji2
6204	3017	3617	4410	2932	0942	7707	0476
帝	乙	歸	妹	以	祉	元	吉

The sovereign Yi gives his daughter in marriage.
This brings happiness and great fortune.

Top Six

cheng2	fu4	yu2	huang2	wu4	yong4	shi1
0380	1992	7592	2295	7208	7567	5760
城	復	于	隍	勿	用	師

zi4	yi4	gao4	ming4	zhen1	lin4
6960	3037	3287	4537	0346	4040
自	邑	告	命	貞	吝

The wall falls back into the pit. Do not use the army now! Proclaim your
commands only in your own town. The determination brings humiliation.

12. Standstill / Stagnation

Judgment

pi3	zhi1	fei3	ren2	bu4	li4	jun1
1902	0935	1820	3097	5379	3867	1715
否	之	匪	人	不	利	君

zi3	zhen1	da4	wang3	xiao3	lai2
6939	0346	5943	7050	2605	3768
子	貞	大	往	小	來

Standstill.
Worthless people are unfavorable to the determination of the noble.
The great is going away, the petty is coming.

Image

tian1	di4	bu4	jiao1	pi3
6361	6198	5379	0702	1902
天	地	不	交	否

jun1	zi3	yi3	jian3	de2	bi4	nan2
1715	6939	2932	0848	6162	5172	4625
君	子	以	儉	德	辟	難

bu4	ke3	rong2	yi3	lu4
5379	3381	7582	2932	4196
不	可	榮	以	祿

Heaven and earth are not related: The image of Standstill.
Thus the noble, restrains his virtue, and avoids calamities.
He does not accept receiving rank or salary.

First Six

ba2	mao2	ru2	yi3	qi2	hui4	zhen1	ji2	heng1
4848	4364	3139	2932	0525	2349	0346	0476	2099
拔	茅	茹	以	其	彙	貞	吉	亨

When reeds are pulled,
they pull up others of the same kind together with them.
The determination brings good fortune and success.

Second Six

bao1	cheng2	xiao3	ren2	ji2
4937	0386	2605	3097	0476
包	承	小	人	吉

da4	ren2	pi3	heng1
5943	3097	1902	2099
大	人	否	亨

They support and tolerate. Good fortune for the petty.
By accepting the Standstill the great man will have success.

Third Six

bao1	xiu1
4937	2797
包	羞

They bear the shame.

Fourth Nine

you3	ming4	wu2	jiu4	chou2	li2	zhi3
7533	4537	7173	1192	1322	3902	0942
有	命	无	咎	疇	離	祉

Who follows the commands of Heaven will have no defect.
His comrades will share the blessings.

Fifth Nine

xiu1	pi3	da4	ren2	ji2	qi2	wang2
2786	1902	5943	3097	0476	0525	7034
休	否	大	人	吉	其	亡

qi2	wang2	xi4	yu2	bao1	sang1
0525	7034	2458	7592	4941	5424
其	亡	繫	于	苞	桑

The Standstill is stopping.
Good fortune for the great man.
It can fail! It can fail! Tie it to a luxuriant mulberry tree.

Top Nine

qing1	pi3	xian1	pi3	hou4	xi3
1161	1902	2702	1902	2143	2434
傾	否	先	否	後	喜

The Standstill is overthrown.
First standstill, afterwards joy.

13. Fellowship

Judgment

tong2	ren2	yu2	ye3	heng1	li4
6615	3097	7592	7314	2099	3867
同	人	于	野	亨	利

she4	da4	chuan1	li4	jun1	zi3	zhen1
5707	5943	1439	3867	1715	6939	0346
涉	大	川	利	君	子	貞

Fellowship in the fields. Success.
It is advantageous to cross the great river.
The determination brings good fortune for the noble.

Image

tian1	yu3	huo3	tong2	ren2
6361	7615	2395	6615	3097
天	與	火	同	人

jun1	zi3	yi3	lei4	zu2	bian4	wu4
1715	6939	2932	4244	6830	5240	7209
君	子	以	類	族	辨	物

Heaven and fire: The image of the Fellowship.
Thus the noble organizes the clans
and discriminates among things.

First Nine

tong2	ren2	yu2	men2	wu2	jiu4
6615	3097	7592	4418	7173	1192
同	人	于	門	无	咎

Fellowship in the front door. No defect.

Second Six

tong2	ren2	yu2	zong1	lin4
6615	3097	7592	6896	4040
同	人	于	宗	吝

Fellowship in the clan. Shame.

Third Nine

fu2	rong2	yu2	mang3	sheng1		
1964	3181	7592	4354	5745		
伏	戎	于	莽	升		

qi2	gao1	ling2	san1	sui4	bu4	xing1
0525	3290	4067	5415	5538	5379	2753
其	高	陵	三	歲	不	興

He hides weapons in the bush and climbs the high hill,
but for three years he will not rise.

Fourth Nine

cheng2	qi2	yong1	fu2	ke4	gong1	ji2
0398	0525	7578	1981	3320	3699	0476
乘	其	墉	弗	克	攻	吉

He climbs to his wall he but cannot attack. Good fortune.

Fifth Nine

tong2	ren2	xian1	hao4	tao2	er2	hou4	xiao4
6615	3097	2702	2064	6152	1756	2143	2615
同	人	先	號	咷	而	後	笑

da4	shi1	ke4	xiang1	yu4		
5943	5760	3320	2562	7625		
大	師	克	相	遇		

The men in Fellowship first weep and mourn, but then laugh.
Great armies come across.

Top Nine

tong2	ren2	yu2	jiao1	wu2	hui3
6615	3097	7592	0714	7173	2336
同	人	于	郊	无	悔

Fellowship in the field. No repentance.

14. Great Possession

Judgment

da4	you3	yuan2	heng1
5943	7533	7707	2099
大	有	元	亨

Great Possession. Outstanding success.

Image

huo3	zai4	tian1	shang4	da4	you3	
2395	6657	6361	5669	5943	7533	
火	在	天	上	大	有	

jun1	zi3	yi3	e4	e4	yang2	shan4
1715	6939	2932	4812	4809	7259	5657
君	子	以	遏	惡	揚	善

shun4	tian1	xiu1	ming4
5935	6361	2786	4537
順	天	休	命

Fire at the top of heaven: The image of Great Possession.
Thus the noble punishes evil and promotes good,
following the good will of Heaven.

First Nine

wu2	jiao1	hai4	fei3	jiu4
7173	0702	2015	1820	1192
无	交	害	匪	咎

jian1	ze2	wu2	jiu4
0834	6746	7173	1192
艱	則	无	咎

No relationship with harmful things. No defect.
There will be hardship but no defect.

Second Nine

da4	che1	yi3	zai4	you3	you1	wang3
5943	0280	2932	6653	7533	7519	7050
大	車	以	載	有	攸	往

wu2	jiu4
7173	1192
无	咎

A great carriage for carrying things.
One has a goal. No defect.

Third Nine

gong1	yong4	heng1	yu2	tian1	zi3
3701	7567	2099	7592	6361	6939
公	用	亨	于	天	子

xiao3	ren2	fu2	ke4
2605	3097	1981	3320
小	人	弗	克

A prince presents his offerings to the Son of Heaven.
A petty man is not able to do so.

Fourth Nine

fei3	qi2	peng2	wu2	jiu4
1820	0525	5060	7173	1192
匪	其	彭	无	咎

He is not arrogant.
No defect.

Fifth Six

jue2	fu2	jiao1	ru2	wei1	ru2	ji2
1680	1936	0702	3137	7051	3137	0476
厥	孚	交	如	威	如	吉

His sincerity will earn the trust and respect of others.
Good fortune.

Top Nine

zi4	tian1	you4	zhi1	ji2	wu2	bu4	li4
6960	6361	7543	0935	0476	7173	5379	3867
自	天	祐	之	吉	无	不	利

He has the protection of Heaven. Good fortune.
Nothing that is not favorable.

15. Modesty

```
▬▬ ▬▬
▬▬ ▬▬
▬▬▬▬▬
▬▬ ▬▬
▬▬ ▬▬
▬▬ ▬▬
```

Judgment

qian1	heng1	jun1	zi3	you3	zhong1
0885	2099	1715	6939	7533	1500
謙	亨	君	子	有	終

Modesty. Success.
The noble carries things to completion.

Image

di4	zhong1	you3	shan1	qian1		
6198	1504	7533	5630	0885		
地	中	有	山	謙		
jun1	zi3	yi3	shuai1	duo1	yi4	gua3
1715	6939	2932	5908	6416	3052	3517
君	子	以	衰	多	益	寡
cheng1	wu4	ping2	shi1			
0383	7209	5303	5768			
稱	物	平	施			

A Mountain in the middle of the earth: The image of Modesty.
Thus the noble reduces what is excessive and increases what is insufficient.
Weighs and distributes things evenly.

First Six

qian1	qian1	jun1	zi3	
0885	0885	1715	6939	
謙	謙	君	子	
yong4	she4	da4	chuan1	ji2
7567	5707	5943	1439	0476
用	涉	大	川	吉

An extremely modest noble can cross the great river.
Good fortune.

Second Six

ming2	qian1	zhen1	ji2
4535	0885	0346	0476
鳴	謙	貞	吉

Modesty expresses itself.
The determination is fortunate.

Third Nine

lao2	qian1	jun1	zi3	you3	zhong1	ji2
3826	0885	1715	6939	7533	1500	0476
勞	謙	君	子	有	終	吉

A noble meritorious for his modesty carries things to completion.
Good fortune.

Fourth Six

wu2	bu4	li4	hui1	qian1
7173	5379	3867	2356	0885
无	不	利	撝	謙

Nothing that is not favorable for manifested modesty.

Fifth Six

bu4	fu4	yi3	qi2	lin2	li4	yong4
5379	1952	2932	0525	4033	3867	7567
不	富	以	其	鄰	利	用

qin1	fa1	wu2	bu4	li4
1108	1765	7173	5379	3867
侵	伐	无	不	利

Without wealth can employ his neighbors.
It is advantageous to take the offensive.
Nothing that is not favorable.

Top Six

ming2	qian1	li4	yong4	xing2	shi1
4535	0885	3867	7567	2754	5760
鳴	謙	利	用	行	師

zheng1	yi4	guo2
0352	3037	3738
征	邑	國

Manifest Modesty.
It is favorable to launch armies
to punish the capital city.

16. Enthusiasm

Judgment

yu4	li4	jian4	hou2	xing2	shi1
7603	3867	0853	2135	2754	5760
豫	利	建	侯	行	師

Enthusiasm.
It is favorable to appoint officers and to set the army in motion.

Image

lei2	chu1	di4	fen4	yu4		
4236	1409	6198	1874	7603		
雷	出	地	奮	豫		
xian1	wang2	yi3	zuo4	le4	chong2	de2
2702	7037	2932	6780	4129	1528	6162
先	王	以	作	樂	崇	德
yin1	jian4	zhi1	shang4	di4		
7423	0872	0935	5669	6204		
殷	薦	之	上	帝		
yi3	pei4	zu3	kao3			
2932	5019	6815	3299			
以	配	祖	考			

Thunder comes out from the earth: The image of Enthusiasm.
So the kings of old made music to honor merit, and lavishly offered it to the Supreme Lord to be worthy of their dead ancestors.

First Six

ming2	yu4	xiong1
4535	7603	2808
鳴	豫	凶

Manifest Enthusiasm is ominous.

Second Six

jie4	yu2	shi2	bu4	zhong1	ri4
0629	7592	5813	5379	1500	3124
介	于	石	不	終	日
zhen1	ji2				
0346	0476				
貞	吉				

Solid as a rock.
His chance will come before the end of the day.
The determination brings good fortune.

Third Six

xu1	yu4	hui3	chi2	you3	hui3
2819	7603	2336	1024	7533	2336
盱	豫	悔	遲	有	悔

Enthusiasm that looks upward brings repentance. Hesitation brings remorse.

Fourth Nine

you2	yu4	da4	you3	de2	wu4	yi2
7513	7603	5943	7533	6161	7208	2940
由	豫	大	有	得	勿	疑

peng2	he2	zan1
5054	2119	6679
朋	盍	簪

Enthusiasm causes great things.
Do not hesitate. Friends are quick to join your side.

Fifth Six

zhen1	ji2	heng2	bu4	si3
0346	0492	2107	5379	5589
貞	疾	恆	不	死

Determination. Persistently ill but not dying.

Top Six

ming2	yu4	cheng2	you3	yu2	wu2	jiu4
4528	7603	0379	7533	7635	7173	1192
冥	豫	成	有	渝	无	咎

Confused Enthusiasm.
But if one changes course after it is over, there will be no defect.

17. Following

Judgment

sui2	yuan2	heng1	li4	zhen1	wu2	jiu4
5523	7707	2099	3867	0346	7173	1192
隨	元	亨	利	貞	无	咎

Following has outstanding success.
The determination is favorable.
No defect.

Image

ze2	zhong1	you3	lei2	sui2			
0277	1504	7533	4236	5523			
澤	中	有	雷	隨			
jun1	zi3	yi3	xiang4	hui4	ru4	yan4	xi1
1715	6939	2932	2561	2337	3152	7364	2495
君	子	以	嚮	晦	入	宴	息

In the middle of the lake is the thunder: The image of Following.
Thus the noble, at dusk, enters and rests in peace.

First Nine

guan1	you3	yu2	zhen1	ji2
3552	7533	7635	0346	0476
官	有	渝	貞	吉
chu1	men2	jiao1	you3	gong1
1409	4418	0702	7533	3698
出	門	交	有	功

The situation is changing.
The determination is favorable.
Going outside to find associates is worthwhile.

Second Six

xi4	xiao3	zi3	shi1	zhang4	fu1
2424	2605	6939	5806	0200	1908
係	小	子	失	丈	夫

He clings to the boy and lets go the strong man.

Third Six

xi4	zhang4	fu1	shi1	xiao3	zi3
2424	0200	1908	5806	2605	6939
係	丈	夫	失	小	子

sui2	you3	qiu2	de2	li4	ju1	zhen1
5523	7533	1217	6161	3867	1535	0346
隨	有	求	得	利	居	貞

He is involved with the strong man and lets go the boy.
By following one gets what one seeks for.
The determination is favorable.

Fourth Nine

sui2	you3	huo4	zhen1	xiong1
5523	7533	2412	0346	2808
隨	有	獲	貞	凶

you3	fu2	zai4	dao4	yi3	ming2
7533	1936	6657	6136	2932	4534
有	孚	在	道	以	明

he2	jiu4
2109	1192
何	咎

By following there will be a catch.
The determination is ominous.
He is truthful and bright on the way.
How could there be defect in this?

Fifth Nine

fu2	yu2	jia1	ji2
1936	7592	0592	0476
孚	于	嘉	吉

Sincerity leads to excellence.
Good fortune.

Top Six

ju1	xi4	zhi1	nai3	cong2	wei2	zhi1
1542	2424	0935	4612	6919	7067	0935
拘	係	之	乃	從	維	之

wang2	yong4	heng1	yu2	xi1	shan1
7037	7567	2099	7592	2460	5630
王	用	亨	于	西	山

Strong ties between those who follow the same path.
The king makes an offering in the Western Mountain.

18. Correcting Decay / Corruption

Judgment

gu3	yuan2	heng1	li4	she4	da4	chuan1
3475	7707	2099	3867	5707	5943	1439
蠱	元	亨	利	涉	大	川

xian1	jia3	san1	ri4	hou4	jia3	san1	ri4
2702	0610	5415	3124	2143	0610	5415	3124
先	甲	三	日	後	甲	三	日

Correcting Decay has outstanding success.
It is favorable to cross the great river.
Before the first day three days.
After the first day three days.

Image

shan1	xia4	you3	feng1	gu3
5630	2520	7533	1890	3475
山	下	有	風	蠱

jun1	zi3	yi3	zhen4	min2	yu4	de2
1715	6939	2932	0313	4508	7687	6162
君	子	以	振	民	育	德

Under the mountain is (blows) the wind: The image of Corruption.
Thus the noble puts in motion the people and cultivates their moral values.

First Six

gan4	fu4	zhi1	gu3	you3	zi3
3235	1933	0935	3475	7533	6939
幹	父	之	蠱	有	子

kao3	wu2	jiu4	li4	zhong1	ji2
3299	7173	1192	3906	1500	0476
考	无	咎	厲	終	吉

Correcting the decay left by his father.
Since there is a son the father will have no defect.
Danger. Good fortune in the end.

Second Nine

gan4	mu3	zhi1	gu3	bu4	ke3	zhen1
3235	4582	0935	3475	5379	3381	0346
幹	母	之	蠱	不	可	貞

Correcting the decay left by his mother.
Cannot be determined.

Third Nine

gan4	fu4	zhi1	gu3	xiao3	you3	hui3
3235	1933	0935	3475	2605	7533	2336
幹	父	之	蠱	小	有	悔

wu2	da4	jiu4
7173	5943	1192
无	大	咎

Correcting the decay left by his father.
There will be some regrets, but no great defect.

Fourth Six

yu4	fu4	zhi1	gu3	wang3	jian4	lin4
7667	1933	0935	3475	7050	0860	4040
裕	父	之	蠱	往	見	吝

Tolerating the decay left by his father.
He will regret going this way.

Fifth Six

gan4	fu4	zhi1	gu3	yong4	yu4
3235	1933	0935	3475	7567	7617
幹	父	之	蠱	用	譽

Correcting the decay left by his father.
You get praises.

Top Nine

bu4	shi4	wang2	hou2
5379	5787	7037	2135
不	事	王	侯

gao1	shang4	qi2	shi4
3290	5670	0525	5787
高	尚	其	事

Does not serve kings or lords.
He seeks much higher goals.

19. Approach / Leadership

Judgment

lin2	yuan2	heng1	li4	zhen1	
4027	7707	2099	3867	0346	
臨	元	亨	利	貞	

zhi4	yu2	ba1	yue4	you3	xiong1
0982	7592	4845	7696	7533	2808
至	于	八	月	有	凶

Approach. Outstanding Success.
The determination is favorable.
On the eighth month there will be misfortune.

Image

ze2	shang4	you3	di4	lin2		
0277	5669	7533	6198	4027		
澤	上	有	地	臨		

jun1	zi3	yi3	jiao1	si1	wu2	qiong2
1715	6939	2932	0719	5580	7173	1247
君	子	以	教	思	无	窮

rong2	bao3	min2	wu2	jiang1		
7560	4946	4508	7173	0643		
容	保	民	无	疆		

Above the lake is the earth: The image of Approach.
Thus the noble is tireless in his efforts to educate the people
and doesn't know boundaries in protecting and supporting them.

First Nine

xian2	lin2	zhen1	ji2
2666	4027	0346	0476
咸	臨	貞	吉

Joint approach.

The determination is favorable.

Second Nine

xian2	lin2	ji2	wu2	bu4	li4
2666	4027	0476	7173	5379	3867
咸	臨	吉	无	不	利

Joint approach.
Good fortune.
Everything is favorable

Third Six

gan1	lin2	wu2	you1	li4	ji4	you1	zhi1
3223	4027	7173	7519	3867	0453	7508	0935
甘	臨	无	攸	利	既	憂	之

wu2	jiu4
7173	1192
无	咎

Sweet approach.
No goal is favorable.
If he becomes anxious about it, there will be no defect.

Fourth Six

zhi4	lin2	wu2	jiu4
0982	4027	7173	1192
至	臨	无	咎

Approach reaches its climax.
No defect.

Fifth Six

zhi1	lin2	da4	jun1	zhi1	yi2	ji2
0932	4027	5943	1715	0935	2993	0476
知	臨	大	君	之	宜	吉

Wise approach.
It is fitting for a lord.
Good fortune.

Top Six

dun1	lin2	ji2	wu2	jiu4
6571	4027	0476	7173	1192
敦	臨	吉	无	咎

Sincere and generous approach.
Good fortune. No defect.

20. Contemplation

Judgment

guan1	guan4	er2	bu4	jian4
3575	3569	1756	5379	0872
觀	盥	而	不	薦

you3	fu2	yong2	ruo4
7533	1936	8008	3126
有	孚	顒	若

Contemplation.
The ablution was done but not yet the offering.
His dignified appearance inspires confidence.

Image

feng1	xing2	di4	shang4	guan1	xian1	wang2
1890	2754	6198	5669	3575	2702	7037
風	行	地	上	觀	先	王

yi3	xing3	fang1	guan1	min2	she4	jiao4
2932	5744	1802	3575	4508	5711	0719
以	省	方	觀	民	設	教

The wind moves upon the earth: The image of Contemplation.
Thus the ancient kings inspected all regions looking at the people and giving instruction.

First Six

tong2	guan1	xiao3	ren2	wu2	jiu4
6626	3575	2605	3097	7173	1192
童	觀	小	人	无	咎

jun1	zi3	lin4
1715	6939	4040
君	子	吝

Childish contemplations.
No defect for the small man.
For the noble is humiliating.

Second Six

kui1	guan1	li4	nu3	zhen1
3649	3575	3867	4776	0346
闚	觀	利	女	貞

Furtive contemplation.
The determination is favorable for a woman.

Third Six

guan1	wo3	sheng1	jin4	tui4
3575	4778	5738	1091	6568
觀	我	生	進	退

Looking at the progress and setbacks in my life.

Fourth Six

guan1	guo2	zhi1	guang1
3575	3738	0935	3583
觀	國	之	光

li4	yong4	bin1	yu2	wang2
3867	7567	5259	7592	7037
利	用	賓	于	王

Contemplation of the glory of the kingdom.
It is favorable to act as a guest of a king.

Fifth Nine

guan1	wo3	sheng1	jun1	zi3	wu2	jiu4
3575	4778	5738	1715	6939	7173	1192
觀	我	生	君	子	无	咎

Contemplation of my life.
The noble has no defect.

Top Nine

guan1	qi2	sheng1	jun1	zi3	wu2	jiu4
3575	0525	5738	1715	6939	7173	1192
觀	其	生	君	子	无	咎

Contemplation of his life.
The noble has no faults.

21. Biting Through

Judgment

shi4	he2	heng1	li4	yong4	yu4
5764	2120	2099	3867	7567	7685
噬	嗑	亨	利	用	獄

Biting Through is successful.
It is favorable to administer justice.

Image

lei2	dian4	shi4	he2
4236	6358	5764	2120
雷	電	噬	嗑

xian1	wang2	yi3	ming2	fa2	chi4	fa3
2702	7037	2932	4534	1769	1050	1762
先	王	以	明	罰	敕	法

Thunder and lightning: The image of the Biting Through.
Thus the ancient kings applied punishments with intelligence and enacted laws.

First Nine

ju4	xiao4	mie4	zhi3	wu2	jiu4
1572	0706	4483	0944	7173	1192
屨	校	滅	趾	无	咎

His feet are trapped by fetters and his toes are mangled.
No defect.

Second Six

shi4	fu1	mie4	bi2	wu2	jiu4
5764	1958	4483	5100	7173	1192
噬	膚	滅	鼻	无	咎

Biting Through tender flesh, the nose is destroyed.
No defect.

Third Six

shi4	xi1	rou4	yu4	du2
5764	3763	3153	7625	6509
噬	腊	肉	遇	毒

xiao3	lin4	wu2	jiu4
2605	4040	7173	1192
小	吝	无	咎

Biting Through dried meat finds poison. A little humiliation. No defect.

Fourth Nine

shi4	gan1	zi3	de2	jin1	shi3
5764	3233	6950	6161	1057	5784
噬	乾	胏	得	金	矢

li4	jian1	zhen1	ji2
3867	0834	0346	0476
利	艱	貞	吉

Biting Through bone-dry meat he gets metal arrows.
It is favorable fortitude under trying conditions.
Good fortune.

Fifth Six

shi4	gan1	rou4	de2	huang2	jin1
5764	3233	3153	6161	2297	1057
噬	乾	肉	得	黃	金

zhen1	li4	wu2	jiu4
0346	3906	7173	1192
貞	厲	无	咎

Biting Through dry meat he gets yellow metal.
The determination is dangerous.
No defect.

Top Nine

he4	xiao4	mie4	er3	xiong1
2109	0706	4483	1744	2808
何	校	滅	耳	凶

He carries a yoke that make his ears disappear.
Ominous.

22. Elegance / Adornment

Judgment

bi4	heng1	xiao3	li4	you3	you1	wang3
5027	2099	2605	3867	7533	7519	7050
賁	亨	小	利	有	攸	往

Elegance. Success
It is favorable to have a goal in minor matters.

Image

shan1	xia4	you3	huo3	bi4	
5630	2520	7533	2395	5027	
山	下	有	火	賁	
jun1	zi3	yi3	ming2	shu4	zheng4
1715	6939	2932	4534	5874	0355
君	子	以	明	庶	政
wu2	gan3	zhe2	yu4		
7173	3229	0267	7685		
无	敢	折	獄		

Fire at the foot of the mountain: The image of Elegance.
Thus the noble regulates the crowds with enlightenment.
But doesn't dare to decide criminal cases.

First Nine

bi4	qi2	zhi3	she3	che1	er2	tu2
5027	0525	0944	5699	0280	1756	6536
賁	其	趾	舍	車	而	徒

He gives Elegance to his feet,
leaves the carriage and walks.

Second Six

bi4	qi2	xu1
5027	0525	2847
賁	其	須

He gives Elegance to his beard.

Third Nine

bi4	ru2	ru2	ru2	yong3	zhen1	ji2
5027	3137	3149	3137	7589	0346	0476
賁	如	濡	如	永	貞	吉

Adorned with moisture.
Long-term determination is fortunate.

58

Fourth Six

bi4	ru2	po2	ru2	bai2	ma3	han4
5027	3137	5351	3137	4975	4310	2042
賁	如	皤	如	白	馬	翰

ru2	fei3	kou4	hun1	gou4
3137	1820	3444	2360	3426
如	匪	寇	婚	媾

Adorned in white. A white horse soaring.
He is not a robber, but a suitor.

Fifth Six

bi4	yu2	qiu1	yuan2	shu4	bo2	jian1
5027	7592	1213	7731	5891	4979	0866
賁	于	丘	園	束	帛	戔

jian1	lin4	zhong1	ji2
0866	4040	1500	0476
戔	吝	終	吉

Elegance in hills and gardens.
The silk bundle is meager.
Humiliation, but good fortune at the end.

Top Nine

bai2	bi4	wu2	jiu4
4975	5027	7173	1192
白	賁	无	咎

Simple elegance.
No defect.

23. Splitting Apart

Judgment

bo1	bu4	li4	you3	you1	wang3
5337	5379	3867	7533	7519	7050
剝	不	利	有	攸	往

Splitting Apart. It is not favorable to go anywhere.

Image

shan1	fu4	yu2	di4	bo1	
5630	1924	7643	6198	5337	
山	附	於	地	剝	

shang4	yi3	hou4	xia4	an1	zhai2
5669	2932	2147	2520	0026	0275
上	以	厚	下	安	宅

The mountain lies on earth: The image of Splitting Apart.
Thus by means of being munificent with those below them,
the superiors secure the peace and stability of their own position.

First Six

bo1	chuang2	yi3	zu2	mie4	zhen1	xiong1
5337	1459	2932	6824	4485	0346	2808
剝	牀	以	足	蔑	貞	凶

Splitting Apart the legs of the bed.
Determination leads to destruction.
Ominous.

Second Six

bo1	chuang2	yi3	bian4	mie4	zhen1	xiong1
5337	1459	2932	5240	4485	0346	2808
剝	牀	以	辨	蔑	貞	凶

Splitting Apart the bed's frame.
Determination leads to destruction.
Ominous.

Third Six

bo1	zhi1	wu2	jiu4
5337	0935	7173	1192
剝	之	无	咎

Splitting Apart them.
No defect.

Fourth Six

bo1	chuang2	yi3	fu1	xiong1
5337	1459	2932	1958	2808
剝	牀	以	膚	凶

The bed is peeled down to the skin.
Ominous.

Fifth Six

guan4	yu2	yi3	gong1	ren2	chong3
3566	7668	2932	3705	3097	1534
貫	魚	以	宮	人	寵

wu2	bu4	li4
7173	5379	3867
无	不	利

A string of fishes.
Favors by means of the ladies of palace.
Nothing that is not favorable.

Top Nine

shuo4	guo3	bu4	shi2	jun1	zi3	de2
5815	3732	5379	5810	1715	6939	6161
碩	果	不	食	君	子	得

yu2	xiao3	ren2	bo1	lu2
7618	2605	3097	5337	4158
輿	小	人	剝	廬

A large fruit still uneaten.
The noble gets a carriage;
the petty man shelter is split apart.

24. Return

Judgment

fu4	heng1	chu1	ru4	wu2	ji2	peng2
1992	2099	1409	3152	7173	0492	5054
復	亨	出	入	无	疾	朋

lai2	wu2	jiu4	fan3	fu4	qi2	dao4	
3768	7173	1192	1781	1992	0525	6136	
來	无	咎	反	復	其	道	

qi1	ri4	lai2	fu4	li4	you3	you1	wang3
0579	3124	3768	1992	3867	7533	7519	7050
七	日	來	復	利	有	攸	往

Return. Success.

Exit and entry without harm.

Friends come.

No defect.

Back and forth along the way.

In seven days will return.

It is favorable to have where to go.

Image

lei2	zai4	di4	zhong1	fu4	xian1	wang2
4236	6657	6198	1504	1992	2702	7037
雷	在	地	中	復	先	王

yi3	zhi4	ri4	bi4	guan1	shang1	lu3
2932	0982	3124	5092	3571	5673	4286
以	至	日	閉	關	商	旅

bu4	xing2	hou4	bu4	xing3	fang1
5379	2754	2144	5379	5744	1802
不	行	后	不	省	方

The thunder in the middle of the earth: The image of Return.

So on the day of the solstice,

the ancient kings closed the border crossings.

Merchants and travelers did not travel and the ruler did not visit his dominions.

First Nine

bu4	yuan3	fu4	wu2	zhi1	hui3	yuan2	ji2
5379	7734	1992	7173	0952	2336	7707	0476
不	遠	復	无	祗	悔	元	吉

Returning before going too far.

There will be no need for repentance.

Outstanding good fortune.

Second Six

xiu1	fu4	ji2
2786	1992	0476
休	復	吉

Quiet return. Good fortune.

Third Six

pin2	fu4	li4	wu2	jiu4
5275	1992	3906	7173	1192
頻	復	厲	无	咎

Repeated return. Danger.
No repentance.

Fourth Six

zhong1	xing2	du2	fu4
1504	2754	6512	1992
中	行	獨	復

Returns alone by the middle of the road.

Fifth Six

dun1	fu4	wu2	hui3
6571	1992	7173	2336
敦	復	无	悔

Earnest return. No defect.

Top Six

mi2	fu4	xiong1	you3	zai1	sheng3
4450	1992	2808	7533	6652	5741
迷	復	凶	有	災	眚

yong4	xing2	shi1	zhong1	you3	da4	bai4
7567	2754	5760	1500	7533	5943	4866
用	行	師	終	有	大	敗

yi3	qi2	guo2	jun1	xiong1	zhi4	yu2
2932	0525	3738	1715	2808	0982	7592
以	其	國	君	凶	至	于

shi2	nian2	bu4	ke4	zheng1
5807	4711	5379	3320	0352
十	年	不	克	征

The return goes astray. Ominous.
Calamities and errors.
If he puts armies on the march, in the end will suffer a great defeat, whose misfortune will extend to the ruler of the state.
For ten years he will not be able to attack.

25. Innocence / No expectations

Judgment

wu2	wang4	yuan2	heng1	li4	zhen1
7173	**7035**	7707	2099	3867	0346
无	妄	元	亨	利	貞

qi2	fei3	zheng4	you3	sheng3
0525	1820	0351	7533	5741
其	匪	正	有	眚

bu4	li4	you3	you1	wang3
5379	3867	7533	7519	7050
不	利	有	攸	往

Innocence. Outstanding success.
The determination is favorable.
If one is not honest he has misfortune.
It is favorable to have a goal.

Image

tian1	xia4	lei2	xing2
6361	2520	4236	2754
天	下	雷	行

wu4	yu3	wu2	wang4
7209	7615	7173	7035
物	與	无	妄

xian1	wang2	yi3	mao4	dui4	shi2	yu4	wan4	wu4
2702	7037	2932	4580	6562	5780	7687	7030	7209
先	王	以	茂	對	時	育	萬	物

The thunder moves under heaven
and all things partake of innocence.
Thus the ancient kings, in excellent harmony with the seasons,
nurtured all beings.

First Nine

wu2	wang4	wang3	ji2
7173	7035	7050	0476
无	妄	往	吉

Going forward with innocence
brings good fortune.

Second Six

bu4	geng1	huo4	bu4	zi1	yu2
5379	3343	2207	5379	6932	7606
不	耕	穫	不	菑	畲

ze2	li4	you3	you1	wang3
6746	3867	7533	7519	7050
則	利	有	攸	往

Harvest without plowing.
The fields are ready for use without having been prepared.
It is favorable to have a goal.

Third Six

wu2	wang4	zhi1	zai1	huo4	xi4	zhi1
7173	7035	0935	6652	2402	2458	0935
无	妄	之	災	或	繫	之

niu2	xing2	ren2	zhi1	de2
4737	2754	3097	0935	6161
牛	行	人	之	得

yi4	ren2	zhi1	zai1
3037	3097	0935	6652
邑	人	之	災

Unexpected disaster.
The cow tied by someone,
is the traveler's gain and the villager's misfortune.

Fourth Nine

ke3	zhen1	wu2	jiu4
3381	0346	7173	1192
可	貞	无	咎

Can be determined.
No defect.

Fifth Nine

wu2	wang4	zhi1	ji2	wu4	yao4	you3	xi3
7173	7035	0935	0492	7208	7501	7533	2434
无	妄	之	疾	勿	藥	有	喜

Unexpected illness.
Do not take medicine
and you will rejoice.

Top Nine

wu2	wang4	xing2	you3	sheng3	wu2	you1	li4
7173	7035	2754	7533	5741	7173	7519	3867
无	妄	行	有	眚	无	攸	利

Innocent action brings misfortune.
No place is favorable.

26. Great Accumulation

Judgment

da4	chu4	li4	zhen1	bu4	jia1	shi2
5943	1412	3867	0346	5379	0594	5810
大	畜	利	貞	不	家	食

ji2	li4	she4	da4	chuan1
0476	3867	5707	5943	1439
吉	利	涉	大	川

Great Accumulation.

The determination is favorable.

Not eating at home brings good fortune.

It is favorable to cross the great river.

Image

tian1	zai4	shan1	zhong1	da4	chu4	
6361	6657	5630	1504	5943	1412	
天	在	山	中	大	畜	

jun1	zi3	yi3	duo1	shi2	qian2	yan2
1715	6939	2932	6416	5825	0919	7334
君	子	以	多	識	前	言

wang3	xing2	yi3	chu4	qi2	de2
7050	2754	2932	1412	0525	6162
往	行	以	畜	其	德

Heaven in the middle of the mountain: The image of Great Accumulation.
Thus, the noble is acquainted with many words and deeds of the past
and cultivates his character.

First Nine

you3	li4	li4	yi3
7533	3906	3867	2930
有	厲	利	已

Danger. It is best to halt.

Second Nine

yu2	tuo1	fu4
7618	5939	1997
輿	說	輹

The axle brackets are removed from the carriage.

Third Nine

liang2	ma3	zhu2	li4	jian1	zhen1	yue1
3941	4310	1383	3867	0834	0346	7694
良	馬	逐	利	艱	貞	曰

xian2	yu2	wei4	li4	you3	you1	wang3
2679	7618	7089	3867	7533	7519	7050
閑	輿	衛	利	有	攸	往

Good horses that run one after another.

Fortitude under trying conditions.

Exercise every day with chariots and defensive measures.

It is favorable to have a goal.

Fourth Six

tong2	niu2	zhi1	gu4	yuan2	ji2
6626	4737	0935	8003	7707	0476
童	牛	之	牿	元	吉

The protective covering of the horns of the calf.

Outstanding good fortune.

Fifth Six

fen2	shi3	zhi1	ya2	ji2
1873	5766	0935	7214	0476
豶	豕	之	牙	吉

The tusks of a castrated boar.

Good fortune.

Top Nine

he2	tian1	zhi1	qu2	heng1
2109	6361	0935	1611	2099
何	天	之	衢	亨

Attains the way of Heaven.

Success.

27. Nourishment / The Jaws

Judgment

yi2	zhen1	ji2	guan1	yi2
2969	0346	0476	3575	2969
頤	貞	吉	觀	頤

zi4	qiu2	kou3	shi2
6960	1217	3434	5821
自	求	口	實

Nourishment.

Determination brings good fortune.

Watch what you nourish and what you are looking to fill your mouth with.

Image

shan1	xia4	you3	lei2	yi2	jun1	zi3
5630	2520	7533	4236	2969	1715	6939
山	下	有	雷	頤	君	子

yi3	shen4	yan2	yu3	jie2	yin3	shi2
2932	5734	7334	7651	0795	7454	5810
以	愼	言	語	節	飲	食

Under the mountain is the thunder: The image of Nourishment.

Thus the noble is careful with what he says,

and restrained in his drinking and eating.

First Nine

she3	er3	ling2	gui1	guan1	wo3	duo3
5699	1754	4071	3621	3575	4778	6419
舍	爾	靈	龜	觀	我	朵

yi2	xiong1
2969	2808
頤	凶

You let your magic turtle go and look at me with your jaws hanging. Misfortune.

Second Six

dian1	yi2	fu2	jing1	yu2	qiu1
6337	2969	1986	1123	7592	1213
顛	頤	拂	經	于	丘

yi2	zheng1	xiong1
2969	0352	2808
頤	征	凶

Forages in the summit.

Turns away from the path and goes to the summit for Nourishment.

Going forward brings misfortune.

Third Six

fu2	yi2	zhen1	xiong1
1986	2969	0346	2808
拂	頤	貞	凶

shi2	nian2	wu4	yong4	wu2	you1	li4
5807	4711	7208	7567	7173	7519	3867
十	年	勿	用	无	攸	利

Rejects Nourishment.
The determination brings misfortune.
Do not act for ten years.
Nothing at all is favorable.

Fourth Six

dian1	yi2	ji2	hu3	shi4	dan1	dan1
6337	2969	0476	2161	5789	6028	6028
顛	頤	吉	虎	視	眈	眈

qi2	yu4	zhu2	zhu2	wu2	jiu4
0525	7671	1383	1383	7173	1192
其	欲	逐	逐	无	咎

Forages in the summit.
Staring like a tiger,
with greed and insatiable desire to chase.
No defect.

Fifth Six

fu2	jing1	ju1	zhen1	ji2
1986	1123	1535	0346	0476
拂	經	居	貞	吉

bu4	ke3	she4	da4	chuan1
5379	3381	5707	5943	1439
不	可	涉	大	川

Moving away from the path.
The determination brings good fortune.
He cannot cross the great river.

Top Nine

you2	yi2	li4	ji2	li4	she4	da4	chuan1
7513	2969	3906	0476	3867	5707	5943	1439
由	頤	厲	吉	利	涉	大	川

The source of Nourishment.
Danger, but good fortune.
It is favorable to cross the great river.

28. Great Excess

Judgment

da4	guo4	dong4	nao2
5943	3730	6607	3087
大	過	棟	橈

li4	you3	you1	wang3	heng1
3867	7533	7519	7050	2099
利	有	攸	往	亨

Great Excess.

The main beam sags. It is favorable to have a goal.

Success.

Image

ze2	mie4	mu4	da4	guo4
0277	4483	4593	5943	3730
澤	滅	木	大	過

jun1	zi3	yi3	du2	li4	bu4	ju4
1715	6939	2932	6512	3921	5379	1560
君	子	以	獨	立	不	懼

dun4	shi4	wu2	men4
6586	5790	7173	4420
遯	世	无	悶

The lake covers the trees: The image of Great Excess.

Thus the noble remains alone without fear and can retreat from the world without regret.

First Six

jie4	yong4	bai2	mao2	wu2	jiu4
0767	7567	4975	4364	7173	1192
藉	用	白	茅	无	咎

Use a white mat of reeds offerings.

No defect.

Second Nine

ku1	yang2	sheng1	ti2	lao3	fu1	de2
3492	7261	5738	6252	3833	1908	6161
枯	楊	生	稊	老	夫	得

qi2	nu3	qi1	wu2	bu4	li4
0525	4776	0555	7173	5379	3867
其	女	妻	无	不	利

New shoots grow from a withered willow.
An old man gets a young wife.
Nothing that is not favorable.

Third Nine

dong4	nao2	xiong1
6607	3087	2808
棟	橈	凶

The main beam sags.
Misfortune.

Fourth Nine

dong4	long2	ji2
6607	4255	0476
棟	隆	吉

you3	tuo1	lin4
7533	6439	4040
有	它	吝

The main beam bulges upward.
Good fortune.
If there is something else, it will be regretful.

Fifth Nine

ku1	yang2	sheng1	hua2	lao3	fu4	de2
3492	7261	5738	2217	3833	1963	6161
枯	楊	生	華	老	婦	得

qi2	shi4	fu1	wu2	jiu4	wu2	yu4
0525	5776	1908	7173	1192	7173	7617
其	士	夫	无	咎	无	譽

A withered willow produces flowers.
An old woman gets a young husband.
Neither failure nor praise.

Top Six

guo4	she4	mie4	ding3	xiong1	wu2	jiu4
3730	5707	4483	6390	2808	7173	1192
過	涉	滅	頂	凶	无	咎

Excess when fording the river.
The water covers the top of the head.
Misfortune.
No defect.

29. Pit doubled / Pit within a pit

Judgment

xi2	kan3	you3	fu2	wei2	xin1	heng1
2499	3245	7533	1936	7067	2735	2099
習	坎	有	孚	維	心	亨

xing2	you3	shang4
2754	7533	5670
行	有	尚

The Pit doubled.

If you follow what you feel in your heart you will succeed.

Moving forward brings rewards.

Image

shui3	jian4	zhi4	xi2	kan3	jun1	zi3
5922	0880	0982	2499	3245	1715	6939
水	洊	至	習	坎	君	子

yi3	chang2	de2	xing2	xi2	jiao1	shi4
2932	0221	6162	2754	2499	0719	5787
以	常	德	行	習	教	事

The water flows to reach the goal: The image of the Pit doubled.

Thus the noble maintains constantly his virtuous conduct,

and practices the job of teaching.

First Six

xi2	kan3	ru4	yu2	kan3	dan4
2499	3245	3152	7592	3245	8002
習	坎	入	于	坎	窞

xiong1
2808
凶

The Pit doubled.

One falls into a pit at the bottom of the cave.

Misfortune.

Second Nine

kan3	you3	xian3	qiu2	xiao3	de2
3245	7533	2689	1217	2605	6161
坎	有	險	求	小	得

The Pit is dangerous.

Seek small gains.

Third Six

lai2	zhi1	kan3	kan3	xian3	qie3	zhen3
3768	0935	3245	3245	2689	0803	0308
來	之	坎	坎	險	且	枕

ru4	yu2	kan3	dan4	wu4	yong4
3152	7592	3245	8002	7208	7567
入	于	坎	窞	勿	用

Coming to the Pit.
Deep and dangerous Pit.
Enters a pit in the cave.
Do nothing.

Fourth Six

zun1	jiu3	gui3	er4	yong4	fou3
6886	1208	3633	1752	7567	1905
樽	酒	簋	貳	用	缶

na4	yue1	zi4	you3	zhong1	wu2	jiu4
4607	7493	6960	7507	1500	7173	1192
納	約	自	牖	終	无	咎

A jug of wine over a bowl of rice.
Using clay pots,
delivered jointly by the window.
At the end there will be no defect.

Fifth Nine

kan3	bu4	ying2	zhi1	ji4	ping2	wu2	jiu4
3245	5379	7474	0952	0453	5303	7173	1192
坎	不	盈	祇	既	平	无	咎

The Pit does not overflow.
Only is filled to the brim.
No defect.

Top Six

xi4	yong4	hui1	mo4	zhi4	yu2	cong2
2424	7567	2354	4387	0976	7592	6921
係	用	徽	纆	寘	于	叢

ji2	san1	sui4	bu4	de2	xiong1
0486	5415	5538	5379	6161	2808
棘	三	歲	不	得	凶

Tied with a braided rope and a black cord.
Abandoned in a thorny bush.
For three years you get nothing.
Misfortune.

30. The Clinging / Fire

Judgment

li2	li4	zhen1	heng1	chu4	pin4	niu2	ji2
3902	3867	0346	2099	1412	5280	4737	0476
離	利	貞	亨	畜	牝	牛	吉

The Clinging.
The determination is favorable.
Taming a cow brings good fortune.

Image

ming2	liang3	zuo4	li2	da4	ren2	yi3
4534	3953	6780	3902	5943	3097	2932
明	兩	作	離	大	人	以

ji4	ming2	zhao4	yu2	si4	fang1
0452	4534	0238	7592	5598	1802
繼	明	照	于	四	方

Brightness duplicated: The image of The Clinging.
Thus the great man maintains its clarity illuminating the four cardinal points.

First Nine

lu3	cuo4	ran2	jing4	zhi1	wu2	jiu4
3893	6793	3072	1138	0935	7173	1192
履	錯	然	敬	之	无	咎

Walking with hesitant and cautious steps.
If you are respectful there will be no defect.

Second Six

huang2	li2	yuan2	ji2
2297	3902	7707	0476
黃	離	元	吉

Yellow glow.
Outstanding good fortune.

Third Nine

ri4	ze4	zhi1	li2	bu4	gu3	fou3
3124	6755	0935	3902	5379	3479	1905
日	昃	之	離	不	鼓	缶

er2	ge1	ze2	da4	die2	zhi1
1756	3364	6746	5943	6314	0935
而	歌	則	大	耋	之

jie1   xiong1
0763   2808
嗟   凶

In the light of the setting sun,
if one docs not drum the pot and sing,
he will regret the approach of old age.
Misfortune.

Fourth Nine

tu1	ru2	qi2	lai2	ru2	fen2	ru2
6540	3137	0525	3768	3137	1866	3137
突	如	其	來	如	焚	如

si3	ru2	qi4	ru2
5589	3137	0550	3137
死	如	棄	如

Comes abruptly,
as with fire and death
and thus is discarded.

Fifth Six

chu1	ti4	tuo2	ruo4	qi1	jie1	ruo4	ji2
1409	6250	6442	3126	0575	0763	3126	0476
出	涕	沱	若	戚	嗟	若	吉

Torrents of tears
with sorrow and lamentations.
Good fortune.

Top Nine

wang2	yong4	chu1	zheng1	you3	jia1	zhe2
7037	7567	1409	0352	7533	0592	0267
王	用	出	征	有	嘉	折

shou3	huo4	fei3	qi2	chou3	wu2	jiu4
5839	2412	1820	0525	1327	7173	1192
首	獲	匪	其	醜	无	咎

The king sends him to attack.
It is worthwhile to execute the leaders
and capture those that are not
of the same evil sort.
No defect.

31. Influence / Reciprocity

Judgment

xian2	heng1	li4	zhen1	qu3	nu3	ji2
2666	2099	3867	0346	1615	4776	0476
咸	亨	利	貞	取	女	吉

Influence.
Success. The determination is favorable.
Taking a wife brings good fortune.

Image

shan1	shang4	you3	ze2	xian2
5630	5669	7533	0277	2666
山	上	有	澤	咸

jun1	zi3	yi3	xu1	shou4	ren2
1715	6939	2932	2821	5840	3097
君	子	以	虛	受	人

A lake on the mountain: The image of Influence.

Thus the noble is open-minded and welcoming for people.

First Six

xian2	qi2	mu3
2666	0525	4584
咸	其	拇

Influence in the big toe of the foot.

Second Six

xian2	qi2	fei2	xiong1	ju1	ji2
2666	0525	1830	2808	1535	0476
咸	其	腓	凶	居	吉

Influence in the calves.
Misfortune.
Keeping still brings good fortune.

Third Nine

xian2	qi2	gu3	zhi2	qi2	sui2	wang3	lin4
2666	0525	3467	0996	0525	5523	7050	4040
咸	其	股	執	其	隨	往	吝

Influence on the thighs.
He holds close to what he follows.
Going ahead causes humiliation.

Fourth Nine

zhen1	ji2	hui3	wang2	chong1	chong1	wang3
0346	0476	2336	7034	1529	1529	7050
貞	吉	悔	亡	憧	憧	往

lai2	peng2	cong2	er3	si1
3768	5054	6919	1754	5580
來	朋	從	爾	思

The determination brings good fortune.
Regret vanishes.
Restless and indecisive comes and goes,
his friends can follow his thoughts.

Fifth Nine

xian2	qi2	mei2	wu2	hui3
2666	0525	8004	7173	2336
咸	其	脢	无	悔

Influence in the back of the neck.
There is no repentance.

Top Six

xian2	qi2	fu3	jia2	she2
2666	0525	1945	0614	5705
咸	其	輔	頰	舌

Influence in the jaws, cheeks and tongue.

32. Duration / Constancy

Judgment

heng2	heng1	wu2	jiu4	li4	zhen1
2107	2099	7173	1192	3867	0346
恆	亨	无	咎	利	貞

li4	you3	you1	wang3
3867	7533	7519	7050
利	有	攸	往

Duration. Success.

No defect.

The determination is favorable.

It is favorable to have a place to go.

Image

lei2	feng1	heng2
4236	1890	2107
雷	風	恆

jun1	zi3	yi3	li4	bu4	yi4	fang1
1715	6939	2932	3921	5379	2952	1802
君	子	以	立	不	易	方

Thunder and wind: The image of the Duration.

Thus the noble stands up and does not change its course.

First Six

jun4	heng2	zhen1	xiong1	wu2	you1	li4
1729	2107	0346	2808	7173	7519	3867
浚	恆	貞	凶	无	攸	利

He goes too far.

The determination brings misfortune.

No target is favorable.

Second Nine

hui3	wang2
2336	7034
悔	亡

Regret disappears.

Third Nine

bu4	heng2	qi2	de2	huo4	cheng2	zhi1
5379	2107	0525	6162	2402	0386	0935
不	恆	其	德	或	承	之

xiu1	zhen1	lin4
2797	0346	4040
羞	貞	吝

His character is not constant.
He may have to bear the shame.
The determination is humiliating.

Fourth Nine

tian2	wu2	qin2
6362	7173	1100
田	无	禽

No animals in the hunt.

Fifth Six

heng2	qi2	de2	zhen1	fu4	ren2	ji2
2107	0525	6162	0346	1963	3097	0476
恆	其	德	貞	婦	人	吉

fu1	zi3	xiong1
1908	6939	2808
夫	子	凶

Perseverance in constancy is auspicious for a wife but wrong for a master.

Top Six

zhen4	heng2	xiong1
0313	2107	2808
振	恆	凶

Constantly agitated.
Misfortune.

33. Retreat

Judgment

dun4	heng1	xiao3	li4	zhen1
6586	2099	2605	3867	0346
遯	亨	小	利	貞

The Retreat.
Success.
Determination in small matters is favorable.

Image

tian1	xia4	you3	shan1	dun4	jun1	zi3
6361	2520	7533	5630	6586	1715	6939
天	下	有	山	遯	君	子

yi3	yuan3	xiao3	ren2	bu4	e4	er2	yan2
2932	7734	2605	3097	5379	4809	1756	7347
以	遠	小	人	不	惡	而	嚴

Mountain under heaven: The image of Retreat.
Thus the noble keeps the petty afar,
not with hatred but with reserve.

First Six

dun4	wei3	li4
6586	7109	3906
遯	尾	厲

wu4	yong4	you3	you1	wang3
7208	7567	7533	7519	7050
勿	用	有	攸	往

At the tail of the Retreat. Danger.
Do not try to undertake anything.

Second Six

zhi2	zhi1	yong4	huang2	niu2	zhi1	ge2
0996	0935	7567	2297	4737	0935	3314
執	之	用	黃	牛	之	革

mo4	zhi1	sheng4	tuo1
4557	0935	5754	5939
莫	之	勝	說

Clutching a yellow ox leather
no one can remove.

Third Nine

xi4	dun4	you3	ji2	li4
2424	6586	7533	0492	3906
係	遯	有	疾	厲

chu4	chen2	qie4	ji2
1412	0327	0814	0476
畜	臣	妾	吉

An entangled retreat is
stressing and dangerous.
It is favorable to take charge of servants and maids.

Fourth Nine

hao3	dun4	jun1	zi3	ji2	xiao3	ren2	pi3
2062	6586	1715	6939	0476	2605	3097	1902
好	遯	君	子	吉	小	人	否

Retreats from what he is fond of.
Good fortune for the noble,
decline for the vulgar.

Fifth Nine

jia1	dun4	zhen1	ji2
0592	6586	0346	0476
嘉	遯	貞	吉

Excellent retreat.
The determination is favorable.

Top Nine

fei2	dun4	wu2	bu4	li4
1839	6586	7173	5379	3867
肥	遯	无	不	利

Fruitful retreat.
Nothing that is not favorable.

34. Great Power

Judgment

da4	zhuang4	li4	zhen1
5943	1453	3867	0346
大	壯	利	貞

Great Power.
The determination is favorable.

Image

lei2	zai4	tian1	shang4	da4	zhuang4	
4236	6657	6361	5669	5943	1453	
雷	在	天	上	大	壯	

jun1	zi3	yi3	fei1	li3	fu2	lu3
1715	6939	2932	1819	3886	1981	3893
君	子	以	非	禮	弗	履

The thunder at the top of the sky: The image of Great Power.
Thus the noble does not tread any path
that deviates from the established order.

First Nine

zhuang4	yu2	zhi3	zheng1	xiong1	you3	fu2
1453	7592	0944	0352	2808	7533	1936
壯	于	趾	征	凶	有	孚

Power in the toes.
To push ahead brings misfortune.
Have confidence.

Second Nine

zhen1	ji2
0346	0476
貞	吉

The determination is favorable.

Third Nine

xiao3	ren2	yong4	zhuang4	jun1	zi3	yong4
2605	3097	7567	1453	1715	6939	7567
小	人	用	壯	君	子	用

wang3	zhen1	li4	di1	yang2	chu4	fan1
7045	0346	3906	6195	7247	1416	1800
罔	貞	厲	羝	羊	觸	藩

lei2	qi2	jiao3
4240	0525	1174
羸	其	角

A common man uses the power.
The noble does not act like that.
The determination is dangerous.
A ram butts the fence and his horns get stuck.

Fourth Nine

zhen1	ji2	hui3	wang2	fan1	jue2	bu4
0346	0476	2336	7034	1800	1697	5379
貞	吉	悔	亡	藩	決	不

lei2	zhuang4	yu2	da4	yu2	zhi1	fu4
4240	1453	7592	5943	7618	0935	1997
羸	壯	于	大	輿	之	輹

The determination is favorable.
Regret vanishes.
The fence is broken and will not entangle you anymore.
The power lies in the axle-brace of a great carriage.

Fifth Six

sang4	yang2	yu2	yi4	wu2	hui3
5429	7247	7592	2952	7173	2336
喪	羊	于	易	无	悔

Loses the goat at Yi.
There is no repentance.

Top Six

di1	yang2	chu4	fan1	bu4	neng2	tui4
6195	7247	1416	1800	5379	4648	6568
羝	羊	觸	藩	不	能	退

bu4	neng2	sui4	wu2	you1	li4	jian1
5379	4648	5530	7173	7519	3867	0834
不	能	遂	无	攸	利	艱

ze2	ji2
6746	0476
則	吉

The ram butts the fence.
Cannot retreat and cannot push through.
Nothing is favorable.
Fortitude under trying conditions.
Good fortune.

35. Progress / Advance

Judgment

jin4	kang1	hou2	yong4	xi1	ma3	fan2
1088	3278	2135	7567	2505	4310	1798
晉	康	侯	用	錫	馬	蕃

shu4	zhou4	ri4	san1	jie1
5874	1302	3124	5415	0800
庶	晝	日	三	接

Progress.
The Marquis of Kang is honored with numerous horses.
On the same day he is received three times.

Image

ming2	chu1	di4	shang4	jin4	jun1	zi3
4534	1409	6198	5669	1088	1715	6939
明	出	地	上	晉	君	子

yi3	zi4	zhao1	ming2	de2
2932	6960	0236	4534	6162
以	自	昭	明	德

The brightness of the sun rises over the earth: The image of Progress.
Thus the noble himself makes clear his talents.

First Six

jin4	ru2	cui1	ru2	zhen1	ji2
1088	3137	6866	3137	0346	0476
晉	如	摧	如	貞	吉

wang3	fu2	yu4	wu2	jiu4
7045	1936	7667	7173	1192
罔	孚	裕	无	咎

Progressing but repressed.
The determination is favorable.
Be tolerant of lack of confidence.
No defect.

Second Six

jin4	ru2	chou2	ru2	zhen1	ji2	shou4
1088	3137	1325	3137	0346	0476	5840
晉	如	愁	如	貞	吉	受

zi1	jie4	fu2	yu2	qi2	wang2	mu3
6935	0629	1978	7592	0525	7037	4582
茲	介	福	于	其	王	母

Progressing with grief.
The determination is favorable.
Receives a great blessing from her ancestor.

Third Six

zhong4	yun3	hui3	wang2
1517	7759	2336	7034
衆	允	悔	亡

All agree and trust.
Regret disappears.

Fourth Nine

jin4	ru2	shi2	shu3	zhen1	li4
1088	3137	5816	5871	0346	3906
晉	如	鼫	鼠	貞	厲

Progressing as a squirrel.
The determination is dangerous.

Fifth Six

hui3	wang2	shi1	de2	wu4	xu4
2336	7034	5806	6161	7208	2862
悔	亡	失	得	勿	恤

wang3	ji2	wu2	bu4	li4
7050	0476	7173	5379	3867
往	吉	无	不	利

Regret disappears.
Do not worry about loss or gain.
Going forward brings happiness.
Nothing that is not favorable.

Top Nine

jin4	qi2	jiao3	wei2	yong4	fa1	yi4
1088	0525	1174	7067	7567	1765	3037
晉	其	角	維	用	伐	邑

li4	ji2	wu2	jiu4	zhen1	lin4
3906	0476	7173	1192	0346	4040
厲	吉	无	咎	貞	吝

Progressing with the horns.
Use them only to punish your own city.
Danger, but there will be good fortune.
No defect.
The determination is humiliating.

36. Suppressed Light

Judgment

ming2	yi2	li4	jian1	zhen1
4534	2982	3867	0834	0346
明	夷	利	艱	貞

Suppressed Light.
Fortitude under trying conditions brings good fortune.

Image

ming2	ru4	di4	zhong1	ming2	yi2	jun1	zi3
4534	3152	6198	1504	4534	2982	1715	6939
明	入	地	中	明	夷	君	子

yi3	li4	zhong4	yong4	hui4	er2	ming2
2932	3912	1517	7567	2337	1756	4534
以	涖	衆	用	晦	而	明

Light has come into the earth: The image of the Suppressed Light.
Thus the noble deals with the masses,
concealing his talents, but still illuminating.

First Nine

ming2	yi2	yu2	fei1	chui2	qi2	yi4
4534	2982	7592	1850	1478	0525	3051
明	夷	于	飛	垂	其	翼

jun1	zi3	yu2	xing2	san1	ri4	bu4	shi2
1715	6939	7592	2754	5415	3124	5379	5810
君	子	于	行	三	日	不	食

you3	you1	wang3	zhu3	ren2	you3	yan2
7533	7519	7050	1336	3097	7533	7334
有	攸	往	主	人	有	言

Suppressed Light during flight.
He lowers his wings.
The noble goes along the road for three days without food,
but has somewhere to go.
The host gossips about him.

Second Six

ming2	yi2	yi2	yu2	zuo3	gu3
4534	2982	2982	7592	6774	3467
明	夷	夷	于	左	股

yong4	zheng3	ma3	zhuang4	ji2
7567	0360	4310	1453	0476
用	拯	馬	壯	吉

Suppressed Light.
Wounded in the left thigh. Rescued by a powerful horse.
Good fortune.

Third Nine

ming2	yi2	yu2	nan2	shou4	de2	qi2	da4
4534	2982	7592	4620	5845	6161	0525	5943
明	夷	于	南	狩	得	其	大

shou3	bu4	ke3	ji2	zhen1
5839	5379	3381	0492	0346
首	不	可	疾	貞

Suppressed Light during the hunt in the south.
The great leader is caught.
Cannot be hurriedly determined.

Fourth Six

ru4	yu2	zuo3	fu4	huo4	ming2	yi2
3152	7592	6774	1994	2412	4534	2982
入	于	左	腹	獲	明	夷

zhi1	xin1	yu2	chu1	men2	ting2
0935	2735	7592	1409	4418	6405
之	心	于	出	門	庭

Enters the left side of the belly.
Grasps the heart of the Suppressed Light.
Leaves the gate and courtyard.

Fifth Six

ji1	zi3	zhi1	ming2	yi2	li4	zhen1
0402	6939	0935	4534	2982	3867	0346
箕	子	之	明	夷	利	貞

Suppressed Light (as) Prince Ji.
The determination is favorable.

Top Six

bu4	ming2	hui4	chu1	deng1	yu2	tian1
5379	4534	2337	1390	6167	7592	6361
不	明	晦	初	登	于	天

hou4	ru4	yu2	di4
2143	3152	7592	6198
後	入	于	地

No light, but darkness.
First ascended to heaven.
Later sank into the earth.

37. The Family / The Clan

Judgment

jia1	ren2	li4	nu3	zhen1
0594	**3097**	3867	4776	0346
家	人	利	女	貞

The Family.
The determination is favorable for a woman.

Image

feng1	zi4	huo3	chu1	jia1	ren2	jun1	zi3
1890	6960	2395	1409	0594	3097	1715	6939
風	自	火	出	家	人	君	子

yi3	yan2	you3	wu4	er2	xing2	you3	heng2
2932	7334	7533	7209	1756	2754	7533	2107
以	言	有	物	而	行	有	恆

The wind comes from the fire: The image of The Family.
So the noble's words have substance
and his actions duration.

First Nine

xian2	you3	jia1	hui3	wang2
2679	7533	0594	2336	7034
閑	有	家	悔	亡

With firm boundaries in The Family
regret vanishes.

Second Six

wu2	you1	sui4	zai4	zhong1	kui4	zhen1	ji2
7173	7519	5530	6657	1504	3669	0346	0476
无	攸	遂	在	中	饋	貞	吉

Unpretentious.
Stays inside preparing food.
The determination is favorable.

Third Nine

jia1	ren2	he4	he4	hui3	li4	ji2
0594	3097	2134	2134	2336	3906	0476
家	人	嗃	嗃	悔	厲	吉

fu4	zi3	xi1	xi1	zhong1	lin4
1963	6939	2436	2436	1500	4040
婦	子	嘻	嘻	終	吝

A family run with stern severity will cause regrets,
but there will be good fortune.
Women and children chuckling and giggling
will end in shame.

Fourth Six

fu4	jia1	da4	ji2
1952	0594	5943	0476
富	家	大	吉

A thriving family.
Great good fortune.

Fifth Nine

wang2	jia3	you3	jia1	wu4	xu4	ji2
7037	0599	7533	0594	7208	2862	0476
王	假	有	家	勿	恤	吉

The king approaches his family.
Do not worry.
Good fortune.

Top Nine

you3	fu2	wei1	ru2	zhong1	ji2
7533	1936	7051	3137	1500	0476
有	孚	威	如	終	吉

He inspires confidence and awe.
At the end there will be good fortune.

38. Antagonism / Opposition

Judgment

kui2	xiao3	shi4	ji2
3660	2605	5787	0476
睽	小	事	吉

Antagonism.
Good fortune in small matters.

Image

shang4	huo3	xia4	ze2	kui2	
5669	2395	2520	0277	3660	
上	火	下	澤	睽	

jun1	zi3	yi3	tong2	er2	yi4
1715	6939	2932	6615	1756	3009
君	子	以	同	而	異

Fire is above, lake below: The image of Antagonism.
Thus the noble is companionable, but maintains its uniqueness.

First Nine

hui3	wang2	sang4	ma3	wu4	zhu2	zi4
2336	7034	5429	4310	7208	1383	6960
悔	亡	喪	馬	勿	逐	自

fu4	jian4	e4	ren2	wu2	jiu4	
1992	0860	4809	3097	7173	1192	
復	見	惡	人	无	咎	

Repentance fades.
Do not chase the horse that got away. It will return on its own.
You will find bad people, but you will not make mistakes.

Second Nine

yu4	zhu3	yu2	xiang4	wu2	jiu4
7625	1336	7592	2553	7173	1192
遇	主	于	巷	无	咎

He meets his master in an alley.
No defect.

Third Six

jian4	yu2	yi4	qi2	niu2	che4	qi2
0860	7618	3008	0525	4737	0282	0525
見	輿	曳	其	牛	掣	其

ren2	tian1	qie3	yi4	wu2	chu1	you3	zhong1
3097	6361	0803	3013	7173	1390	7533	1500
人	天	且	劓	无	初	有	終

He sees his cart pulled back.

His oxen and his men arrested, marked and mutilated.

There is no (a good) start but (a good) end.

Fourth Nine

kui2	gu1	yu4	yuan2	fu1	jiao1	fu2	li4	wu2	jiu4
3660	3470	7625	7707	1908	0702	1936	3906	7173	1192
睽	孤	遇	元	夫	交	孚	厲	无	咎

Isolated by antagonism.

One meets an outstanding man (that can become a) truthful partner.

Danger. No defect.

Fifth Six

hui3	wang2	jue2	zong1	shi4	fu1	wang3	he2	jiu4
2336	70 34	1680	6896	5764	1958	7050	2109	1192
悔	亡	厥	宗	噬	膚	往	何	咎

Repentance fades.

In the temple of the clan they eat meat.

How could it be a mistake to go there?

Top Nine

kui2	gu1	jian4	shi3	fu4	tu2	zai4
3660	3470	0860	5766	1956	6525	6653
睽	孤	見	豕	負	塗	載

gui3	yi1	che1	xian1	zhang1	zhi1	hu2
3634	3016	0280	2702	0195	0935	2184
鬼	一	車	先	張	之	弧

hou4	tuo1	zhi1	hu2	fei3	kou4	hun1
2143	5939	0935	2184	1820	3444	2360
後	說	之	弧	匪	寇	婚

gou4	wang3	yu4	yu3	ze2	ji2
3426	7050	7625	7662	6746	0476
媾	往	遇	雨	則	吉

Isolated by antagonism.

He sees (the other as) a pig covered with mud, a carriage full of demons.

First tenses his bow, but then puts it aside.

It is not a robber but a marriage suitor.

Going forward rain falls.

Good fortune.

39. Hampered / Obstruction

≡≡ (hexagram)

Judgment

jian3	li4	xi1	nan2	bu4	li4	dong1
0843	3867	2460	4620	5379	3867	6605
蹇	利	西	南	不	利	東

bei3	li4	jian4	da4	ren2	zhen1	ji2
4974	3867	0860	5943	3097	0346	0476
北	利	見	大	人	貞	吉

Hampered.
The south-west is favorable;
the north-east is not advantageous.
It is favorable to see the great man.
Determination brings good fortune.

Image

shan1	shang4	you3	shui3	jian3
5630	5669	7533	5922	0843
山	上	有	水	蹇

jun1	zi3	yi3	fan3	shen1	xiu1	de2
1715	6939	2932	1781	5718	2795	6162
君	子	以	反	身	脩	德

Above the mountain there is water: The image of Hampered.
Thus the noble goes back to himself to cultivate his nature.

First Six

wang3	jian3	lai2	yu4
7050	0843	3768	7617
往	蹇	來	譽

Going forward is Hampered, going back brings praise.

Second Six

wang2	chen2	jian3	jian3	fei3	gong1	zhi1	gu4
7037	0327	0843	0843	1820	3704	0935	3455
王	臣	蹇	蹇	匪	躬	之	故

The king's servant (is struggling with) difficulties.
Not because of himself.

Third Nine

wang3	jian3	lai2	fan3
7050	0843	3768	1781
往	蹇	來	反

Going forward is Hampered.
He comes back.

Fourth Six

wang3	jian3	lai2	lian2
7050	0843	3768	4009
往	蹇	來	連

Going forward is Hampered.
Coming back meets companions.

Fifth Nine

da4	jian3	peng2	lai2
5943	0843	5054	3768
大	蹇	朋	來

When the Obstruction is greater, friends will come over.

Top Six

wang3	jian3	lai2	shuo4	ji2
7050	0843	3768	5815	0476
往	蹇	來	碩	吉

li4	jian4	da4	ren2
3867	0860	5943	3097
利	見	大	人

Going forward is Hampered,
coming back brings great good fortune.
It is favorable to see the great man.

40. Liberation

Judgment

jie3 0626 解	li4 3867 利	xi1 2460 西	nan2 4620 南	wu2 7173 无	suo3 5465 所	wang3 7050 往
qi2 0525 其	lai2 3768 來	fu4 1992 復	ji2 0476 吉	you3 7533 有	you1 7519 攸	wang3 7050 往
su4 5502 夙	ji2 0476 吉					

Liberation.

The south-west is favorable.

If there is nowhere to go return brings good fortune.

If there is somewhere to go, to be early brings good fortune.

Image

lei2 4236 雷	yu3 7662 雨	zuo4 6780 作	jie3 0626 解			
jun1 1715 君	zi3 6939 子	yi3 2932 以	she4 5702 赦	guo4 3730 過	you4 7536 宥	zui4 6860 罪

Thunder and rain in action: The image of Liberation.

Thus the noble forgives excesses and excuses offenses.

First Six

wu2 7173 无	jiu4 1192 咎

No defect.

Second Nine

tian2 6362 田	huo4 2412 獲	san1 5415 三	hu2 2185 狐	de2 6161 得	huang2 2297 黃	shi3 5784 矢
zhen1 0346 貞	ji2 0476 吉					

One catches three foxes in the hunt
and gets a yellow arrow.
Determination brings good fortune.

Third Six

fu4	qie3	cheng2	zhi4	kou4	zhi4	zhen1	lin4
1956	0803	0398	0984	3444	0982	0346	4040
負	且	乘	致	寇	至	貞	吝

One who bears a burden on his back but rides on a carriage
attracts bandits.
The determination is humiliating.

Fourth Nine

jie3	er2	mu3	peng2	zhi4	si1	fu2
0626	1756	4584	5054	0982	5574	1936
解	而	拇	朋	至	斯	孚

Deliver yourself from your big toe.
Then a trusty companion will come.

Fifth Six

jun1	zi3	wei2	you3	jie3	ji2
1715	6939	7067	7533	0626	0476
君	子	維	有	解	吉

you3	fu2	yu2	xiao3	ren2
7533	1936	7592	2605	3097
有	孚	于	小	人

Only the noble can have liberation.
Good fortune.
Inferior people trust him.

Top Six

gong1	yong4	she4	sun3	yu2	gao1	yong1
3701	7567	5703	1487	7592	3290	7578
公	用	射	隼	于	高	墉

zhi1	shang4	huo4	zhi1	wu2	bu4	li4
0935	5669	2412	0935	7173	5379	3867
之	上	獲	之	无	不	利

The prince shoots at a hawk on a high wall
and hits the target.
Nothing that is not favorable.

41. Decrease

Judgment

sun3	you3	fu2	yuan2	ji2	wu2	jiu4
5548	7533	1936	7707	0476	7173	1192
損	有	孚	元	吉	无	咎
ke3	zhen1	li4	you3	you1	wang3	he2
3381	0346	3867	7533	7519	7050	2122
可	貞	利	有	攸	往	曷
zhi1	yong4	er4	gui3	ke3	yong4	xiang3
0935	7567	1751	3633	3381	7567	2552
之	用	二	簋	可	用	享

Decrease with sincerity brings outstanding good fortune.
No defect.
Can be determined.
It is favorable to have somewhere to go.
What should be done?
Two bowls can be used for the offering

Image

shan1	xia4	you3	ze2	sun3		
5630	2520	7533	0277	5548		
山	下	有	澤	損		
jun1	zi3	yi3	cheng2	fen4	zhi4	yu4
1715	6939	2932	0384	1854	0994	7671
君	子	以	懲	忿	窒	欲

Down the mountain is the lake: The image of the Decrease.
Thus the noble controls his anger and restrains his passions.

First Nine

si4	shi4	chuan2	wang3	wu2	jiu4	zhuo2	sun3	zhi1
5590	5787	1444	7050	7173	1192	1257	5548	0935
巳	事	遄	往	无	咎	酌	損	之

There is no defect if after finishing your work you go quickly,
but think about how much you can sacrifice.

Second Nine

li4	zhen1	zheng1	xiong1	fu2	sun3	yi4	zhi1
3867	0346	0352	2808	1981	5548	3052	0935
利	貞	征	凶	弗	損	益	之

The determination is favorable.
Going forward with violence brings misfortune.
Without loss one may increase.

Third Six

san1	ren2	xing2	ze2	sun3	yi1	ren2
5415	3097	2754	6746	5548	3016	3097
三	人	行	則	損	一	人

yi1	ren2	xing2	ze2	de2	qi2	you3
3016	3097	2754	6746	6161	0525	7540
一	人	行	則	得	其	友

Three men walking along the road together are decreased,
but one man walking gains a companion.

Fourth Six

sun3	qi2	ji2	shi3	chuan2	you3	xi3
5548	0525	0492	5770	1444	7533	2434
損	其	疾	使	遄	有	喜

wu2	jiu4
7173	1192
无	咎

As a result of reducing his anxiety, he will have joy quickly.
No defect.

Fifth Six

huo4	yi4	zhi1	shi2	peng2	zhi1	gui1
2402	3052	0935	5807	5054	0935	3621
或	益	之	十	朋	之	龜

fu2	ke4	wei2	yuan2	ji2
1981	3320	7093	7707	0476
弗	克	違	元	吉

Someone increases him by ten pairs of tortoise shells.
Nobody can resist.
Outstanding happiness.

Top Nine

fu2	sun3	yi4	zhi1	wu2	jiu4	zhen1	ji2
1981	5548	3052	0935	7173	1192	0346	0476
弗	損	益	之	无	咎	貞	吉

li4	you3	you1	wang3	de2	chen2	wu2	jia1
3867	7533	7519	7050	6161	0327	7173	0594
利	有	攸	往	得	臣	无	家

There is no Decrease but increase.
No defect.
The determination brings good fortune.
It is favorable to have where to go.
One gets servants but not a household.

42. Increase

Judgment

yi4	li4	you3	you1	wang3	li4	she4	da4	chuan1
3052	3867	7533	7519	7050	3867	5707	5943	1439
益	利	有	攸	往	利	涉	大	川

Increase.
It is favorable to have where to go.
It is favorable to cross the great river.

Image

feng1	lei2	yi4	jun1	zi3	yi3	jian4
1890	4236	3052	1715	6939	2932	0860
風	雷	益	君	子	以	見

shan4	ze2	qian1	you3	guo4	ze2	gai3
5657	6746	0911	7533	3730	6746	3196
善	則	遷	有	過	則	改

Wind and thunder: The image of Increase.
Thus the noble moves toward the good when he sees it;
and corrects any excesses.

First Nine

li4	yong4	wei2	da4	zuo4	yuan2	ji2	wu2	jiu4
3867	7567	7059	5943	6780	7707	0476	7173	1192
利	用	爲	大	作	元	吉	无	咎

It is favorable to begin great endeavors.
Outstanding good fortune. No defect.

Second Six

huo4	yi4	zhi1	shi2	peng2	zhi1	gui1
2402	3052	0935	5807	5054	0935	3621
或	益	之	十	朋	之	龜

fu2	ke4	wei2	yong3	zhen1	ji2
1981	3320	7093	7589	0346	0476
弗	克	違	永	貞	吉

wang2	yong4	xiang3	yu2	di4	ji2
7037	7567	2552	7592	6204	0476
王	用	享	于	帝	吉

Someone increases him by ten pairs of tortoise shells.
Nobody can resist.
Long-term determination brings good fortune.
Used by the king in an offering to the Divine Ruler. Good fortune.

Third Six

yi4	zhi1	yong4	xiong1	shi4	wu2	jiu4
3052	0935	7567	2808	5787	7173	1192
益	之	用	凶	事	无	咎

you3	fu2	zhong1	xing2	gao4	gong1	yong4	gui1
7533	1936	1504	2754	3287	3701	7567	3609
有	孚	中	行	告	公	用	圭

Increased by unfortunate events.

If your service is sincere there is no defect.

Walk in the middle and report to the prince with a jade baton.

Fourth Six

zhong1	xing2	gao4	gong1	cong2
1504	2754	3287	3701	6919
中	行	告	公	從

li4	yong4	wei2	yi1	qian1	guo2
3867	7567	7059	2990	0911	3738
利	用	爲	依	遷	國

If you walk in the middle and report to the prince, he will follow.

It is favorable to be assigned to relocate the capital.

Fifth Nine

you3	fu2	hui4	xin1	wu4	wen4	yuan2	ji2
7533	1936	2339	2735	7208	7141	7707	0476
有	孚	惠	心	勿	問	元	吉

you3	fu2	hui4	wo3	de2
7533	1936	2339	4778	6162
有	孚	惠	我	德

If you have a sincere and kind heart you do not need to ask.

Outstanding good fortune.

One has sincerity and is favored with spiritual power.

Top Nine

mo4	yi4	zhi1	huo4	ji1	zhi1
4557	3052	0935	2402	0481	0935
莫	益	之	或	擊	之

li4	xin1	wu4	heng2	xiong1
3921	2735	7208	2107	2808
立	心	勿	恆	凶

He increases no one.

Perhaps somebody will attack him.

Doesn't keep his heart constant. Misfortune.

43. Breakthrough / Resoluteness / Parting

≡≡

Judgment

guai4	yang2	yu2	wang2	ting2	fu2
3535	7259	7592	7037	6405	1936
夬	揚	于	王	庭	孚

hao4	you3	li4	gao4	zi4	yi4	bu4
2064	7533	3906	3287	6960	3037	5379
號	有	厲	告	自	邑	不

li4	ji2	rong2	li4	you3	you1	wang3
3867	0495	3181	3867	7533	7519	7050
利	卽	戎	利	有	攸	往

Breakthrough.
Proclaim the matter truthfully in the king's court.
Danger.
Report to your own city.
It is not favorable to resort to weapons.
It is favorable to have where to go.

Image

ze2	shang4	yu2	tian1	guai4	jun1	zi3	yi3	shi1
0277	5669	7643	6361	3535	1715	6939	2932	5768
澤	上	於	天	夬	君	子	以	施

lu4	ji2	xia4	ju1	de2	ze2	ji4
4196	0468	2520	1535	6162	6746	0432
祿	及	下	居	德	則	忌

The lake rises above the heaven: The image of the Breakthrough.
Thus the noble distributes benefits downward,
while avoiding presumption of virtue.

First Nine

zhuang4	yu2	qian2	zhi3	wang3	bu4	sheng4	wei2	jiu4
1453	7592	0919	0944	7050	5379	5754	7059	1192
壯	于	前	趾	往	不	勝	爲	咎

Powerful in the toes.
He goes forward but cannot triumph, and makes a mistake.

Second Nine

ti4	hao4	mo4	ye4	you3	rong2	wu4	xu4
6263	2064	4557	7315	7533	3181	7208	2862
惕	號	莫	夜	有	戎	勿	恤

Cries of alarm at evening and night.
If you are armed there is nothing to fear.

Third Nine

zhuang4	yu2	qiu2	you3	xiong1	jun1	zi3
1453	7592	8007	7533	2808	1715	6939
壯	于	頄	有	凶	君	子

guai4	guai4	du2	xing2	yu4	yu3	ruo4
3535	3535	6512	2754	7625	7662	3126
夬	夬	獨	行	遇	雨	若

u2	you3	yun4	wu2	jiu4
3149	7533	7766	7173	1192
濡	有	慍	无	咎

To be powerful in the cheeks
brings misfortune.
The noble is perfectly resolved.
Walks alone in the rain,
wet and grieved.
No defect.

Fourth Nine

tun2	wu2	fu1	qi2	xing2	ci4	qie3
6602	7173	1958	0525	2754	6980	0803
臀	无	膚	其	行	次	且

qian1	yang2	hui3	wang2	wen2	yan2	bu4	xin4
0881	7247	2336	7034	7142	7334	5379	2748
牽	羊	悔	亡	聞	言	不	信

There is no flesh on his buttocks.
Walks haltingly and leading a sheep.
Regret disappears.
Hearing complaints, not to be believed.

Fifth Nine

xian4	lu4	guai4	guai4	zhong1	xing2	wu2	jiu4
2686	4191	3535	3535	1504	2754	7173	1192
莧	陸	夬	夬	中	行	无	咎

A goat mountain breaks through and goes along the middle of the road.
No defect.

Top Six

wu2	hao4	zhong1	you3	xiong1
7173	2064	1500	7533	2808
无	號	終	有	凶

There is no cry.
At the end there will be misfortune.

44. Close Encounter / Meeting

☰
☴

Judgment

gou4	nu3	zhuang4	wu4	yong4	qu3	nu3
3422	4776	1453	7208	7567	1615	4776
姤	女	壯	勿	用	取	女

Close encounter.
The woman is powerful.
Do not take her as wife.

Image

tian1	xia4	you3	feng1	gou4
6361	2520	7533	1890	3422
天	下	有	風	姤

hou4	yi3	shi1	ming4	gao4	si4	fang1
2144	2932	5768	4537	3288	5598	1802
后	以	施	命	誥	四	方

Under the sky is the wind: The image of Close Encounter.
Thus the sovereign dispenses his orders to the four corners of the world.

First Six

xi4	yu2	jin1	ni3	zhen1	ji2	you3
2458	7592	1057	4659	0346	0476	7533
繫	于	金	梔	貞	吉	有

you1	wang3	jian4	xiong1
7519	7050	0860	2808
攸	往	見	凶

lei2	shi3	fu2	zhi2	zhu2
4240	5766	1936	8000	1388
羸	豕	孚	蹢	躅

Tie it to a metal brake.
The determination brings good fortune.
Has where to go but sees pitfalls.
When one relies on a skinny pig it will falter.

Second Nine

bao1	you3	yu2	wu2	jiu4	bu4	li4	bin1
4937	7533	7668	7173	1192	5379	3867	5259
包	有	魚	无	咎	不	利	賓

There is a fish in the wrapping
No defect.
Not fitting for guests.

Third Nine

tun2	wu2	fu1	qi2	xing2	ci4	qie3
6602	7173	1958	0525	2754	6980	0803
臀	无	膚	其	行	次	且

li4	wu2	da4	jiu4
3906	7173	5943	1192
厲	无	大	咎

There is no flesh on his buttocks
and and he walks unsteadily.
Danger.
There will be no great defect.

Fourth Nine

bao1	wu2	yu2	qi3	xiong1
4937	7173	7668	0548	2808
包	无	魚	起	凶

There are no fish in the wrapping.
This causes misfortune.

Fifth Nine

yi3	qi3	bao1	gua1	han2	zhang1
2932	0547	4937	3504	2017	0182
以	杞	包	瓜	含	章

you3	yun3	zi4	tian1
7533	7756	6960	6361
有	隕	自	天

A melon wrapped in willow leaves.
Hidden brilliance.
It falls from Heaven.

Top Nine

gou4	qi2	jiao3	lin4	wu2	jiu4
3422	0525	1174	4040	7173	1192
姤	其	角	吝	无	咎

Close encounter with his horns.
Humiliation.
No defect.

45. Gathering together

Judgment

cui4	heng1	wang2	jia3	you3	miao4	li4
6880	2099	7037	0599	7533	4473	3867
萃	亨	王	假	有	廟	利
jian4	da4	ren2	heng1	li4	zhen1	yong4
0860	5943	3097	2099	3867	0346	7567
見	大	人	亨	利	貞	用
da4	sheng1	ji2	li4	you3	you1	wang3
5943	5739	0476	3867	7533	7519	7050
大	牲	吉	利	有	攸	往

Gathering together. Success.
The king approaches his temple.
It is favorable to see the great man. Success.
The determination is favorable. Offering great sacrifices brings good fortune.
It is favorable to have where to go.

Image

ze2	shang4	yu2	di4	cui4	jun1	zi3
0277	5669	7643	6198	6880	1715	6939
澤	上	於	地	萃	君	子
yi3	chu2	rong2	qi4	jie4	bu4	yu2
2932	1391	3181	0549	0627	5379	7648
以	除	戎	器	戒	不	虞

The lake rises above earth: The image of Gathering together.
Thus the noble gets his weapons in order,
to be on guard against the unexpected.

First Six

you3	fu2	bu4	zhong1	nai3	luan4	nai3
7533	1936	5379	1500	4612	4220	4612
有	孚	不	終	乃	亂	乃
cui4	ruo4	hao4	yi1	wo4	wei2	xiao4
6880	3126	2064	3016	7161	7059	2615
萃	若	號	一	握	爲	笑
wu4	xu4	wang3	wu2	jiu4		
7208	2862	7050	7173	1192		
勿	恤	往	无	咎		

One has confidence but not to the end, hence there will be confusion.
Gathering together. One calls out, after one handclasp he will laugh.
Do not worry. Going has no defect.

Second Six

yin3	ji2	wu2	jiu4
7429	0476	7173	1192
引	吉	无	咎

fu2	nai3	li4	yong4	yue4
1936	4612	3867	7567	7498
孚	乃	利	用	禴

Drawn out. Good fortune.

No defect.

If he is sincere it is favorable to make a small offering.

Third Six

cui4	ru2	jie1	ru2	wu2	you1	li4
6880	3137	0763	3137	7173	7519	3867
萃	如	嗟	如	无	攸	利

wang3	wu2	jiu4	xiao3	lin4
7050	7173	1192	2605	4040
往	无	咎	小	吝

Gathering together between moans. Nothing is favorable.

Going is without defect. Small humiliation.

Fourth Nine

da4	ji2	wu2	jiu4
5943	0476	7173	1192
大	吉	无	咎

Great good fortune. No defect.

Fifth Nine

cui4	you3	wei4	wu2	jiu4	fei3	fu2
6880	7533	7116	7173	1192	1820	1936
萃	有	位	无	咎	匪	孚

yuan2	yong3	zhen1	hui3	wang2
7707	7589	0346	2336	7034
元	永	貞	悔	亡

Gathering together has a good position. No defect. There is no trust.

Having outstanding long term determination regret disappears.

Top Six

ji1	zi1	ti4	yi2	wu2	jiu4
0464	6923	6250	2986	7173	1192
齎	咨	涕	洟	无	咎

Sighing and moaning, copious tears. No defect.

46. Ascending

Judgment

sheng1	yuan2	heng1	yong4	jian4	da4	ren2
5745	7707	2099	7567	0860	5943	3097
升	元	亨	用	見	大	人

wu4	xu4	nan2	zheng1	ji2
7208	2862	4620	0352	0476
勿	恤	南	征	吉

Ascending has outstanding success.
It is useful to see the great man.
Do not worry.
Marching forth toward the south brings good fortune.

Image

di4	zhong1	sheng1	mu4	sheng1	jun1	zi3	
6198	1504	5738	4593	5745	1715	6939	
地	中	生	木	升	君	子	

yi3	shun4	de2	ji1	xiao3	yi3	gao1	da4
2932	5935	6162	0500	2605	2932	3290	5943
以	順	德	積	小	以	高	大

In the middle of the earth grows wood: The image of Ascending.
Thus the noble, with yielding character,
accumulates the small to achieve the great.

First Six

yun3	sheng1	da4	ji2
7759	5745	5943	0476
允	升	大	吉

Trusted and ascending.
Great good fortune.

Second Nine

fu2	nai3	li4	yong4	yue4	wu2	jiu4
1936	4612	3867	7567	7498	7173	1192
孚	乃	利	用	禴	无	咎

If one is sincere it is favorable to present a small offering.
No defect.

Third Nine

sheng1	xu1	yi4
5745	2821	3037
升	虛	邑

One ascends into an empty city.

Fourth Six

wang2	yong4	heng1	yu2	qi2	shan1	ji2
7037	7567	2099	7592	0522	5630	0476
王	用	亨	于	岐	山	吉

wu2	jiu4
7173	1192
无	咎

The King presents an offering on Mount Qi.
Good fortune.
No defect.

Fifth Six

zhen1	ji2	sheng1	jie1
0346	0476	5745	0625
貞	吉	升	階

The determination brings good fortune.
One ascends on stairs.

Top Six

ming2	sheng1
4528	5745
冥	升

li4	yu2	bu4	xi1	zhi1	zhen1
3867	7592	5379	2495	0935	0346
利	于	不	息	之	貞

Ascending in the dark.
It is favorable an untiring determination.

47. Oppression / Besieged / Impasse

▤

Judgment

kun4	heng1	zhen1	da4	ren2	ji2
3688	2099	0346	5943	3097	0476
困	亨	貞	大	人	吉

wu2	jiu4	you3	yan2	bu4	xin4
7173	1192	7533	7334	5379	2748
无	咎	有	言	不	信

Oppression. Success.

The determination brings good fortune to the great man.

No defect. Talk is not to be trusted.

Image

ze2	wu2	shui3	kun4
0277	7173	5922	3688
澤	无	水	困

jun1	zi3	yi3	zhi4	ming4	sui4	zhi4
1715	6939	2932	0984	4537	5530	0971
君	子	以	致	命	遂	志

The lake has no water: The image of Oppression.

Thus the noble will sacrifice his own life to achieve his objective.

First Six

tun2	kun4	yu2	zhu1	mu4	ru4	yu2
6602	3688	7592	1348	4593	3152	7592
臀	困	于	株	木	入	于

you1	gu3	san1	sui4	bu4	di2
7505	3483	5415	5538	5379	6230
幽	谷	三	歲	不	覿

Buttocks oppressed by a tree stump.

Enters a dark valley and is not seen for three years.

Second Nine

kun4	yu2	jiu3	shi2	zhu1	fu2	fang1	lai2
3688	7592	1208	5810	1346	1971	1802	3768
困	于	酒	食	朱	紱	方	來

li4	yong4	xiang3	si4	zheng1	xiong1	wu2	jiu4
3867	7567	2552	5592	0352	2808	7173	1192
利	用	享	祀	征	凶	无	咎

Oppressed between wine and food.

Scarlet knee bands arrive from all sides.

Offering a sacrifice is favorable.

Marching forth will bring misfortune. No defect.

Third Six

kun4	yu2	shi2	ju4	yu2	ji2	li2	ru4
3688	7592	5813	1563	7592	0494	3877	3152
困	于	石	據	于	蒺	藜	入

yu2	qi2	gong1	bu4	jian4	qi2	qi1	xiong1
7592	0525	3705	5379	0860	0525	0555	2808
于	其	宮	不	見	其	妻	凶

Oppressed by stones. Leans on thorny bushes and thistles.

Enters his house but does not see his wife. Misfortune.

Fourth Nine

lai2	xu2	xu2	kun4	yu2	jin1	che1	lin4	you3	zhong1
3768	2841	2841	3688	7592	1057	0280	4040	7533	1500
來	徐	徐	困	于	金	車	吝	有	終

He comes very slowly, oppressed in a metal carriage.

Humiliation, but it will be carried to conclusion.

Fifth Nine

yi4	yue4	kun4	yu2	chi4	fu2	nai3
3013	7697	3688	7592	1048	1971	4612
劓	刖	困	于	赤	紱	乃

xu2	you3	shuo1	li4	yong4	ji4	si4
2841	7533	5939	3867	7567	0465	5592
徐	有	說	利	用	祭	祀

His nose and feet are severed.

Oppressed by scarlet knee bands.

The joy comes slowly. It is favorable to present offerings and libations.

Top Six

kun4	yu2	ge2	lei3	yu2	nie4	wu4
3688	7592	3377	4235	7592	4700	7211
困	于	葛	藟	于	臲	卼

yue1	dong4	hui3	you3	hui3	zheng1	ji2
7694	6611	2336	7533	2336	0352	0476
曰	動	悔	有	悔	征	吉

Oppressed by climbing plants. He is anxious and insecure.

He says to himself that movement will bring regret.

With repentance, marching forth brings good fortune.

48. The Well

Judgment

jing3	gai3	yi4	bu4	gai3	jing3	wu2
1143	3196	3037	5379	3196	1143	7173
井	改	邑	不	改	井	无

sang4	wu2	de2	wang3	lai2	jing3	jing3
5429	7173	6161	7050	3768	1143	1143
喪	无	得	往	來	井	井

qi4	zhi4	yi4	wei4	yu4	jing3
8006	0982	3021	7114	8009	1143
汔	至	亦	未	繘	井

lei2	qi2	ping2	xiong1
4240	0525	5301	2808
羸	其	瓶	凶

The Well.
Changing the town, not changing the well. No loss, no gain.
Going to take water from the well nearly dry.
If the rope does not reach the water or the jar breaks,
misfortune.

Image

mu4	shang4	you3	shui3	jing3
4593	5669	7533	5922	1143
木	上	有	水	井

jun1	zi3	yi3	lao2	min2	quan4	xiang1
1715	6939	2932	3826	4508	1662	2562
君	子	以	勞	民	勸	相

Wood above the water: The image of the Well.
Thus the noble encourages people at their work to cooperate among themselves.

First Six

jing3	ni2	bu4	shi2	jiu4	jing3	wu2	qin2
1143	4660	5379	5810	1205	1143	7173	1100
井	泥	不	食	舊	井	无	禽

One does not drink from a muddy well
There are no animals (birds) in an old well.

Second Nine

jing3	gu3	she4	fu4	weng4	bi4	lou4
1143	3483	5703	1927	7151	5101	4152
井	谷	射	鮒	甕	敝	漏

Shooting fishes in the well.
The jar is broken and leaks.

Third Nine

jing3	xie4	bu4	shi2	wei2	wo3	xin1
1143	6318	5379	5810	7059	4778	2735
井	渫	不	食	爲	我	心

ce4	ke3	yong4	ji2	wang2	ming2
6758	3381	7567	0472	7037	4534
惻	可	用	汲	王	明

bing4	shou4	qi2	fu2
5292	5840	0525	1978
並	受	其	福

The well is cleaned
but its water is not drunk.
Our hearts grieve,
because the water might be drawn out and used.
If the king were clear-minded
all would receive the blessings.

Fourth Six

jing3	zhou4	wu2	jiu4
1143	1305	7173	1192
井	甃	无	咎

The well is lined.
No defect.

Fifth Nine

jing3	lie4	han2	quan2	shi2
1143	3987	2048	1674	5810
井	冽	寒	泉	食

The well has clear, cold
spring water for drinking.

Top Six

jing3	shou1	wu4	mu4	you3	fu2	yuan2	ji2
1143	5837	7208	4559	7533	1936	7707	0476
井	收	勿	幕	有	孚	元	吉

Taking water from the well
Not covering.
It inspires confidence.
Outstanding good fortune.

49. Revolution / Getting rid of

Judgment

ge2	si4	ri4	nai3	fu2	yuan2	heng1
3314	5590	3124	4612	1936	7707	2099
革	巳	日	乃	孚	元	亨

li4	zhen1	hui3	wang2
3867	0346	2336	7034
利	貞	悔	亡

The Revolution is trusted after it has been accomplished.
Outstanding good fortune.
The determination is favorable.
Repentance fades.

Image

ze2	zhong1	you3	huo3	ge2
0277	1504	7533	2395	3314
澤	中	有	火	革

jun1	zi3	yi3	zhi4	li4	ming2	shi2
1715	6939	2932	1021	3931	4534	5780
君	子	以	治	歷	明	時

Within the lake is fire: The image of the Revolution.
Thus the noble regulates the calendar and makes clear the seasons.

First Nine

gong3	yong4	huang2	niu2	zhi1	ge2
3718	7567	2297	4737	0935	3314
鞏	用	黃	牛	之	革

The Revolution is tied with a yellow cow hide.

Second Six

si4	ri4	nai3	ge2	zhi1
5590	3124	4612	3314	0935
巳	日	乃	革	之

zheng1	ji2	wu2	jiu4
0352	0476	7173	1192
征	吉	无	咎

Revolution after the end of the day.
It is favorable to attack.
No defect.

Third Nine

zheng1	xiong1	zhen1	li4	ge2	yan2	san1
0352	2808	0346	3906	3314	7334	5415
征	凶	貞	厲	革	言	三

jiu4	you3	fu2
1210	7533	1936
就	有	孚

Attacking brings misfortune.
The determination is dangerous.
Only after you have spoken about three times
the revolution will be trusted.

Fourth Nine

hui3	wang2	you3	fu2	gai3	ming4	ji2
2336	7034	7533	1936	3196	4537	0476
悔	亡	有	孚	改	命	吉

Repentance fades.
There is confidence.
Reforming the form of government brings good fortune.

Fifth Nine

da4	ren2	hu3	bian4	wei4	zhan1	you3	fu2
5943	3097	2161	5245	7114	0125	7533	1936
大	人	虎	變	未	占	有	孚

The great man changes like a tiger.
Even before asking the oracle he has confidence.

Top Six

jun1	zi3	bao4	bian4	xiao3	ren2	ge2
1715	6939	4954	5245	2605	3097	3314
君	子	豹	變	小	人	革

mian4	zheng1	xiong1	ju1	zhen1	ji2
4497	0352	2808	1535	0346	0476
面	征	凶	居	貞	吉

The noble changes as a leopard.
The petty man changes its face.
Attacking brings misfortune.
The determination brings good fortune.

50. The Caldron

Judgment

ding3	yuan2	ji2	heng1
6392	7707	0476	2099
鼎	元	吉	亨

The Caldron. Outstanding good fortune.
Success.

Image

mu4	shang4	you3	huo3	ding3
4593	5669	7533	2395	6392
木	上	有	火	鼎

jun1	zi3	yi3	zheng4	wei4	ning2	ming4
1715	6939	2932	0351	7116	4732	4537
君	子	以	正	位	凝	命

Fire over wood: The image of the Caldron.
Thus the noble corrects his position to consolidate his fate.

First Six

ding3	dian1	zhi3	li4	chu1	pi3
6392	6337	0944	3867	1409	1902
鼎	顛	趾	利	出	否

de2	qie4	yi3	qi2	zi3	wu2	jiu4
6161	0814	2932	0525	6939	7173	1192
得	妾	以	其	子	无	咎

The Caldron is lying upside down.
It is favorable to remove debris.
One takes a concubine to bear a child.
No defect.

Second Nine

ding3	you3	shi2	wo3	chou2	you3	ji2
6392	7533	5821	4778	1332	7533	0492
鼎	有	實	我	仇	有	疾

bu4	wo3	neng2	ji2	ji2
5379	4778	4648	0495	0476
不	我	能	即	吉

The Caldron is full.
My enemy is anxious, but cannot get at me.
Good fortune.

Third Nine

ding3	er3	ge2	qi2	xing2	se4
6392	1744	3314	0525	2754	5446
鼎	耳	革	其	行	塞

zhi4	gao1	bu4	shi2
0968	3296	5379	5810
雉	膏	不	食

fang1	yu3	kui1	hui3	zhong1	ji2
1802	7662	3650	2336	1500	0476
方	雨	虧	悔	終	吉

The handles of the Caldron are removed.
Progress is impeded.
The fat pheasant meat is not eaten.
Rain falls all around, and regrets disappear.
Finally there will be good fortune.

Fourth Nine

ding3	zhe2	zu2	fu4	gong1	su4
6392	0267	6824	1993	3701	5506
鼎	折	足	覆	公	餗

qi2	xing2	wo4	xiong1
0525	2759	7162	2808
其	形	渥	凶

The Caldron legs are broken.
The stew is spilled and stains the Prince's figure.
Misfortune.

Fifth Six

ding3	huang2	er3	jin1	xuan4	li4	zhen1
6392	2297	1744	1057	2886	3867	0346
鼎	黃	耳	金	鉉	利	貞

The Caldron has yellow handles and metal rings.
The determination is favorable.

Top Nine

ding3	yu4	xuan4	da4	ji2	wu2	bu4	li4
6392	7666	2886	5943	0476	7173	5379	3867
鼎	玉	鉉	大	吉	无	不	利

The Caldron has rings of jade.
Great good fortune.
Nothing that is not favorable.

51. Shock

Judgment

zhen4	heng1	zhen4	lai2	xi4	xi4	xiao4	yan2	e4
0315	2099	0315	3768	2480	2480	2615	7334	7226
震	亨	震	來	虩	虩	笑	言	啞

e4	zhen4	jing1	bai3	li3	bu4	sang4	bi3	chang4
7226	0315	1140	4976	3857	5379	5429	5076	0232
啞	震	驚	百	里	不	喪	匕	鬯

Shock. Success.
The arrival of Shock causes great fear. But afterwards there are laughing words.
Shock terrifies for a hundred li.
But he doesn't drop the libation in the sacrificial ladle.

Image

jian4	lei2	zhen4	jun1	zi3	yi3	kong3	ju4	xiu1	xing3
0880	4236	0315	1715	6939	2932	3721	1560	2795	5744
洊	雷	震	君	子	以	恐	懼	脩	省

The thunder repeated: the image of Shock.
Thus the noble with apprehension and fear,
puts his life in order and evaluates himself.

First Nine

zhen4	lai2	xi4	xi4
0315	3768	2480	2480
震	來	虩	虩

hou4	xiao4	yan2	e4	e4	ji2
2143	2615	7334	7226	7226	0476
後	笑	言	啞	啞	吉

The arrival of Shock causes great fear.
But afterwards there are laughing words. Good fortune.

Second Six

zhen4	lai2	li4	yi4	sang4	bei4	ji1
0315	3768	3906	3042	5429	5005	0461
震	來	厲	億	喪	貝	躋

yu2	jiu3	ling2	wu4	zhu2	qi1	ri4	de2
7592	1198	4067	7208	1383	0579	3124	6161
于	九	陵	勿	逐	七	日	得

Shock comes with risk.
You lose one hundred thousand cowries and climb the nine hills

Do not go in pursuit.
In seven days you will get them.

Third Six

zhen4	su1	su1	zhen4	xing2	wu2	sheng3
0315	5488	5488	0315	2754	7173	5741
震	蘇	蘇	震	行	无	眚

Shock stimulates and terrifies one.
If shock excites one to action, there will be no defect.

Fourth Nine

zhen4	sui4	ni2
0315	5530	4660
震	遂	泥

After Shock mud.

Fifth Six

zhen4	wang3	lai2	li4
0315	7050	3768	3906
震	往	來	厲

yi4	wu2	sang4	you3	shi4
2960	7173	5429	7533	5787
意	无	喪	有	事

Shock comes and goes. Danger.
But nothing is lost. There are things to do.

Top Six

zhen4	suo3	suo3	shi4	jue2	jue2	zheng1	xiong1
0315	5459	5459	5789	1704	1704	0352	2808
震	索	索	視	矍	矍	征	凶

zhen4	bu4	yu2	qi2	gong1	yu2	qi2	lin2
0315	5379	7592	0525	3704	7592	0525	4033
震	不	于	其	躬	于	其	鄰

wu2	jiu4	hun1	gou4	you3	yan2
7173	1192	2360	3426	7533	7334
无	咎	婚	媾	有	言

Shock causes fear and agitation.
One looks around in terror.
Marching forth brings misfortune.
The shock does not reach you but your neighbor.
No defect.
There is talk of marriage.

52. Restraint

Judgment

gen4	qi2	bei4	bu4	huo4	qi2	shen1
3327	0525	4989	5379	2412	0525	5718
艮	其	背	不	獲	其	身

xing2	qi2	ting2	bu4	jian4	qi2	ren2
2754	0525	6405	5379	0860	0525	3097
行	其	庭	不	見	其	人

wu2	jiu4
7173	1192
无	咎

Restraining his back.
Doesn't feel his body.
Goes to his courtyard and doesn't see his people.
No defect.

Image

jian1	shan1	gen4
0830	5630	3327
兼	山	艮

jun1	zi3	yi3	si1	bu4	chu1	qi2	wei4
1715	6939	2932	5580	5379	1409	0525	7116
君	子	以	思	不	出	其	位

Joined mountains: The image of Restraint.
Thus the noble doesn't let his thoughts wander beyond his position.

First Six

gen4	qi2	zhi3	wu2	jiu4	li4	yong3	zhen1
3327	0525	0944	7173	1192	3867	7589	0346
艮	其	趾	无	咎	利	永	貞

Restraining his toes.
No defect.
Long term determination is favorable.

Second Six

gen4	qi2	fei2	bu4	zheng3	qi2	sui2
3327	0525	1830	5379	0360	0525	5523
艮	其	腓	不	拯	其	隨

qi2	xin1	bu4	kuai4
0525	2735	5379	3547
其	心	不	快

Restraining his calves doesn't help the one he follows.
His heart is not happy.

Third Nine

gen4	qi2	xian4	lie4	qi2	yin2
3327	0525	2696	3984	0525	7427
艮	其	限	列	其	夤

li4	xun1	xin1
3906	2906	2735
厲	熏	心

Restraining his hips.
Tears his lumbar area.
Danger.
The heart is suffocated.

Fourth Six

gen4	qi2	shen1	wu2	jiu4
3327	0525	5718	7173	1192
艮	其	身	无	咎

Restrains his torso.
No defect.

Fifth Six

gen4	qi2	fu3	yan2	you3	xu4	hui3	wang2
3327	0525	1945	7334	7533	2851	2336	7034
艮	其	輔	言	有	序	悔	亡

Restrains his jaws.
What he says is orderly.
Repentance fades.

Top Nine

dun1	gen4	ji2
6571	3327	0476
敦	艮	吉

Earnest restrain.
Good fortune.

53. Gradual Development

Judgment

jian4	nu3	gui1	ji2	li4	zhen1
0878	4776	3617	0476	3867	0346
漸	女	歸	吉	利	貞

Gradual Development.
The maiden's marriage brings good fortune.
The determination is favorable.

Image

shan1	shang4	you3	mu4	jian4			
5630	5669	7533	4593	0878			
山	上	有	木	漸			

jun1	zi3	yi3	ju1	xian2	de2	shan4	su2
1715	6939	2932	1535	2671	6162	5657	5497
君	子	以	居	賢	德	善	俗

On the mountain is a tree: The image of Gradual Development.
Thus the noble dwells in virtue and so improves the mores of the people.

First Six

hong2	jian4	yu2	gan1	xiao3	zi3	li4
2386	0878	7592	3211	2605	6939	3906
鴻	漸	于	干	小	子	厲

you3	yan2	wu2	jiu4
7533	7334	7173	1192
有	言	无	咎

The goose gradually moves toward the riverbank.
The child is in danger and will be spoken against. No defect.

Second Six

hong2	jian4	yu2	pan2	yin3	shi2	kan4	kan4	ji2
2386	0878	7592	4904	7454	5810	3252	3252	0476
鴻	漸	于	磐	飲	食	衎	衎	吉

The goose gradually moves toward a big rock.
Eats and drinks joyfully. Good fortune.

Third Nine

hong2	jian4	yu2	lu4	fu1	zheng1	bu4	fu4
2386	0878	7592	4191	1908	0352	5379	1992
鴻	漸	于	陸	夫	征	不	復

fu4	yun4	bu4	yu4	xiong1	li4	yu4	kou4
1963	7765	5379	7687	2808	3867	7665	3444
婦	孕	不	育	凶	利	禦	寇

The goose gradually moves to the highlands.
The man goes on an expedition but does not return;
the woman is pregnant but does not give birth.
Misfortune.
It is favorable to fend off bandits.

Fourth Six

hong2	jian4	yu2	mu4	huo4	de2	qi2	jue2
2386	0878	7592	4593	2402	6161	0525	1175
鴻	漸	于	木	或	得	其	桷

wu2	jiu4
7173	1192
无	咎

The goose gradually moves toward the woods.
It may find a flat branch. No defect.

Fifth Nine

hong2	jian4	yu2	ling2	fu4	san1	sui4
2386	0878	7592	4067	1963	5415	5538
鴻	漸	于	陵	婦	三	歲

bu4	yun4	zhong1	mo4	zhi1	sheng4	ji2
5379	7765	1500	4557	0935	5754	0476
不	孕	終	莫	之	勝	吉

The goose gradually moves toward the top of the hill.
The woman cannot conceive for three years.
Finally, nothing can stop it.
Good fortune.

Top Nine

hong2	jian4	yu2	lu4	qi2	yu3	ke3
2386	0878	7592	4191	0525	7658	3381
鴻	漸	于	陸	其	羽	可

yong4	wei2	yi2	ji2
7567	7059	3003	0476
用	爲	儀	吉

The goose gradually moves toward the highlands.
Its feathers can be used to practice the rites.
Good fortune.

54. The Marrying Maiden

Judgment

gui1	mei4	zheng1	xiong1	wu2	you1	li4
3617	4410	0352	2808	7173	7519	3867
歸	妹	征	凶	无	攸	利

The Marrying Maiden.
Marching forth brings misfortune.
Nothing that is favorable.

Image

ze2	shang4	you3	lei2	gui1	mei4	
0277	5669	7533	4236	3617	4410	
澤	上	有	雷	歸	妹	
jun1	zi3	yi3	yong3	zhong1	zhi1	bi4
1715	6939	2932	7589	1500	0932	5101
君	子	以	永	終	知	敝

On the lake is the thunder: The image of the Marrying Maiden.
Thus the noble persists to the end and knows the cause of the damage.

First Nine

gui1	mei4	yi3	di4	bo3	neng2	lu3
3617	4410	2932	6202	5317	4648	3893
歸	妹	以	娣	跛	能	履
zheng1	ji2					
0352	0476					
征	吉					

She marries as a concubine.
A lame man can walk.
Marching forth brings good fortune.

Second Nine

miao3	neng2	shi4	li4	you1	ren2	zhi1	zhen1
4476	4648	5789	3867	7505	3097	0935	0346
眇	能	視	利	幽	人	之	貞

A one-eyed man can see.
The determination of a secluded man is favorable.

Third Six

gui1	mei4	yi3	xu1	fan3	gui1	yi3	di4
3617	4410	2932	8011	1781	3617	2932	6202
歸	妹	以	嬬	反	歸	以	娣

The Marrying Maiden in servitude.
She returns and marries as a secondary wife.

Fourth Nine

gui1	mei4	qian1	qi2	chi2	gui1	you3	shi2
3617	4410	0889	0526	1024	3617	7533	5780
歸	妹	愆	期	遲	歸	有	時

The Marrying Maiden delays marriage, waiting for the right time.
There will be a late marriage.

Fifth Six

di4	yi3	gui1	mei4	qi2	jun1	zhi1
6204	3017	3617	4410	0525	1715	0935
帝	乙	歸	妹	其	君	之

mei4	bu4	ru2	qi2	di4	zhi1	mei4
4456	5379	3137	0525	6202	0935	4456
袂	不	如	其	娣	之	袂

liang2	yue4	ji1	wang4	ji2
3941	7696	0409	7043	0476
良	月	幾	望	吉

The emperor *Yi* gives his daughter in marriage.
The sleeves of her dress were less gorgeous than her bridesmaid's.
The moon is almost full.
Good fortune.

Top Six

nu3	cheng2	kuang1	wu2	shi2	shi4	kui1
4776	0386	3598	7173	5821	5776	3642
女	承	筐	无	實	士	刲

yang2	wu2	xue4	wu2	you1	li4
7247	7173	2901	7173	7519	3867
羊	无	血	无	攸	利

The woman has a basket, but it contains no fruit.
The man stabs a sheep but it does not bleed.
Nothing is favorable.

55. Abundance / Wholeness

Judgment

feng1	heng1	wang2	jia3	zhi1
1897	2099	7037	0599	0935
豐	亨	王	假	之

wu4	you1	yi2	ri4	zhong1
7208	7508	2993	3124	1504
勿	憂	宜	日	中

Abundance has success.

The king is coming. Do not be sad.

Suitable at midday.

Image

lei2	dian4	jie1	zhi4	feng1
4236	6358	0620	0982	1897
雷	電	皆	至	豐

jun1	zi3	yi3	zhe2	yu4	zhi4	xing2
1715	6939	2932	0267	7685	0984	2755
君	子	以	折	獄	致	刑

Thunder and lightning culminate altogether: The image of Abundance.

Thus the noble decides legal cases and applies punishments.

First Nine

yu4	qi2	pei4	zhu3	sui1	xun2	wu2	jiu4	wang3	you3	shang4
7625	0525	5019	1336	5519	2915	7173	1192	7050	7533	5670
遇	其	配	主	雖	旬	无	咎	往	有	尚

Meets the master that is his match.

Even if they are together for ten days there will be no mistake.

Going forward attains rewards.

Second Six

feng1	qi2	bu4	ri4	zhong1	jian4	dou3	wang3
1897	0525	8001	3124	1504	0860	6472	7050
豐	其	蔀	日	中	見	斗	往

de2	yi2	ji2	you3	fu2	fa1	ruo4	ji2
6161	2940	0492	7533	1936	1768	3126	0476
得	疑	疾	有	孚	發	若	吉

The curtain has such fullness that the Big Dipper could be seen at noon.

Going forwards attains distrust and hatred.

Manifest sincerity will have good fortune.

124

Third Nine

feng1	qi2	pei4	ri4	zhong1	jian4	mei4
1897	0525	5020	3124	1504	0860	4412
豐	其	沛	日	中	見	沬

zhe2	qi2	you4	gong1	wu2	jiu4
0267	0525	7541	3706	7173	1192
折	其	右	肱	无	咎

The covering has such fullness that the star Mei could be seen at noon.
Breaks his right arm. No defect.

Fourth Nine

feng1	qi2	bu4	ri4	zhong1	jian4	dou3
1897	0525	8001	3124	1504	0860	6472
豐	其	蔀	日	中	見	斗

yu4	qi2	yi2	zhu3	ji2
7625	0525	2982	1336	0476
遇	其	夷	主	吉

The curtain has such fullness that the Big Dipper could be seen at noon.
He meets his master in secret.
Good fortune.

Fifth Six

lai2	zhang1	you3	qing4	yu4	ji2
3768	0182	7533	1167	7617	0476
來	章	有	慶	譽	吉

Brilliance is coming.
You will have blessings and fame.
Good fortune.

Top Six

feng1	qi2	wu1	bu4	qi2	jia1
1897	0525	7212	8001	0525	0594
豐	其	屋	蔀	其	家

kui1	qi2	hu4	qu4	qi2	wu2	ren2
3649	0525	2180	1627	0525	7173	3097
闚	其	戶	闃	其	无	人

san1	sui4	bu4	di2	xiong1
5415	5538	5379	6230	2808
三	歲	不	覿	凶

A large canopy hides his house.
He peeks from his door, silent and with no one at his side.
For three years he sees nothing. Misfortune.

56. The Wanderer

Judgment

lu3	xiao3	heng1	lu3	zhen1	ji2
4286	2605	2099	4286	0346	0476
旅	小	亨	旅	貞	吉

The Wanderer.
Success in small things.
The determination of the wanderer brings good fortune.

Image

shan1	shang4	you3	huo3	lu3
5630	5669	7533	2395	4286
山	上	有	火	旅

jun1	zi3	yi3	ming2
1715	6939	2932	4534
君	子	以	明

shen4	yong4	xing2	er2	bu4	liu2	yu4
5734	7567	2755	1756	5379	4083	7685
慎	用	刑	而	不	畱	獄

Above the mountain is fire: The image of the Wanderer.
Thus the noble applies punishments with clarity and doesn't prolong litigations.

First Six

lu3	suo3	suo3	si1	qi2	suo3	qu3	zai1
4286	5466	5466	5574	0525	5465	1615	6652
旅	瑣	瑣	斯	其	所	取	災

The Wanderer is too fussy.
He will bring calamity upon himself.

Second Six

lu3	ji2	ci4	huai2	qi2	zi1
4286	0495	6980	2233	0525	6927
旅	即	次	懷	其	資

de2	tong2	pu2	zhen1
6161	6626	5401	0346
得	童	僕	貞

The Wanderer comes to a resting place.
Keeps his belongings safely
and gets a young and loyal servant.

Third Nine

lu3	fen2	qi2	ci4	sang4	qi2	tong2	pu2	zhen1	li4
4286	1866	0525	6980	5429	0525	6626	5401	0346	3906
旅	焚	其	次	喪	其	童	僕	貞	厲

The Wanderer burns his resting place.
He loses his young servant.
The determination is dangerous.

Fourth Nine

lu3	yu2	chu3	de2	qi2	zi1	fu3
4286	7592	1407	6161	0525	6927	1934
旅	于	處	得	其	資	斧

wo3	xin1	bu4	kuai4
4778	2735	5379	3547
我	心	不	快

The Wanderer stays at one place and obtains property and an ax.
My heart is not happy.

Fifth Six

she4	zhi4	yi1	shi3	wang2	zhong1	yi3	yu4	ming4
5703	0968	3016	5784	7034	1500	2932	7617	4537
射	雉	一	矢	亡	終	以	譽	命

He shoots a pheasant.
Although the first arrow fails
finally he is praised and given employment.

Top Nine

niao3	fen2	qi2	chao2
4688	1866	0525	0253
鳥	焚	其	巢

lu3	ren2	xian1	xiao4	hou4	hao4	tao2
4286	3097	2702	2615	2143	2064	6152
旅	人	先	笑	後	號	咷

sang4	niu2	yu2	yi4	xiong1
5429	4737	7592	2952	2808
喪	牛	于	易	凶

The bird burns its nest.
The Wanderer laughs at first but afterward cries out and weeps.
He loses his cow in Yi.
Misfortune.

57. Gentle Influence / Compliance / Penetrating / The Wind

☴

Judgment

xun4	xiao3	heng1	li4	you3	you1	wang3
5550	2605	2099	3867	7533	7519	7050
巽	小	亨	利	有	攸	往

li4	jian4	da4	ren2
3867	0860	5943	3097
利	見	大	人

Gentle Influence.
Success in small things.
It is favorable to have a place to go.
It is favorable to see the great man.

Image

sui2	feng1	xun4
5523	1890	5550
隨	風	巽

jun1	zi3	yi3	shen1	ming4	xing2	shi4
1715	6939	2932	5712	4537	2754	5787
君	子	以	申	命	行	事

Winds that follow each other: The image of Gentle Influence.
Thus the noble proclaims his commands and acts to carry out his tasks.

First Six

jin4	tui4	li4	wu3	ren2	zhi1	zhen1
1091	6568	3867	7195	3097	0935	0346
進	退	利	武	人	之	貞

Advancing and retreating.
The determination is favorable for a warrior.

Second Nine

xun4	zai4	chuang2	xia4	yong4	shi3	wu1
5550	6657	1459	2520	7567	5769	7164
巽	在	牀	下	用	史	巫

fen1	ruo4	ji2	wu2	jiu4
1859	3126	0476	7173	1192
紛	若	吉	无	咎

Penetration under the bed.
Using invokers and sorcerers in large number brings good fortune. No defect.

Third Nine

pin2	xun4	lin4
5275	5550	4040
頻	巽	吝

Repeated penetration.
Humiliation.

Fourth Six

hui3	wang2	tian2	huo4	san1	pin3
2336	7034	6362	2412	5415	5281
悔	亡	田	獲	三	品

Repentance fades.
Captures three types of prey in hunting.

Fifth Nine

zhen1	ji2	hui3	wang2	wu2	bu4	li4
0346	0476	2336	7034	7173	5379	3867
貞	吉	悔	亡	无	不	利

wu2	chu1	you3	zhong1	xian1	geng1	san1
7173	1390	7533	1500	2702	3339	5415
无	初	有	終	先	庚	三

ri4	hou4	geng1	san1	ri4	ji2
3124	2143	3339	5415	3124	0476
日	後	庚	三	日	吉

The determination is fortunate.
Repentance fades.
Nothing that is not favorable.
There is no beginning, but an end.
Before the seventh day, three days; after the seventh day, three days.
Good fortune.

Top Nine

xun4	zai4	chuang2	xia4	sang4	qi2	zi1
5550	6657	1459	2520	5429	0525	6927
巽	在	牀	下	喪	其	資

fu3	zhen1	xiong1
1934	0346	2808
斧	貞	凶

Penetration under the bed.
He loses his belongings and an ax.
The determination is ominous.

58. Joyousness / The Lake

≣

Judgment

dui4	heng1	li4	zhen1
6560	2099	3867	0346
兌	亨	利	貞

Joyousness.
Success. Determination is favorable.

Image

li4	ze2	dui4	jun1	zi3	yi3	peng2
3914	0277	6560	1715	6939	2932	5054
麗	澤	兌	君	子	以	朋

you3	jiang3	xi2
7540	0645	2499
友	講	習

Two lakes together: The image of Joyousness.
Thus the noble joins his friends
for discussion and training.

First Nine

he2	dui4	ji2
2115	6560	0476
和	兌	吉

Harmonious joy.
Good fortune.

Second Nine

fu2	dui4	ji2	hui3	wang2
1936	6560	0476	2336	7034
孚	兌	吉	悔	亡

Sincere joy.
Good fortune.
Regrets go away.

Third Six

lai2	dui4	xiong1
3768	6560	2808
來	兌	凶

Coming joy.
Misfortune.

Fourth Nine

shang1	dui4	wei4	ning2	jie4	ji2	you3	xi3
5673	6560	7114	4725	0629	0492	7533	2434
商	兌	未	寧	介	疾	有	喜

Haggling joy.
Still not at peace.
After limiting your anxiety there will be happiness.

Fifth Nine

fu2	yu2	bo1	you3	li4
1936	7592	5337	7533	3906
孚	于	剝	有	厲

Trusting degrading influences is dangerous.

Top Six

yin3	dui4
7429	6560
引	兌

Alluring joyousness.

59. Dispersion / Dissolution / The Flood

䷲

Judgment

huan4	heng1	wang2	jia3	you3	miao4
2252	2099	7037	0599	7533	4473
渙	亨	王	假	有	廟

li4	she4	da4	chuan1	li4	zhen1
3867	5707	5943	1439	3867	0346
利	涉	大	川	利	貞

Dispersion. Success.
The king approaches his temple.
It is favorable to cross the great river.
The determination is favorable.

Image

feng1	xing2	shui3	shang4	huan4
1890	2754	5922	5669	2252
風	行	水	上	渙

xian1	wang2	yi3	xiang3	yu2	di4	li4	miao4
2702	7037	2932	2552	7592	6204	3921	4473
先	王	以	享	于	帝	立	廟

Wind moving over the water: The image of Dispersion.
Thus the ancient kings made offerings to the Supreme Lord
and erected temples.

First Six

yong4	zheng3	ma3	zhuang4	ji2
7567	0360	4310	1453	0476
用	拯	馬	壯	吉

Uses the strength of a horse for rescue.
Good fortune.

Second Nine

huan4	ben1	qi2	ji1	hui3	wang2
2252	5028	0525	0411	2336	7034
渙	奔	其	机	悔	亡

Dispersion.
Run to your support.
Repentance fades.

Third Six

huan4	qi2	gong1	wu2	hui3
2252	0525	3704	7173	2336
渙	其	躬	无	悔

Disperses himself.
No repentance.

Fourth Six

huan4	qi2	qun2	yuan2	ji2
2252	0525	1737	7707	0476
渙	其	羣	元	吉

huan4	you3	qiu1	fei3	yi2	suo3	si1
2252	7533	1213	1820	2982	5465	5580
渙	有	丘	匪	夷	所	思

Disperses his group.
Outstanding good fortune.
Dispersion is great.
Common people do not consider that point.

Fifth Nine

huan4	han4	qi2	da4	hao4
2252	2028	0525	5943	2064
渙	汗	其	大	號

huan4	wang2	ju1	wu2	jiu4
2252	7037	1535	7173	1192
渙	王	居	无	咎

Dispersing sweat, proclaiming aloud.
Disperses the king dwelling.
No defect.

Top Nine

huan4	qi2	xue4	qu4	ti4	chu1
2252	0525	2901	1594	6265	1409
渙	其	血	去	逖	出

wu2	jiu4
7173	1192
无	咎

Disperses his blood.
Going away, keeping at a distance, departing.
No defect.

60. Limitation

Judgment

jie2	heng1	ku3	jie2	bu4	ke3	zhen1
0795	2099	3493	0795	5379	3381	0346
節	亨	苦	節	不	可	貞

Limitation
Success.
A severe limitation cannot be applied with persistence.

Image

ze2	shang4	you3	shui3	jie2	jun1	zi3
0277	5669	7533	5922	0795	1715	6939
澤	上	有	水	節	君	子
yi3	zhi4	shu3	du4	yi4	de2	xing2
2932	0986	5865	6504	3006	6162	2754
以	制	數	度	議	德	行

Above the lake is water: The image of Limitation.
Thus the noble establishes the number and measure
and deliberates about morality and conduct.

First Nine

bu4	chu1	hu4	ting2	wu2	jiu4
5379	1409	2180	6405	7173	1192
不	出	戶	庭	无	咎

Not going out of the door to the courtyard.
No defect.

Second Nine

bu4	chu1	men2	ting2	xiong1
5379	1409	4418	6405	2808
不	出	門	庭	凶

Not going out of the gate of the courtyard
Misfortune.

Third Six

bu4	jie2	ruo4	ze2	jie1	ruo4	wu2	jiu4
5379	0795	3126	6746	0763	3126	7173	1192
不	節	若	則	嗟	若	无	咎

Disregarding the limits leads to sorrow.
No defect.

Fourth Six

an1	jie2	heng1
0026	0795	2099
安	節	亨

Contented limitation.
Success.

Fifth Nine

gan1	jie2	ji2	wang3	you3	shang4
3223	0795	0476	7050	7533	5670
甘	節	吉	往	有	尚

Pleasant limitation.
Good fortune.
Going forward has praise.

Top Six

ku3	jie2	zhen1	xiong1	hui3	wang2
3493	0795	0346	2808	2336	7034
苦	節	貞	凶	悔	亡

Bitter limitation.
The determination is ominous.
Repentance fades.

61. Inner Truth

Judgment

zhong1	fu2	tun2	yu2	ji2
1504	1936	6600	7668	0476
中	孚	豚	魚	吉

li4	she4	da4	chuan1	li4	zhen1
3867	5707	5943	1439	3867	0346
利	涉	大	川	利	貞

Inner truth.
Pigs and fishes. Good fortune.
It is favorable to cross the great river.
The determination is favorable.

Image

ze2	shang4	you3	feng1	zhong1	fu2
0277	5669	7533	1890	1504	1936
澤	上	有	風	中	孚

jun1	zi3	yi3	yi4	yu4	huan3	si3
1715	6939	2932	3006	7685	2242	5589
君	子	以	議	獄	緩	死

Above the lake is the wind: The image of Inner Truth.
Thus the noble discusses criminal cases
and delays executions.

First Nine

yu2	ji2	you3	ta1	bu4	yan4
7648	0476	7533	5961	5379	7399
虞	吉	有	他	不	燕

It is auspicious to be prepared.
If there is something else, it is unsettling.

Second Nine

ming2	he4	zai4	yin1	qi2	zi3	he2	zhi1	wo3
4535	2131	6657	7444	0525	6939	2115	0935	4778
鳴	鶴	在	陰	其	子	和	之	我

you3	hao3	jue2	wu2	yu3	er3	mi2	zhi1
7533	2062	1179	7188	7615	1754	4455	0935
有	好	爵	吾	與	爾	靡	之

A crane calling from the shadows.
His young replies.
I have a good cup.
I will share it with you.

Third Six

de2	di2	huo4	gu3	huo4	ba4
6161	6221	2402	3479	2402	4841
得	敵	或	鼓	或	罷

huo4	qi4	huo4	ge1
2402	0563	2402	3364
或	泣	或	歌

Gets a mate.
Sometimes beats the drum, sometimes stops.
Sometimes weeps, sometimes sings.

Fourth Six

yue4	ji1	wang4	ma3	pi3	wang2	wu2	jiu4
7696	0409	7043	4310	5170	7034	7173	1192
月	幾	望	馬	匹	亡	无	咎

The moon is almost full.
One of the team's horses goes away.
No defect.

Fifth Nine

you3	fu2	luan2	ru2	wu2	jiu4
7533	1936	4300	3137	7173	1192
有	孚	攣	如	无	咎

He has truth that links them together.
No defect.

Top Nine

han4	yin1	deng1	yu2	tian1	zhen1	xiong1
2042	7418	6167	7592	6361	0346	2808
翰	音	登	于	天	貞	凶

The cry of the pheasant rises up into heaven.
The determination is ominous.

62. Excess of the Small

Judgment

xiao3	guo4	heng1	li4	zhen1	ke3	xiao3	shi4
2605	3730	2099	3867	0346	3381	2605	5787
小	過	亨	利	貞	可	小	事
bu4	ke3	da4	shi4	fei1	niao3	yi2	zhi1
5379	3381	5943	5787	1850	4688	2995	0935
不	可	大	事	飛	鳥	遺	之
yin1	bu4	yi2	shang4	yi2	xia4	da4	ji2
7418	5379	2993	5669	2993	2520	5943	0476
音	不	宜	上	宜	下	大	吉

The Excess of the Small.

Success. The determination is favorable.

Proper for small matters, not suitable for great matters.

The flying bird leaves the message:

It is not right to ascend, it is fit to go below.

Great good fortune.

Image

shan1	shang4	you3	lei2	xiao3	guo4	jun1	zi3	yi3	xing2	
5630	5669	7533	4236	2605	3730	1715	6939	2932	2754	
山	上	有	雷	小	過	君	子	以	行	
guo4	hu1	gong1	sang4	guo4	hu1	ai1	yong4	guo4	hu1	jian3
3730	2154	3711	5429	3730	2154	0003	7567	3730	2154	0848
過	乎	恭	喪	過	乎	哀	用	過	乎	儉

On top of the mountain is the thunder: The image of the Excess of the Small.

Thus the noble in his behavior is exceedingly reverent,

in mourning is exceedingly sorrow, and in his expenditures is exceedingly frugal.

First Six

fei1	niao3	yi3	xiong1
1850	4688	2932	2808
飛	鳥	以	凶

The flying bird will have misfortune.

Second Six

guo4	qi2	zu3	yu4	qi2	bi3	bu4	
3730	0525	6815	7625	0525	5082	5379	
過	其	祖	遇	其	妣	不	
ji2	qi2	jun1	yu4	qi2	chen2	wu2	jiu4
0468	0525	1715	7625	0525	0327	7173	1192
及	其	君	遇	其	臣	无	咎

Passing by his ancestor, meeting his ancestress.
Not reaching his ruler, meeting his minister. No defect.

Third Nine

fu2	guo4	fang2	zhi1	cong2	huo4	qiang1	zhi1	xiong1
1981	3730	1817	0935	6919	2402	0673	0935	2808
弗	過	防	之	從	或	戕	之	凶

If he is not exceedingly careful, somebody may follow and strike him.
Misfortune.

Fourth Nine

wu2	jiu4	fu2	guo4	yu4	zhi1	wang3
7173	1192	1981	3730	7625	0935	7050
无	咎	弗	過	遇	之	往

li4	bi4	jie4	wu4	yong4	yong3	zhen1
3906	5109	0627	7208	7567	7589	0346
厲	必	戒	勿	用	永	貞

No defect.
Not passing, meeting.
Moving on is dangerous. One must be alert.
Not using long term determination.

Fifth Six

mi4	yun2	bu4	yu3	zi4	wo3	xi1	jiao1
4464	7750	5379	7662	6960	4778	2460	0714
密	雲	不	雨	自	我	西	郊

gong1	yi4	qu3	bi3	zai4	xue2
3701	3018	1615	5093	6657	2899
公	弋	取	彼	在	穴

Heavy clouds but no rain from our western frontier.
The prince catches the one in the cave.

Top Six

fu2	yu4	guo4	zhi1	fei1	niao3	li2
1981	7625	3730	0935	1850	4688	3902
弗	遇	過	之	飛	鳥	離

zhi1	xiong1	shi4	wei4	zai1	sheng3
0935	2808	5794	7079	6652	5741
之	凶	是	謂	災	眚

Passes without finding him.
The flying bird is netted.
Misfortune. This means disaster.

63. Already Across

Judgment

ji4	ji4	heng1	xiao3	li4	zhen1
0453	**0459**	2099	2605	3867	0346
既	濟	亨	小	利	貞

chu1	ji2	zhong1	luan4
1390	0476	1500	4220
初	吉	終	亂

Already Across.
Success.
The determination is favorable for small things.
At first good fortune, at the end chaos.

Image

shui3	zai4	huo3	shang4	ji4	ji4	jun1	
5922	6657	2395	5669	0453	0459	1715	
水	在	火	上	既	濟	君	

zi3	yi3	si1	huan4	er2	yu4	fang2	zhi1
6939	2932	5580	2240	1756	7603	1817	0935
子	以	思	患	而	豫	防	之

Water on the fire: The image of Already Across.
Thus the noble meditates on misfortune in advance to prevent it.

First Nine

yi4	qi2	lun2	ru2	qi2	wei3	wu2	jiu4
3008	0525	4254	3149	0525	7109	7173	1192
曳	其	輪	濡	其	尾	无	咎

Drag his wheels and wets his tail.
No defect.

Second Six

fu4	sang4	qi2	fu2	wu4	zhu2
1963	5429	0525	1989	7208	1383
婦	喪	其	茀	勿	逐

qi1	ri4	de2
0579	3124	6161
七	日	得

The woman loses the curtain of her carriage.
Do not chase it; you will get it in seven days.

Third Nine

gao1	zong1	fa1	gui3	fang1	san1	nian2
3290	6896	1765	3634	1802	5415	4711
高	宗	伐	鬼	方	三	年

ke4	zhi1	xiao3	ren2	wu4	yong4
3320	0935	2605	3097	7208	7567
克	之	小	人	勿	用

The eminent ancestor attacks the Land of the Devil,
after three years conquests it.
Petty men must not be used.

Fourth Six

xu1	you3	yi1	ru2	zhong1	ri4	jie4
2845	7533	2989	3140	1500	3124	0627
繻	有	衣	袽	終	日	戒

He has torn silk and caulking rags.
Be cautious until the end of the day.

Fifth Nine

dong1	lin2	sha1	niu2	bu4	ru2	xi1
6605	4033	5615	4737	5379	3137	2460
東	鄰	殺	牛	不	如	西

lin2	zhi1	yue4	ji4	shi2	shou4	qi2	fu2
4033	0935	7498	0465	5821	5840	0525	1978
鄰	之	禴	祭	實	受	其	福

The eastern neighbor sacrifices an ox,
but this falls short of the neighbor in the west
with his small offering,
whose sincerity receives blessings.

Top Six

ru2	qi2	shou3	li4
3149	0525	5839	3906
濡	其	首	厲

He soaks his head.
Danger.

64. Before Crossing

Judgment

wei4	ji4	heng1	xiao3	hu2	qi4	ji4
7114	0459	2099	2605	2185	8006	0459
未	濟	亨	小	狐	汔	濟

ru2	qi2	wei3	wu2	you1	li4
3149	0525	7109	7173	7519	3867
濡	其	尾	无	攸	利

Before Crossing.
Success.
The little fox tail gets wet when finishes fording the river.
Nothing is favorable.

Image

huo3	zai4	shui3	shang4	wei4	ji4
2395	6657	5922	5669	7114	0459
火	在	水	上	未	濟

jun1	zi3	yi3	shen4	bian4	wu4	ju1	fang1
1715	6939	2932	5734	5240	7209	1535	1802
君	子	以	慎	辨	物	居	方

Fire over water: The image of Before Crossing.
The noble is careful discriminating things,
so that each one is left in place.

First Six

ru2	qi2	wei3	lin4
3149	0525	7109	4040
濡	其	尾	吝

He wets his tail. Humiliation.

Second Nine

yi4	qi2	lun2	zhen1	ji2
3008	0525	4254	0346	0476
曳	其	輪	貞	吉

Dragging his wheels. The determination is fortunate.

Third Six

wei4	ji4	zheng1	xiong1	li4
7114	0459	0352	2808	3867
未	濟	征	凶	利

she4	da4	chuan1
5707	5943	1439
涉	大	川

Before Crossing.
Attack brings misfortune.
It is favorable to ford the great river.

Fourth Nine

zhen1	ji2	hui3	wang2	zhen4	yong4	fa1
0346	0476	2336	7034	0315	7567	1765
貞	吉	悔	亡	震	用	伐

gui3	fang1	san1	nian2	you3	shang3
3634	1802	5415	4711	7533	5672
鬼	方	三	年	有	賞

yu2	da4	guo2
7592	5943	3738
于	大	國

The determination is fortunate.
Repentance fades.
Shock to conquer the Land of the Devil.
Three years of reward from the great kingdom.

Fifth Six

zhen1	ji2	wu2	hui3
0346	0476	7173	2336
貞	吉	无	悔

jun1	zi3	zhi1	guang1	you3	fu2	ji2
1715	6939	0935	3583	7533	1936	0476
君	子	之	光	有	孚	吉

The determination is fortunate. There is no repentance.
The glory of the noble is true. Good fortune.

Top Nine

you3	fu2	yu2	yin3	jiu3	wu2	jiu4
7533	1936	7592	7454	1208	7173	1192
有	孚	于	飲	酒	无	咎

ru2	qi2	shou3	you3	fu2	shi1	shi4
3149	0525	5839	7533	1936	5806	5794
濡	其	首	有	孚	失	是

They drink wine in confidence.
No defect.
But confidence will be lost if your head gets wet.

DICTIONARY

Karlgren: 550h
PinYin: ai1
Rad./Strokes: 30+6

0003

Grief, sorrow, regret; mourn, lament; to wail, to pity or have compassion for other person or oneself; alas!

 Karlgren: 146a
PinYin: an1
Rad./Strokes: 40+3

0026

Quiet, at peace, calm; tranquility, safety, security; settled, comfort, contentment. Related with **7364** 宴: feast, leisure, repose.

 Karlgren: 618a
PinYin: zhan1
Rad./Strokes: 25+3

0125

Divine by casting lots, prognosticating; observe signs; foretell by looking at an augury or using yarrow wands *(Achillea sibirica* or *mongolica).*

 Karlgren: 147r
PinYin: zhan4
Rad./Strokes: 62+12

0147

Battle, struggle, fight, war, combat; hostilities.

章 **Karlgren:** 723a
PinYin: zhang1
Rad./Strokes: 117+6

0182

Brilliance, splendor, refinement, distinction; ornament, emblem of distinction, jade tablet; amulet.
Its short form, with the jade radical, means "jade baton".
Wilhelm/Baynes translates it as *lines,* but most other translators use words as *elegancy, splendor, brilliant qualities,* etc.

 Karlgren: 721h
PinYin: zhang1
Rad./Strokes: 57+8

0195

Draw taut (a bow), string the bow; stretch, extend. Has many other related meanings but only the first ones are pertinent.
From 弓, "bow" and **0213** 長, phonetic.

丈 **Karlgren:** 722a
PinYin: zhang4
Rad./Strokes: 1+2

0200

Strong, mature, a married man; responsible; respectable; gentleman. One to be respected.

Karlgren: 721a
PinYin: zhang3
0213 **Rad./Strokes:** 168+0

Eldest, grown-up, senior, superior, leader, chief, maturity, tenured. Long, long lasting; tall.

Karlgren: 725e
PinYin: chang2
0221 **Rad./Strokes:** 50+8

Regular lot or duty; constant, always, lasting; perpetuate; frequent, regular, recurring; a rule or principle.

Karlgren: 719a
PinYin: chang4
0232 **Rad./Strokes:** 192+0

Aromatic spirits, libation, sacrificial spirits made up by fermenting millet *(Panicum miliaceum)* and fragrant herbs.

Shows a chalice, and what is inside it; below there is a **5076** 匕 sacrificial spoon.

Older versions show clearly the chalice filled with a libation:

Karlgren: 1143a
PinYin: zhao1
0233 **Rad./Strokes:** 74+8

Morning, dawn, is the original meaning, but since the king held court at dawn and transacted state business early in the morning, it also means audience.

148

Karlgren: 1131m
PinYin: zhao1
0236 **Rad./Strokes:** 72+5

Bright, brilliant, brightness of the sun; enlighten, display, show, manifest; illustrious.

From **3124** 日, "sun" and 召, "imperial decree; summon", phonetic.
Related with **0238** 照.

Karlgren: 1131o
PinYin: zhao4
0238 **Rad./Strokes:** 86+9

Shine, illumine; enlighten; to look after.
Related with **0236** 昭, but adds "fire" **2395** 灬 (火) below 昭.

Karlgren: 1169a
PinYin: chao2
0253 **Rad./Strokes:** 47+8

Nest, a nest in a tree; haunt, retreat, den.

Shows a tree **4593** 木, a nest **6362** 田 and feathers **1439** 巛.

The characters used for "nest" and "feathers" do not have such meanings, but that is what 巢 means.
Older versions are more graphic:

折

Karlgren: 287a
PinYin: zhe2
0267 **Rad./Strokes:** 64+4

Sever, break; bend, destroy, execute; decide a cause, discriminate, judge.
From 扌 (手), "hand" and 斤, "axe".

Karlgren: 780b
PinYin: zhai2
0275 **Rad./Strokes:** 40+3

Position, residence, dwelling, place for settlement; inhabit; consolidate.
From 宀, "house roof" and 乇, phonetic.

 Karlgren: 790o
PinYin: ze2
0277 **Rad./Strokes:** 85+13

Marsh, pool, pond, lake; flat body of water and the vapors rising from it; enrich, fertilize, benefit; moist, moisten; glossy, polished.
See **6560** 兌 (the ideogram for *The Lake* trigram: ☱ and **9000**, The Trigrams).

 Karlgren: 74a
PinYin: che1
0280 **Rad./Strokes:** 159+0

Chariot, wagon, cart, carriage.
Shows the wheels at the sides of the carriage, older versions in bronze and bone also show the horses:

See also **0398** 乘: ride, mount.

 Karlgren: 335c
PinYin: che4
0282 **Rad./Strokes:** 64+8

Drag, to trail, to hinder, obstruct.
From **0986** 制, "regulate" and 手, "hand".

 Karlgren: 656g
PinYin: zhen3
0308 **Rad./Strokes:** 75+4

Pillow, to use as a pillow; rest, resting place; stop, lean back on, soften, relax; a stake to tether cattle.
Rutt, *Kunst* and *Shaughnessy* replace this character with 沉: deep; to sink; to perish.

 Karlgren: 455p
PinYin: zhen4
0313 **Rad./Strokes:** 64+7

Excite, shake, quake (*Kunst*), arouse action; save help; arrange, to marshal troops; to restore order.
From 扌 (手), "hand" and 辰, phonetic.
Related with **0315** 震.

震 **Karlgren:** 455s
PinYin: zhen4
0315 **Rad./Strokes:** 173+7

Shock; clap of thunder; fear; awe inspiring; stimulation, movement, excitation; to excite, to terrify; to quicken; endow, succor.
Related with **0313** 振 and with the ☳ trigram: The Arousing (Shock, Thunder) (Hex. 51). See **9000**: The Eight Trigrams.

臣 **Karlgren:** 377a
PinYin: chen2
0327 **Rad./Strokes:** 131+0

Servant, retainer, vassal, statesman, officer (41.6); male slave, male bondservant or may be a slave couple (33.3).
7037 王臣: 39.2: king minister.
1715 君臣: 62.2: prince minister.

149

0346

Karlgren: 834g
PinYin: zhen1
Rad./Strokes: 154+2

Perseverance, persistence, determination, steadiness, firmness; straight, correct, verified, certain; pure, loyal.

This ideogram is the most repeated in the *YiJing* and also one of the most important to understand the meaning of the text.

In the last decades of the XX century the study of old oracular bone inscriptions shed new light on the original meaning of 貞.

貞 defines the divination act. Originally meant "to determine an uncertain matter through divination". This determination of the propitiousness of external factors, with time changed to an interior determination, subjective commitment to do what is right (*Kunst*). The oldest character versions show a metal incense container in which the divination cracks were made on ox shoulder blades (scapulimancy) or the under-parts of turtle-shells (plastromancy) (See **3621** 龜: turtle):

貞 is also one of the "four cardinal virtues": *yuan heng li zhen*: **7707** 元 **2099** 亨 **3867** 利 貞.
See also **9001**: *The four cardinal virtues.*
It appears 111 times.

正

0351

Karlgren: 833j
PinYin: zheng4
Rad./Strokes: 77+1

Correct, proper, upright, straight; correct, regulate, chief, ruler; just, exactly.

150

征

0352

Karlgren: 833o
PinYin: zheng1
Rad./Strokes: 60+5

Punishing expedition ("to correct"), to reduce to submission, attack, punish, attack; to levy taxes; comes, brings.

 0476: brings good fortune (appears at: 11.1, 46.0, 47.6, 49.2 and 54.1).

征凶 **2808**: brings misfortune (appears at: 9.6, 27.2, 34.1, 41.2, 47.2, 49.3, 49.6, 51.6, 54.0 and 64.3).

政

0355

Karlgren: 833r
PinYin: zheng4
Rad./Strokes: 66+5; 66+4

Standard, law (civil, not criminal), regulation, government.
From **0351** 正, "correct" and 攵 (支), "beat".
See also **7685** 獄: criminal lawsuits.

拯

0360

Karlgren: 896i
PinYin: zheng3
Rad./Strokes: 64+6

Relief, rescue, to lift up, to raise; geld, remove (*Kunst, Rutt*).

成

0379

Karlgren: 818a
PinYin: cheng2
Rad./Strokes: 62+2; 62+3

Accomplish, achieve, finish, complete a task, fulfill; completed, perfect, fully developed, mature; peace making.

城

0380

Karlgren: 818e
PinYin: cheng2
Rad./Strokes: 32+6

City walls; battlements, place fortified for defence; city, citadel.

0383

Karlgren: 894g
PinYin: cheng1
Rad./Strokes: 115+9

Evaluate, weigh, assess, appraise.
From 禾, "grain" and 冉, "a ⊓ hand holding 冉 scales": weighing the grain.

 0384

Karlgren: 891b
PinYin: cheng2
Rad./Strokes: 61+15

Restrain, curb; correct, chastise, reprimand, corrective punishment; a warning.

 0386

Karlgren: 896c
PinYin: cheng2
Rad./Strokes: 64+4

- Support (12.2, 32.3).
- Assist, bear, serve, to present (54.6).
- Receive, inherit: 承家 **0594** (7.6).

 0398

Karlgren: 895a
PinYin: cheng2
Rad./Strokes: 4+9

Ride (40.3), mount, ascend, climb up (13.4).

乘馬 **4310**: a team of four horses (3.2, 3.4, 3.6).

Riding horses was not practised until the fifth century BC in China, long after the ZhouYi was written; before then horses were only used to draw chariots and carriages.

乘 is the image of a war chariot. See also **0280** 車. An ancient representation is shown below:

箕 **0402**

Karlgren: 952f
PinYin: ji1
Rad./Strokes: 118+8

Although this character means winnowing basket, sieve, separate grain from chaff, winnow, it is also the name of an ancient *Shang* State and the name of a prince or viscount.

It only appears in 36.5 along with other character:

箕子 **6939**: *Jizi*, Viscount *Ji* was a minister, and the uncle of the last *Shang* king. He was imprisoned for refusing to serve as minister and reproaching the king for his bad actions. It is told that he simulated madness to keep his life.

幾 **0409**

Karlgren: 547a
PinYin: ji1
Rad./Strokes: 52+9

Almost; imminent, nearly; occasion; minutiae, first subtle signs; approaches.

机 **0411**

Karlgren: 602c
PinYin: ji1
Rad./Strokes: 75+2

Support, stool, low or small table.

己 **0429**

Karlgren: 953a
PinYin: ji3
Rad./Strokes: 49+0

Self, oneself, personal, private.
Cyclic character. 6th heavenly stem.
See **2915** 旬: the ten days week.

Wilhelm replaces **5590** 巳 with 己 in 41.1 and 49.0.

Karlgren: 953s
PinYin: ji4
0432 **Rad./Strokes:** 61+3

Avoid, kept distant, shun, hate; prevent, abstain from, taboo; superstitious fear. From **2735** 心, "heart" and **0429** 己, "private": keep apart.

 Karlgren: 1241b
PinYin: ji4
0452 **Rad./Strokes:** 120+14

Perpetuate, continue, carry on; consecutive, connected, line of succession; to follow.

既 **Karlgren:** 515c
PinYin: ji4
0453 **Rad./Strokes:** 71+7; 71+5

Already, consummated, completed, finished; to be done with, get done. Shows a man 旡 facing away a pot of food 皀, already having eaten.

 Karlgren: 593o
PinYin: ji4
0459 **Rad./Strokes:** 85+14

Ford, cross a stream at a shallow place; complete a task, fulfill, consummate; increase; help. Appears in the hexagrams 63, **0453** 既濟, *After Crossing* and 64, **7114** 未濟, *Before Crossing*, both them related with crossing a river.

蹟 **Karlgren:** 593p
PinYin: ji1
0461 **Rad./Strokes:** 157+14

Climb, ascend, scale, go up, rise; steep.

 Karlgren: 593u
PinYin: ji1
0464 **Rad./Strokes:** 154+14

Sigh; bring, give a present.

 Karlgren: 337a
PinYin: ji4
0465 **Rad./Strokes:** 113+6

Sacrifice, offering to gods or spirits, worship. From **7696** 月 (**3153** 肉), "meat", 又, "hand" and 示, "altar": putting the sacrificial meat on the altar.

及 **Karlgren:** 681a
PinYin: ji2
0468 **Rad./Strokes:** 29+2

Reach, come to, draw out, approach to. From **3097** 人, "man, person" and 又 (ヨ), "hand": hand grabbing a person The hand is more visible in ancient versions of this character:

 Karlgren: 681h
PinYin: ji2
0472 **Rad./Strokes:** 85+4

Draw water (from a well or an underground water body); pull towards oneself. Shows the radical 85, 氵 (**5922** 水), "water" and **0468** 及, "approach".

吉 **Karlgren:** 393a
PinYin: ji2
0476 **Rad./Strokes:** 30+3

Good fortune, auspicious, promising,

fortunate, lucky, advantageous, happiness, good auspices.

It is the only single ideogram meaning good luck in the *YiJing*. Its opposite is **2808** 凶. Frequently appears at the end of a line, as the result of following the oracle advice.

In some cases it goes along **5943** 大, "great" or **7707** 元, "outstanding".

Other modifiers of 吉 are **1390** 初 *(6.0, 7.2)*, **1504** 中 and **1500** 終 *(5.2, 5.6, 6.1, 6.3, 10.4, 15.3, 18.1, 22.5, 37.6, 50.3)*.

It appears 147 times and is the second most frequent character in the *YiJing*, usually translated as "lucky" or "good fortune".

Karlgren: 854b
PinYin: ji1
0481   **Rad./Strokes:** 64+13

Strike, repel, beat, attack.

Karlgren: 911a
PinYin: ji2
0486   **Rad./Strokes:** 75+8

Thorny shrubs, jujube *(Zizyphus jujuba)*, thorns; harassing, painful, distress.

It only appears in the hexagram 29, *The Pit;* which can be viewed as a pit dug in the ground to keep prisoners, as used in ancient China.

6921 叢棘: 29.6: keep a prisoner captive in a place (a pit in this case).

Older versions show clearly the thorns:

See also **0494** 蒺.

Karlgren: 494a
PinYin: ji2
0492   **Rad./Strokes:** 104+5

Ill, harm, defect, stress; hurry; hate.

Ancient representations show an arrow hitting a person:

Karlgren: 494d
PinYin: ji2
0494   **Rad./Strokes:** 140+10

Thorns, spiny shrubs, *Tribulus terrestris*. *Tribulus terrestris* is a flowering plant in the family *Zygophyllaceae*, native to warm temperate and tropical regions of the Old World in southern Europe, southern Asia, throughout Africa, and Australia. Like many weedy species, this plant has many common names, including bindii, bullhead, burra gokharu, caltrop, cat's head, devil's eyelashes, devil's thorn, devil's weed, goathead, puncturevine, and tackweed.

See also **0486** 棘.

Karlgren: 923a
PinYin: ji2
0495   **Rad./Strokes:** 26+7

Approach, come to; promptly.

Shows a 皀, "rice pot" and to the right 卩, "a man": a person looking at a pot of rice, about to eat.

Karlgren: 868t
PinYin: ji1
0500   **Rad./Strokes:** 115+11

Accumulate, store up, hoard provisions.

Shows 禾, "grain" and 責, "store up grain", phonetic.

0522

Karlgren: 864h
PinYin: qi2
Rad./Strokes: 46+4

Name of a mountain, the home of the ancestors of the *Zhou* Dinasty. Also means split, fork in the road.
From **5630** 山, "mountain" and 支, phonetic.

0525

Karlgren: 952a
PinYin: qi2
Rad./Strokes: 12+6

Their, his, its, the; this, that. A demonstrative and possessive pronoun.
Shuowen says winnowing basket. The character is a drawing of a basket, but is not used in this sense in the *YiJing*.
Appears 112 times.

0526

Karlgren: 952k
PinYin: qi1
Rad./Strokes: 74+8

Period, time limit, a full fixed time, a year, seasons.
From **0525** 其, phonetic and **7696** 月, "lunar month": time measured in moons.

0538

Karlgren: 867i
PinYin: zhi3
Rad./Strokes: 113+4

The spirit of god of the earth; need (24.1); only (29.5).
Most *YiJing* versions use this character instead de **0952** 祇 in the two places where it appears in 周易折中 *ZhouYi Zhezhong*, the famous imperial edition of 1715, used as source for many *YiJing* translations, including this book.

154

0547

Karlgren: 953l
PinYin: qi3
Rad./Strokes: 75+3

Willow leaves; willow *(Lycium chinense)*.
See also **7261** 楊: willow, poplar.

0548

Karlgren: 953r
PinYin: qi3
Rad./Strokes: 156+3

Originate, begin; rise, go up.

0549

Karlgren: 536a
PinYin: qi4
Rad./Strokes: 30+13

Tools, artifact, weapon; ability, talent.
Appears only one time:
3181 戎器: 45.X: weapons.

0550

Karlgren: 535a
PinYin: qi4
Rad./Strokes: 75+8

Thrown away, abandoned, forgotten, discarded.

0555

Karlgren: 592a
PinYin: qi1
Rad./Strokes: 38+5

Wife, consort. A legal wife (first wife).
See **0814** 妾: secondary wife, concubine.

0563

Karlgren: 694h
PinYin: qi4
Rad./Strokes: 85+5

Weep, tears, sob, to weep silent tears, broken heart.

Karlgren: 1031f
PinYin: qi1
0575 **Rad./Strokes:** 62+7

Grieved, lamenting; distressed; mourn; pitiful.

Karlgren: 400a
PinYin: qi1
0579 **Rad./Strokes:** 1+1

Seven, seventh; seventh day when the moon reaches a major phase after the new moon.

Karlgren: 15g
PinYin: jia1
0592 **Rad./Strokes:** 30+11

Good, excellent, joyful; commendations, approbation; admirable, praiseworthy;

Karlgren: 32a
PinYin: jia1
0594 **Rad./Strokes:** 40+7

Family, household, clan; home, to keep a home.
House (宀, "roof") where you have domestic animals (豕, "pig" **5766**) (*Karlgren*).
The Chinese used to associate prosperity and money with pigs because in ancient times, only rich families were able to afford pork to eat. Since numerous progeny was equated with "a lucky family life," pigs with their large litters were seen as a symbol of luck. "A pig in the house" 家 symbolized good luck in many aspects for the family.
See **7212** 屋: house.

Character used in the first part of the hexagram 37.

Karlgren: 33c
PinYin: jia3
0599 **Rad./Strokes:** 9+9

Approaches, goes to, attains (55).

Karlgren: 629a
PinYin: jia3
0610 **Rad./Strokes:** 102+0

First day of the ten day week; the day to issue new commands; cyclical character; shell, buff coat.
Cyclical character; the first of the Ten Celestial Stems, first heavenly branch. See **2915** 旬: the ten days week.
Ancient versions resemble a shield or a turtle shell:

Karlgren: 630h
PinYin: jia2
0614 **Rad./Strokes:** 181+7

Cheeks; jowls.
See 輔 **1945**, with similar meaning.

Karlgren: 599a
PinYin: jie1
0620 **Rad./Strokes:** 106+4

Altogether; everybody; in accord; together; complete.
May be originally meant two men together talking:

   5076 匕 is **3097** 人, "man, person", inverted.

   4975 白, "white" may have been **7694** 曰, "talk".

155

0625
Karlgren: 599d
PinYin: jie1
Rad./Strokes: 170+9

Steps, stairs; stages; degree; rank.
From 阝 (when placed to the left 阝 is an abbreviation for the radical 170 阜, "hill") and **0620** 皆, phonetic.

 0626
Karlgren: 861a
PinYin: jie3
Rad./Strokes: 148+6

Deliver, deliverance; untie, loosen; untangle; disjoin.
Tag for hexagram 40, it only appears there.
From **1174** 角, "horn", 刀, "knife" and **4737** 牛, "cow, ox": the knife separates the bovine from its horns.

 0627
Karlgren: 990a
PinYin: jie4
Rad./Strokes: 62+3

Warn, caution, limit, on guard, wary.
Two hands 廾 holding a weapon 戈: warning.

0628
Karlgren: 990c
PinYin: jie4
Rad./Strokes: 149+7

Warn, admonish, compel, coerce; to be on guard, to be frightened, frighten, to mistrust.
From **7334** 言, "words" and **0627** 戒, "prohibition, advertence, guard against".
The *Mawangdui* manuscript replaces this character with **0627** 戒: advertence.

 0629
Karlgren: 327a
PinYin: jie4
Rad./Strokes: 9+2

Firm (16), great (35), curb (58); limit, restriction, boundary; armor; protect, assist, depend on, support; great, important, solid.
The ancient oracle bone graph is a drawing of a man, **3097** 亻 (人) protected by an armor made of slips:

 0643
Karlgren: 710h
PinYin: jiang1
Rad./Strokes: 102+14

Limit, boundary, restriction.
The ancient form was 畺.
 6362 田, "fields" with **5415** 三, "boundary lines" *(Karlgren)*.

0645
Karlgren: 1198a
PinYin: jiang3
Rad./Strokes: 149+10

Conversation, explication, study; to discuss, to speak, to preach.
Related with **7334** 言, "words".

0668
Karlgren: 710e
PinYin: qiang2
Rad./Strokes: 57+13

Strong, stubborn, uncompromising, violent, fierce, demanding, coercive, dominant.

 0673
Karlgren: 727g
PinYin: qiang1
Rad./Strokes: 62+4

Strike, kill, injure, violent assault, maltreat.

From 爿 *qiang,* phonetic and 戈, "weapon".

 0702
Karlgren: 1166a
PinYin: jiao1
Rad./Strokes: 8+4

Union, relation, meeting; exchange, do business; share; contact; have relations with; to hand in or over.

 0706
Karlgren: 1166i
PinYin: xiao4
Rad./Strokes: 75+6

Shackles, yoke; foot fetters; punitive restraint; imprison.
See also **0993** 桎 and **3484** 梏.

 0714
Karlgren: 1166n
PinYin: jiao1
Rad./Strokes: 163+6

Countryside, suburbs, outskirts, frontier; suburban altar and sacrifice.
From **0702** 交, phonetic, and 阝, which is an abbreviation for **3037** 邑, "city" when it appears on the right.

 0719
Karlgren: 1167h
PinYin: jiao1, jiao4
Rad./Strokes: 66+7

Depending on the tone may be used as a verb or noun (though the distinction is not strictly observed):

jiao1: verb: teach instruct.

jiao4: noun: teaching, instruction, doctrine.

 0763
Karlgren: 5n
PinYin: jie1
Rad./Strokes: 30+10

Lament, sigh, interjection of regret or sorrow, alas, groan.

From **3434** 口, "mouth" and 差, phonetic.

 0767
Karlgren: 798b'
PinYin: jie4
Rad./Strokes: 140+14

Offering mat, usually made of straw. Sacrifices or gifts to the gods or the dead ancestors were placed over it.

節 **0795**
Karlgren: 399e
PinYin: jie2
Rad./Strokes: 118+8

Regulate, moderate, articulate, rule; moral integrity; degree, rank; regular division; juncture, circumstance; baton, token of authority. *Lit.:* Knot, node, joint, in bamboo of other plants.
Tag for the hexagram 60.

接 **0800**
Karlgren: 635e
PinYin: jie1
Rad./Strokes: 64+8

Receive, welcome, grant audience; to take with the hand; to accept; inherit; to succeed to.
From 扌, "hand" and **0814** 妾, "concubine", phonetic.

 0803
Karlgren: 46a
PinYin: qie3
Rad./Strokes: 1+4

And; meanwhile; moreover; also; both; alternatively.
Wilhelm/Baynes always translates it as "and" in 29, 38, 40, 43 and 44.

Karlgren: 635a
PinYin: qie4
Rad./Strokes: 38+5

0814

Concubine (secondary wife), hand-maiden, servant girl, slave woman.
See **0555** 妻: first wife.
The woman **4776** 女 is a slave because committed a crime 辛, here abbreviated as **3921** 立 (*Karlgren*).

Karlgren: 368c
PinYin: jian1
Rad./Strokes: 32+8

0825

Solid, firm, strong, hard, resolute, obstinate; durable, hardened, solidified.
Originally it was written as 臤, "subject, servant" (as opposite to **1715** 君, "prince"), plus 又, "hand". The meaning is that a prince has his subjects **0327** 臣 firmly controlled. To stress the meaning of solidity, 土, "earth" was added.

Karlgren: 627a
PinYin: jian1
Rad./Strokes: 12+8

0830

Adjacent, joined, connected, combined; together both, equally, double; at the same time.
It shows two 禾 "grain stalks" joined in the hand. The character 彐, is the ancient form for 又, "hand" (*Karlgren*, 1923).

Karlgren: 480c
PinYin: jian1
Rad./Strokes: 138+11

0834

Hardship, distressing, difficult, laborious.
艱貞 **0346**: fortitude under trying conditions.

Karlgren: 143f
PinYin: jian3
Rad./Strokes: 157+10

0843

Hobble, stumble, limp, proceed haltingly; impasse, obstruction, impediment, obstacle, troubles, difficulties.
Tag for the hexagram 39, which is the only place where this character appears.

Karlgren: 613e
PinYin: jian3
Rad./Strokes: 9+13

0848

Thrift, temperate, restricted, frugal, meager; poor harvest.

Karlgren: 249a
PinYin: jian4
Rad./Strokes: 54+6

0853

Establish, found, appoint, confirm a position.
From 聿, "a hand holding a pen, writing on paper" and 廴, phonetic.

Karlgren: 249g
PinYin: jian4
Rad./Strokes: 9+9

0854

Constant, tenacious, continuous; strong, healthy, dynamic.

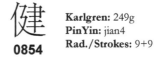

Karlgren: 241a
PinYin: jian4
Rad./Strokes: 147+0

0860

See, observe, look at, to be seen; cause to appear; be exposed to, display, reveal; interview, visit or call on, meet.
From **4596** 目, "eye" and 儿, "person".

0866

Karlgren: 155a
PinYin: jian1
Rad./Strokes: 62+4

Meager, small, insignificant, shabby; narrow, prejudiced.

0872

Karlgren: 477a
PinYin: jian4
Rad./Strokes: 140+13

Offer in sacrifice, offering, worship.

7423 殷薦: 16.X: exalted worship; intensified feelings of praise and awe.

0878

Karlgren: 611f
PinYin: jian4
Rad./Strokes: 85+11

Gradual development, gradually, increasingly; advance by degrees; moisten, dip down into, imbue, influence. Advance like the water, infiltrating gradually.
From **5922** 氵, "water" and 斬, phonetic.
Tag for the hexagram 53.

0880

Karlgren: 432d
PinYin: jian4
Rad./Strokes: 85+6

Continuous flow, repeated, for a second time; flowing water.
From **5922** 氵, "water" and 存, "store, preserve, accumulate".

0881

Karlgren: 366k
PinYin: qian1
Rad./Strokes: 93+7

Lead by hand, lead; haul, drag; to drag into an affair, to connect.
Pull an **4737** 牛, "ox", with a **2881** 玄, "rope".

0885

Karlgren: 627f
PinYin: qian1
Rad./Strokes: 149+10

Modest, humble, yielding, self-effacing attitude, unassuming, reverent.
Some translators, like *Kunst* and *Rutt*, replace this character with his homonymous, 嗛, translating it as "rat, hamster".

> "Partly because of their infestation of dwellings and foodstores, rodents are a rich source of omen material." *(Rutt)*.

Tag for the hexagram 15, which is the only place where it appears.

0889

Karlgren: 197b
PinYin: qian1
Rad./Strokes: 61+9

Exceed, pass the limit; error, transgression.

0911

Karlgren: 206c
PinYin: qian1
Rad./Strokes: 162+12

Move, remove, shift, change, transfer; promotion or change of position or job.

0918

Karlgren: 660n
PinYin: qian2
Rad./Strokes: 85+12

Submerged, hidden (below water); to secret oneself, concealed, to retire.
From **5922** 氵, "water" and 朁, phonetic.
When the *Zhouyi* was written, during the twilight in midwinter, the *Green Dragon* stars cluster was below the horizon, supposedly hidden under water.
See **4258** 龍: dragon.

前
0919
Karlgren: 245a
PinYin: qian2
Rad./Strokes: 18+7

Ahead, front (5), foremost, forward (43), formerly, before, come before in time, anterior, ancient (26).
Ancient representations: 歬, showed a 止, "foot", over a 舟, "boat".
"Prow of a boat" *(Karlgren)* or "A boat going forward".

知
0932
Karlgren: 863a
PinYin: zhi1
Rad./Strokes: 111+3

Wise (19), knows (54), understand, informed.
From **5784** 矢, "arrow" and **3434** 口, "mouth" : To be wise in speech. "Speak so as to hit the mark" *(Karlgren)*.

之
0935
Karlgren: 962a
PinYin: zhi1
Rad./Strokes: 4+3

Personal pronoun, he she, it; this, that, these, etc.; often used as a possessive.

祉
0942
Karlgren: 961k
PinYin: zhi3
Rad./Strokes: 113+4

Blessings, happiness, gratification, good luck, prosperity.
See **1167** 慶, with similar meaning.

趾
0944
Karlgren: 961g
PinYin: zhi3
Rad./Strokes: 157+4

Toes, feet, hoof, paw. Legs (of animals or furniture), footprints, tracks.

From 𤴔 (**6824** 足), "foot" and 止, which shows a left footprint.

祗
0952
Karlgren: 590p
PinYin: zhi1
Rad./Strokes: 113+5

Respect, revere, take as a model.
From 礻 (示), "altar" and 氐, phonetic.
Most *YiJing* versions replace this character by 祇 in the two places where it appears in 周易折中, *Zhouyi Zhezhong*, the famous imperial edition of 1715, used as source for many *YiJing* translations, including this book.
The usual meanings for 祇 are: 29.5, "only" and 24.1, "need".
See **0538** 祇 for more information.

雉
0968
Karlgren: 560e
PinYin: zhi4
Rad./Strokes: 172+5

Pheasant. Bird associated with the trigram Li, ☲ *The Adherent, the Fire.*
See **9000**: The Eight Trigrams.
A 隹, "bird" that is hunted with **5784** 矢, "arrows".
See also **2982** 夷.

志
0971
Karlgren: 962e
PinYin: zhi4
Rad./Strokes: 61+3

Purpose, will, determination, goal; keep the mind on target; treaty; annals.

寘
0976
Karlgren: 375x
PinYin: zhi4
Rad./Strokes: 40+10

Put aside, abandon, to place.

0982
Karlgren: 413a
PinYin: zhi4
Rad./Strokes: 133+0

Arrive, culminate, reach the highest point, utmost, superlative.
"Picture of an arrow (**5784** 矢) that has reached its target" *(Lindqvist)*.
Ancient representations show the arrow clearly:

致 **0984**
Karlgren: 413d
PinYin: zhi4
Rad./Strokes: 133+3

Bring about, cause; involve, induce; present, offer, hand over; send, transmit; extend, apply; carry on to the limit.

制 **0986**
Karlgren: 335a
PinYin: zhi4
Rad./Strokes: 18+6

Make, create, establish; institute, law, regulation; limit, restrain; tailor, trim.
From a modified version of **7114** 未, "tree", and 刂, "knife": Carve a shape with a knife.

桎 **0993**
Karlgren: 413i
PinYin: zhi4
Rad./Strokes: 75+6

Fetters, leg shackles, handcuffs; restrain movement.
See **0706** 校 and **3484** 梏.

窒 **0994**
Karlgren: 413h
PinYin: zhi4
Rad./Strokes: 116+6

Obstruct, block, restrain; block headed; frightened.
From **2899** 穴, "cave, hole" and **0982** 至, phonetic: "struck in a cave or hole".

執 **0996**
Karlgren: 685a
PinYin: zhi2
Rad./Strokes: 32+8

Catch, hold, size, capture; keep, retain; direct, control, manage.
Originally 幸 meant "criminal", and 丸 shows a hand holding an object: criminal and hold.

直 **1006**
Karlgren: 919a
PinYin: zhi2
Rad./Strokes: 109+3

Straight, direct, outspoken, honorable.
An **4596** 目, "eye", that sees in a straight line..
Ancient forms show an eye with a line:

治 **1021**
Karlgren: 976z
PinYin: zhi4
Rad./Strokes: 85+5

Regulate, govern, direct, rule, put in order.
From **5922** 氵, "water" and 台, phonetic: regulate the flow of a river.

遲 **1024**
Karlgren: 596d
PinYin: chi2
Rad./Strokes: 162+12

Hesitation, delay, slow, dilatory, late, procrastinate.

Karlgren: 870b
PinYin: chi3
1028 **Rad./Strokes:** 145+10

Take off, strip off (rank), deprive off, tear off; undress (by force).
From **2989** 衤, "dress" and 虒, phonetic.

Karlgren: 793a
PinYin: chi4
1048 **Rad./Strokes:** 155+0

Purple, red; the color of the fire, associated with the South; sign of official rank.

Karlgren: 917a
PinYin: chi4
1050 **Rad./Strokes:** 66+7

Imperial decree, compel obedience; ordain, dispose, correct, warn. An order from the highest authority.
From **5891** 束, "bind, restrain, control" and 攵, "beat": imperial commands are enforced by tying and beating the people.

金
Karlgren: 652a
PinYin: jin1
1057 **Rad./Strokes:** 167+0

Metal, bronze, gold, golden; money, riches.
When the first part of the *YiJing* was written *(Zhouyi)*, one thousand years BC, gold was a rarity. Shining and polished bronze was a precious metal an a sign of riches. It was also used for metal weapons.

162

晉
Karlgren: 378a
PinYin: jin4
1088 **Rad./Strokes:** 72+6

Progress, advance, promotion, flourishing.
Ancient representations showed two arrows pointing down to what seems to be the sun (**3124** 日). The image below shows an ancient representation in oracular bones.

Tag for the hexagram 35, which is the only one where this ideogram appears.

進
Karlgren: 379a
PinYin: jin4
1091 **Rad./Strokes:** 162+8

Advance, to urge forward, progress; present, introduce, recommend, propose.
From 辶, "walk, go" and 隹, "a bird, probably some kind of dove": indicates advance, like a bird flying forward.

禽
Karlgren: 651j
PinYin: qin2
1100 **Rad./Strokes:** 114+8

Game, animals, birds, prey; quarry, captives, capture. It may be a deer, but it is not its specific meaning.
The bottom part of the character 离, originally was the picture of a net for catching birds, the top part 今 is a phonetic element.

Karlgren: 382o
PinYin: qin1
1107 **Rad./Strokes:** 147+9

Parents, relatives, near, intimate, love, to be fond of, to relate, attach to.

From 亲, phonetic, and **0860** 見, "see": people that one sees every day.

1108
Karlgren: 661c
PinYin: qin1
Rad./Strokes: 9+7

Invade, encroach, appropriate, surprise attack, usurp (The ancient meaning was to approach gradually).

侵伐 **1765**: (15.5): send an army to cross the frontier and raid the enemy.

1123
Karlgren: 831c
PinYin: jing1
Rad./Strokes: 120+7

Classic works; canon, regulate. Lit. the warp of a fabric, pass through. The original meaning was "warp in a loom". In 27.2 and 27.5 it is usually translated as "path".
From 糸 (糸), "silk" and 巠, phonetic, possibly it was the picture of a loom.

經綸 **4252** (3.X) "Thus the noble sorts the threads of the warp and woof": this is a metaphor for the act of government.

It is one of the two characters in *YiJing* **2952** 易經.

1138
Karlgren: 813a
PinYin: jing4
Rad./Strokes: 66+9

Respect, take care of, careful; honor; a present; reverent attention to; good manners.

1140
Karlgren: 813g
PinYin: jing1
Rad./Strokes: 187+13

Frighten, to be afraid, alarmed, startled; stampede.
From **1138** 敬, "respect", over **4310** 馬, "horse": to startle a horse.

1143
Karlgren: 819a
PinYin: jing3
Rad./Strokes: 7+2

Water well; source.
Some older versions of this ideogram show a dot in its center:

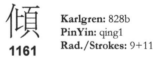

In ancient times the wells were placed in the center of a grid of nine fields. The central field, which had the well, was property of the feudal lord and the eight families living around it cultivated that field in common in benefit of his lord and had shared use of the well.
Tag for the hexagram 48.

1161
Karlgren: 828b
PinYin: qing1
Rad./Strokes: 9+11

To collapse, overturn, upset, overthrown, subvert, bend, exhaust, incline the head; short time *(Kunst)*.

慶
1167
Karlgren: 753a
PinYin: qing4
Rad./Strokes: 61+11

Blessings, good luck; rejoice, happiness; congratulate with gifts, reward.
From **4203** 鹿, "deer" (abbreviated), **2735** 心, "heart" and 夂, "walk slowly": "To come and present a deer to express one's good wishes" *(Karlgren)*.
See **0942** 祉.

1174

Karlgren: 1225a
PinYin: jiao3
Rad./Strokes: 148+0

Horns, in the *YiJing*, symbol of violence and power, not always well employed.

Ancient representations in oracular bones are more graphic:

1175

Karlgren: 1225d
PinYin: jue2
Rad./Strokes: 75+7

Flat or horizontal branch; rafter, roof beams.

From **4593** 木, "tree" and **1174** 角, phonetic.

爵

1179

Karlgren: 1121a
PinYin: jue2
Rad./Strokes: 87+14

Goblet, libation cup, wine cup for ritual libations with bird shaped lid. A cup with tree legs and two handles; sparrow; rank of nobility.

Ancient oracular bones ideograms show clearly a three legged cup:

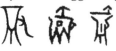

咎

1192

Karlgren: 1068a
PinYin: jiu4
Rad./Strokes: 30+5

Fault, blame, mistake, wrong; inauspicious; misfortune, bad luck, calamity; reproach, censure.

The original meaning of this character was "disaster, illness, harm", but the

meaning has evolved over time adding new meanings, a subjective, moral element as "blame, mistake". Probably the word "fault" is the more adequate for this character, since its covers both the original and the added moral meanings. 咎 appears 100 times in the *YiJing*, but in most cases, along another character (**7173** 无): 无咎, meaning "without fault". Notice that this prognostication doesn't promise success, it only says that there will be neither blame nor calamity.

This character also appears two times in the expression 无大咎 (no big fault). The middle character (**5943** 大) means "big":

> "No big fault", "there will be no great defect" (18.3, 44.3).

It only appears preceded by (18.3, 44.3) **1820** 匪 once.:

> "No defect" (14.1, where 咎 it appears two times).

咎 is preceded two times by **2109** 何:

> "How could there be defect in this?", "How could it be a mistake to go there?" (17.4, 38.5).

Another expression, that appears only once is **2109** 何其 **0525** 咎:

> "How could it be wrong?" (9.1).

Other characters commonly used to indicate trouble are:

4040 吝: humiliation, regret;

3906 厲: danger, threat;

2336 悔: repent, remorse, and

2808 凶: misfortune, pitfall, ominous. This is the worse prognostic possible.

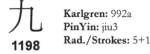

九
1198
Karlgren: 992a
PinYin: jiu3
Rad./Strokes: 5+1

The number nine, nine times, ninth.

舊
1205
Karlgren: 1067c
PinYin: jiu4
Rad./Strokes: 134+12

Ancient, old; past, long ago, for a long time; obsolete. It is used for people, places and things.

酒
1208
Karlgren: 1096k
PinYin: jiu3
Rad./Strokes: 164+3

Drink, wine, liquor, spirits.
From **5922** 氵, "water" and 酉, "wine".
Ancient representations in bronze and oracular bones show clearly a jar:

就
1210
Karlgren: 1093a
PinYin: jiu4
Rad./Strokes: 43+9

Approach, come to, go to, go-around; proceed; follow; accomplish, finish.

丘
1213
Karlgren: 994a
PinYin: qiu1
Rad./Strokes: 1+4

Hill, mound, small hill; great; waste, ruins.
Ancient representations in oracle bones show two hills:

求
1217
Karlgren: 1066a
PinYin: qiu2
Rad./Strokes: 85+2

Seek, strive; ask, implore, beg, pray; desire.

窮
1247
Karlgren: 1006h
PinYin: qiong2
Rad./Strokes: 116+10

Exhaust, worn out, impoverished; gone too far, reduced to extremity; dead end.
From **2899** 穴, "cave" and **3704** 躬, phonetic: poor as those living in caves

酌
1257
Karlgren: 1120d
PinYin: zhuo2
Rad./Strokes: 164+3

Consider, think about, deliberate, consult; pour out wine in a cup.
From 酉, "wine cup" and 勺, "ladle": serve wine to open discussion.

晝
1302
Karlgren: 1075a
PinYin: zhou4
Rad./Strokes: 72+7

Day, time of daylight.
晝日 **3124**: (35.5): day, a day.

甃
1305
Karlgren: 1092h
PinYin: zhou4
Rad./Strokes: 98+9

To repair a well, brickwork of a well, to line a well.

疇
1322
Karlgren: 1090l
PinYin: chou2
Rad./Strokes: 102+14

Comrades, mates; class, category; plowed field, arable land.
From **6362** 田, "cultivated field" and 壽, phonetic

1325
Karlgren: 1092i
PinYin: chou2
Rad./Strokes: 61+9

Anxious, in sorrow; fearful, melancholic, gloomy; mourning.
From 秋, phonetic, and **2735** 心, "heart".

 1327
Karlgren: 1089a
PinYin: chou3
Rad./Strokes: 164+10

Ugly (physically or morally); evil, vile; disgraceful, ominous; drunken, drunk; category, class; enemies. Possessed for an evil spirit.
From **3634** 鬼, "devil", and 酉, "drunk" *(Karlgren)*.

仇 **1332**
Karlgren: 992p
PinYin: chou2
Rad./Strokes: 9+2

Comrade, mate; antagonist, enemy, antagonist; feud, hate.
This character only appears in 50.2 and because of its dual meaning some translations differ:

"My *enemy* dislikes me" (*Legge*).

"My *comrades* are envious" (*Wilhelm/Baynes*).

 1336
Karlgren: 129a
PinYin: zhu3
Rad./Strokes: 3+4

Master, lord, chief; host, innkeeper.
It shows the image of a lamp with a flame above, symbolizing a master (similar to **7037** 王, "king", plus a stroke above):

朱 **1346**
Karlgren: 128a
PinYin: zhu1
Rad./Strokes: 75+2

Scarlet, red, vermilion; symbol of loyalty and sincerity, honor.

株 **1348**
Karlgren: 128f
PinYin: zhu1
Rad./Strokes: 75+6

Stump, trunk or root of a tree; cane.
From **4593** 木, "tree", and **1346** 朱, phonetic, which also shows a tree shape.

諸 **1362**
Karlgren: 45p
PinYin: zhu1
Rad./Strokes: 149+9

Many, all them, every, each one, several, numerous.

"...kept close relations with many/all the feudal lords" (8.X).

From **7334** 言, "words", and 者, phonetic.

逐 **1383**
Karlgren: 1022a
PinYin: zhu2
Rad./Strokes: 162+7

Chase, run after, hunt; expel, push out; in order, in succession; one by one.

"Staring like a tiger, with greed and insatiable desire to *chase*."(27.4).

"Greed and insatiable desire to chase" is written with three characters:

7671 欲, "intense desire" 逐逐: notice how 逐 is repeated twice to remark the passion for the chase.

From **5766** 豕, "pig", and 辶, "go, walk": to chase a pig.

1388

Karlgren: 1224h
PinYin: zhu2
Rad./Strokes: 157+13

Stop walking; falter, limping; halter, hesitate; stamp the foot, fight, struggle. It only appears in 44.1:

8000 蹢躅: "falter, rage around".

"He will be (like) a lean pig, which is sure to keep *jumping about*." *(Legee).*

1390

Karlgren: 87a
PinYin: chu1
Rad./Strokes: 18+5

At first, beginning, initial, incipient, in the early stages.
From **2989** 衤, "clothes", and 刀, "knife": you start to make cloths by cutting the cloth.

1391

Karlgren: 82m
PinYin: chu2
Rad./Strokes: 170+7

Store up, save for future use, put aside, hide in a safe place; eliminate, remove, deduct, divide.

1407

Karlgren: 85a
PinYin: chu3
Rad./Strokes: 141+5

Rest, stop, stay; dwell in a place for a while.
This character originally only included 夂, "man walking slowly" and 几 "small table". A 虍, "tiger" was added later for no clear reason.

1409

Karlgren: 496a
PinYin: chu1
Rad./Strokes: 17+3

Go out, came out, appear, departure; arise, emerge; bring out, take out, expel, leave, get rid of; produce, beget.
Its original shape was a 止, "foot" coming out from an enclosure 凵, as old representations from oracle bones show:

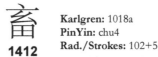

The actual shape is composed by a mountain **5630** 山 repeated two times.

1412

Karlgren: 1018a
PinYin: chu4
Rad./Strokes: 102+5

Accumulate, nurture, support, cultivate, domesticate.
From **2881** 玄 "black" and **6362** 田, "cultivated land": black fertile soil.
Used as a one of the characters in the tags of the hexagrams 9 and 26, both of which are composed by two characters.

1416

Karlgren: 1224g
PinYin: chu4
Rad./Strokes: 148+13

Butt, rush, charge, knock against; strike with the horns; offend or insult.
From **1174** 角, "horn" and 蜀, phonetic.
In the *YijJing* it always indicates an unpropitious action.

1439

Karlgren: 462a
PinYin: chuan1
Rad./Strokes: 47+0

River, flowing water; flood.
Both the *Mawangdui* manuscript and the stone *YiJing* from the *Han* dinasty use

the character 川 as tag for the hexagram 2 (**3684** 坤 is the usual character). *Shaughnessy* says that "water flowing smoothly within a channel" may have been the original meaning. Both *Karlglen* and *Rutt* say that anciently this character was written as 巛 and this is a variant for the three lines used to draw the duplicated trigram that compose the hexagram 2: ☷.
See **9000**: *The Eight Trigrams*.
Compare with **5922** 水, *shui3*: "water, river, stream".

1444

Karlgren: 168m
PinYin: chuan2
Rad./Strokes: 162+9

Quickly, hurry, rapid, rushed, with dispatch.
From 辶, "go, walk" and 耑, phonetic

1453

Karlgren: 727n
PinYin: zhuang4
Rad./Strokes: 33+4

Power, strength, strong, robust, big, full grown male, in the prime of life; injure.
From 爿, "wood" and **5776** 士, "officer, warrior, gentleman".
Used as the second character in the hexagram 34 tag.

1459

Karlgren: 727r
PinYin: chuang2
Rad./Strokes: 90+4

Bed, couch; platform, place to sleep.
Rutt says: "bed, means a platform on which other things rest, such as offerings before a spirit table".
From 爿, "wood" and **4593** 木, "tree".

168

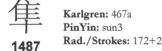

1478

Karlgren: 31a
PinYin: chui2
Rad./Strokes: 32+5

Hang down, (let) drop, lower; bow.

1487

Karlgren: 467a
PinYin: sun3
Rad./Strokes: 172+2

Hawk, bird of prey.
"隹 "bird" on **5807** 十, a kind of roost: captive falcon" *(Karlgren)*.

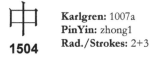

1500

Karlgren: 1002e
PinYin: zhong1
Rad./Strokes: 120+5

End, finish, complete; for ever; end of a cycle; carried to conclusion, consummation, closure; death. The original meaning was: tied-off end of a thread.
From 糸, "silk" and 冬, "eleventh lunar month, winter and the end of the year".

1504

Karlgren: 1007a
PinYin: zhong1
Rad./Strokes: 2+3

Center, inner, in the inside, middle; hit the center, hit target; balanced, central, correct.
Used as the first character in the hexagram 61 tag.

1517

Karlgren: 1010a
PinYin: zhong4
Rad./Strokes: 143+6

Multitude, all, the whole of, majority.
Variant of 眾, which has the same meaning. Ancient representations show three people side by side below an eye

or sun: all people on sight or all people under the sun.

The character for "eye, see" is **4596** 目 and the character for sun is **3124** 日, but its former shape was ☉.

崇
1528
Karlgren: 1003h
PinYin: chong2
Rad./Strokes: 46+8

Extol, honor, reference, esteem; lofty, noble.
From **5630** 山, "mountain" and **6896** 宗, "ancestor": the highest respect (since ancestors were venerated).

憧
1529
Karlgren: 1188b
PinYin: chong1
Rad./Strokes: 61+12

Agitated, unsettled, irresolute. It only appears once (31.4), but duplicated, which intensifies its meaning.
From 忄 (**2735** 心), "heart" and **6626** 童, "child", phonetic.

寵
1534
Karlgren: 1193p
PinYin: chong3
Rad./Strokes: 40+16

Favor, kindness, grace, esteem, affection; receive or give gifts; win favor; to favor (a concubine); concubine.
From 宀, "roof" over **4258** 龍, "dragon", which was a symbol of the emperor.
"Imperial favorite; favour; to love – the one in the imperial chamber" *(Karlgren)*.
Ancient representations show a dragon under a roof (See **4258**, "dragon", to

compare its ancient representations with this character):

居
1535
Karlgren: 49c'
PinYin: ju1
Rad./Strokes: 44+5

Remain; rest (in); abides, dwell; to occupy a position or place; overbearing, arrogant.

拘
1542
Karlgren: 108p
PinYin: ju1
Rad./Strokes: 64+5

Grasp, seize, arrest, catch; to embrace (a person or an idea), to hold in the arms.
From 扌 (手, "hand") and 句, phonetic: grasp with the hand.

懼
1560
Karlgren: 96i
PinYin: ju4
Rad./Strokes: 61+18

Fear, dread, alarm, apprehension.
Only appears in 28.X and 51.X.
3721 恐 has a similar meaning.
From 忄 (**2735** 心, "heart") and 瞿, "startled, scared looks", phonetic.

據
1563
Karlgren: 803f
PinYin: ju4
Rad./Strokes: 64+13

Grasp, seize; lean on, depend on.
From 扌 (手, "hand") and 豦, phonetic.

Karlgren: 123q
PinYin: ju4
1572 **Rad./Strokes:** 44+14

Wear on feet, footwear, shoes; walk on, tread on.
From **5756** 尸, "person", 彳, "walk" and 婁, "to wear": a man who goes on the road with shoes.

Karlgren: 642a
PinYin: qu4
1594 **Rad./Strokes:** 28+3

Go away, leave, depart; remove, put away, eliminate, reject. "Said to be a picture of a cup with a removable lid: that which gets off, is removed" *(Karlgren):*

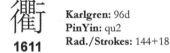

Karlgren: 122c
PinYin: qu1
1602 **Rad./Strokes:** 187+11

Beaters, mounted game flushers; drive horses; chase, expel, to drive away.
From **4310** 馬, "horse" and 區, phonetic.

Karlgren: 96d
PinYin: qu2
1611 **Rad./Strokes:** 144+18

Main road, highway, thoroughfare; a point where many roads meet; crossroads. It only appears in 26.6. Some authors replace it with 祜: blessing, happiness, prosperity. From **2754** 行, "go" and 瞿, phonetic.

Karlgren: 131a
PinYin: qu3
1615 **Rad./Strokes:** 29+6

Take, take a wife, obtain, lay hold of, grasp.

From **1744** 耳, "hear, handle" and 又, "hand": take with the hand, hear and grasp (the meaning).

Karlgren: 860d
PinYin: qu4
1627 **Rad./Strokes:** 169+9

Quiet, alone, silent, lonely; deserted, abandoned.
From **4418** 門, "door" and 臭, phonetic, which combines the characters of **4596** 目 "eye" over 犬 "dog".

Karlgren: 158s
PinYin: quan4
1662 **Rad./Strokes:** 19+18; 19+17

Encourage, exhort, stimulate, urge, advice, persuade.
From 雚, phonetic, and 力, "force, power".

Karlgren: 237a
PinYin: quan2
1674 **Rad./Strokes:** 85+5

Spring, fountain.

Karlgren: 301c
PinYin: jue2
1680 **Rad./Strokes:** 27+10

Their, his, its.

Karlgren: 312b
PinYin: jue2
1697 **Rad./Strokes:** 85+4

Burst open, break, rupture; open a passage for and lead forth a stream; break through an obstacle and scatter; determine, judge, decide.

Karlgren: 778a
PinYin: jue2
1704 **Rad./Strokes:** 109+15

Terrified, look around in fright or alarm, wild-eyed. The doubled character intensifies its meaning.

Karlgren: 459a
PinYin: jun1
1715 **Rad./Strokes:** 30+4

Noble, prince, aristocrat, lord, chief, gentleman; honorable, a highly principled person, superior man.

Most times, this character appears alongside another one, forming the word *JunZi*, whose original meaning was "son of a prince or ruler":

君子**6939**: nobleman.

The "princes" were the feudal nobility of the *Zhou* era, but the word also was applied to the minor aristocracy offspring.

With time, more meanings were added to the word:

- A person of noble character.
- An honorific word used for women to refer to her husband.
- The Confucian philosophy added the "superior man" meaning, which is the one used in some translations (like *Wilhelm/Baynes*).

In many cases *JunZi* is translated as "superior man", following Confucian guidelines, but the word "noble" is more inclusive, since it covers both the original meaning of the word and also gives the idea of "high principles". To translate *JunZi* as "superior man" is anachronistic, since this meaning was coined several centuries after the *YiJing* was written.

A word with a similar meaning is: **5943** 大人**3097**, "big men".
The opposite to 君子 is **2605** 小人 **3097**, "small men".

Karlgren: 468a'
PinYin: jun4
1729 **Rad./Strokes:** 85+7

Deep, deepen, dredge, dig out, dive (in deep water); profound, wise, recondite. It only appears in 32.1.

浚恆**2107** (32.1): ask too much; overstep, go beyond.

Karlgren: 459d
PinYin: qun2
1737 **Rad./Strokes:** 123+7

Group, herd, flock, crowd, host, multitude, congregation.

Karlgren: 981a
PinYin: er3
1744 **Rad./Strokes:** 128+0

Ear/s, handle/s; that which is at the side (as handles).

Karlgren: 564a
PinYin: er4
1751 **Rad./Strokes:** 7+0

Two, twice, the second, to divide en two, dual.

Karlgren: 564g
PinYin: er4
1752 **Rad./Strokes:** 154+5

Supplement, double, secondary, spare; repeat.

Karlgren: 359a
PinYin: er3
Rad./Strokes: 89+10

1754

Your, you.

Karlgren: 982a
PinYin: er2
Rad./Strokes: 126+0

1756

And, then, but, nevertheless, also, only. Join and contrasts two words.

Karlgren: 642k
PinYin: fa3
Rad./Strokes: 85+5

1762

Law, statute; regulations, plan or method; model.

Karlgren: 307a
PinYin: fa1
Rad./Strokes: 9+4

1765

Attack, punish (rebels), submit; beat, cut down, fell.
From 亻 (**3097** 人) "person" and 戈 "battle axe".

Karlgren: 275c
PinYin: fa1
Rad./Strokes: 105+7

1768

Develop, expand, open, manifest, send out, emit, arouse.

Karlgren: 308a
PinYin: fa2
Rad./Strokes: 122+9

1769

Penalty, fine, punish, penalize.

Karlgren: 262a
PinYin: fan3
Rad./Strokes: 29+2

1781

Turn, reverse, come back, return.

Karlgren: 195m
PinYin: fan2
Rad./Strokes: 140+12

1798

Numerous; prosper, propagate, breed, luxurious growth of vegetation, multiply.

Karlgren: 195s
PinYin: fan1
Rad./Strokes: 140+15

1800

Hedge(row), fence, boundary, frontier; to protect.

Karlgren: 740a
PinYin: fang1
Rad./Strokes: 70+0

1802

Square, squarely, directly, straightforward, honest; a place, a region; on all sides; direction, trend, method; suddenly, quick, definite; take a place, occupy; sacrifice to the spirits of the four quarters.

Karlgren: 740z
PinYin: fang2
Rad./Strokes: 170+4

1817

Prevent, careful, protect against; embankment, erect a protective barrier; withstand, be a match for.

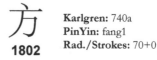

Karlgren: 579a
PinYin: fei1
Rad./Strokes: 175+0

1819

No, strong negative, oppose; wrong, bad; to blame or condemn.

Karlgren: 579c
PinYin: fei3
Rad./Strokes: 22+8

1820

No, strong negative.

1830
Karlgren: 579q
PinYin: fei2
Rad./Strokes: 130+8

Calves of the legs.

1839
Karlgren: 582a
PinYin: fei2
Rad./Strokes: 130+4

Fat, rich, abundant (cheerful); fertile, fruitful.

1850
Karlgren: 580a
PinYin: fei1
Rad./Strokes: 183+0

Fly, flying, soaring; go quickly.

1854
Karlgren: 471g
PinYin: fen4
Rad./Strokes: 61+4

Anger, fury, resentment, exasperation.

1859
Karlgren: 471h
PinYin: fen1
Rad./Strokes: 120+4

Numerous, many; mixed, assorted; confused, scattered, tangled, confusion, disorder.

1866
Karlgren: 474a
PinYin: fen2
Rad./Strokes: 86+8

Burn, set fire; destroy, overthrow.
From **4022** 林, "forest" and **2395** 火 "fire".

1873
Karlgren: 437r
PinYin: fen2
Rad./Strokes: 152+12; 152+

Gelded (pig), castrated; to geld a pig.

1874
Karlgren: 473a
PinYin: fen4
Rad./Strokes: 37+13

Impetuous (resounding); aroused, excited, spirited, determined.

1890
Karlgren: 625h
PinYin: feng1
Rad./Strokes: 182+0

Wind, breath, air; manners, atmosphere. Wind is one of the symbols of the trigram ☴: *The Wind*.
See **9000**: *The Eight Trigrams*.

1895
Karlgren: 899d
PinYin: ping2
Rad./Strokes: 187+2

Ford, wade, cross a stream (shallow or frozen) without a boat.
From **5283** 冫, "ice", phonetic and 马 (**4310** 馬) "horse".

1897
Karlgren: 1014a
PinYin: feng1
Rad./Strokes: 151+11

Abundance, fullness; abundant, luxurious, bountiful, fruitful.
Tag of the hexagram 55.
豐 (*feng*) also appears in bronze inscriptions as the name of the capital city of the *Zhou*.
Feng was the name both of a city and a river. The city of *Feng* was the name of the *Zhou* capital city before the conquest of the *Shang* empire; afterwards it was abandoned.
According to *Steve Marshall*, the hexagram 55 may have a completely different interpretation if we take 豐 as the

name of a city instead the traditional meaning of "abundance".

For more information about Marshall's interpretation see **2993** 宜.

否 **Karlgren:** 999e
PinYin: pi3
1902 **Rad./Strokes:** 30+4

Standstill, stagnation, obstruction, stoppage, dead end; bad, wrong.
Tag for the hexagram 12.

缶 **Karlgren:** 1107a
PinYin: fou3
1905 **Rad./Strokes:** 121+0

Pot, earthen vessel.

夫 **Karlgren:** 101a
PinYin: fu1
1908 **Rad./Strokes:** 37+1

Man, male adult, husband; this, that, those (hex. 8).

 Karlgren: 136q
PinYin: fu4
1927 **Rad./Strokes:** 195+5

Fish, silver carp, perch, freshwater fish.

父 **Karlgren:** 102a
PinYin: fu4
1933 **Rad./Strokes:** 88+0

Father, progenitor; elder, ruler of the family, patriarchal.

 Karlgren: 102h
PinYin: fu3
1934 **Rad./Strokes:** 69+5; 69+4

An axe; a hatchet.

174

孚 **Karlgren:** 1233a
PinYin: fu2
1936 **Rad./Strokes:** 39+4

Truth; reliable, sincere; to inspire confidence in others; capture, prisoner, plunder.
Used as the second character in the hexagram 61 tag.
In ancient bronze and oracular bone inscriptions 孚 was used mainly as a verb, meaning "prisoners, to capture people or booty in battle".
A king who was able to get plenty of plunder and be victorious after war, was considered dependable, trustworthy by his vassals, he inspired confidence. It is possible that this is the link which explains why with time, 孚 become an adjective: "trustworthy, truthful, confidence", losing its original meaning.

輔 **Karlgren:** 102v
PinYin: fu3
1945 **Rad./Strokes:** 159+7

Jaws, cheeks, cheek bone; protect, help, support.
 0614 has a similar meaning.

富 **Karlgren:** 933r
PinYin: fu4
1952 **Rad./Strokes:** 40+9

Rich, wealth, treasure, abundance, prosperity, to enrich.

負 **Karlgren:** 1000a
PinYin: fu4
1956 **Rad./Strokes:** 154+2

Bear, carry, carry in the back, to shoulder, to carry a burden; covered, caked with.

1958 Karlgren: 69g
PinYin: fu1
Rad./Strokes: 130+11

Skin, flesh; cut meat, tender meat.

1963 Karlgren: 1001a
PinYin: fu4
Rad./Strokes: 38+8

Woman, lady, wife, married woman.

1964 Karlgren: 935a
PinYin: fu2
Rad./Strokes: 9+4

Hide away, conceal; crouch, hide, lie hidden, place an ambush.

1971 Karlgren: 276k
PinYin: fu2
Rad./Strokes: 120+5

Knee bands, knee shields; a silk band in which the seal of office was tied to the waist; a band or ribbon worn about the waist, as for ornament, or over the shoulder as a symbol of rank; ceremonial leather apron.

It is not clear which one of the possible meanings is the correct one, but it is clear that 紱 indicates rank and authority.

1978 Karlgren: 933d
PinYin: fu2
Rad./Strokes: 113+9

Happiness, good fortune, blessings.

1980 Karlgren: 933j
PinYin: fu2
Rad./Strokes: 158+9

The spokes of a wheel.

1981 Karlgren: 500a
PinYin: fu2
Rad./Strokes: 57+2

Not (not able or not willing to), negative.
弗克**3320**: impossible, unable to.

1989 Karlgren: 500k
PinYin: fu2
Rad./Strokes: 140+5

Carriage curtain, carriage blind (women were not kept in seclusion, but protected from prying eyes), veil; head ornament, ornamental hairpin, hairpiece, wig.

 only appears in 63.2 where it is not clear if it means a carriage curtain, a head ornament or a wig.

One of the "Book of Songs" *(ShiJing)* odes (from the same time period than the *YiJing*) tells the history of a carriage blind that get lost and is recovered after seven years; on the other hand, *Zhou* women wore large amounts of additional hair, at least on certain formal occasions *(Rutt)*.

1992 Karlgren: 1034d
PinYin: fu4
Rad./Strokes: 60+9

Return, turn back; repeat, restore, revert, recommence.

Tag for the hexagram 24.

1993 Karlgren: 1034m
PinYin: fu4
Rad./Strokes: 146+13; 146+

Overturn, tip over, spill.

1994
Karlgren: 1034h
PinYin: fu4
Rad./Strokes: 130+9

Belly, stomach, gut: body cavity that contains the heart and the spleen, which were considered the source of the feelings.

1997
Karlgren: 1034g
PinYin: fu4
Rad./Strokes: 159+9

Axle trees, axle-brace, two pieces of wood underneath a cart, which hold the axle firm on both sides.

2015
Karlgren: 314a
PinYin: hai4
Rad./Strokes: 40+7

Harm, harmful; injure; to suffer a disease or harm, to injury, hurt, frighten or destroy.

2017
Karlgren: 651l'
PinYin: han2
Rad./Strokes: 30+4

Hidden, hold in the mouth; contain, restrain, tolerate.

2028
Karlgren: 139t
PinYin: han4
Rad./Strokes: 85+3

Sweat, perspiration.
It only appears in 59.5, along with other character, both of them together mean an imperial edict: **2252** 渙汗.

2042
Karlgren: 140f
PinYin: han4
Rad./Strokes: 124+10

Pheasant feather; wing, winged, in flight, soaring.

2048
Karlgren: 143a
PinYin: han2
Rad./Strokes: 40+9

Cold, icy, chilly, wintry; poor needy.

好
2062
Karlgren: 1044a
PinYin: hao3
Rad./Strokes: 38+3

Good, attractive, fine; to like, to be fond of.

2064
Karlgren: 1041q
PinYin: hao4
Rad./Strokes: 141+7

Weep; cry out, call out, scream, cry for help; signal, command.

號咷 **6152**: to weep noisily; wail, to grieve audibly.

亨
2099
Karlgren: 716b
PinYin: heng1
Rad./Strokes: 8+5

Success, prevalence, smooth progress, growth, consummate, triumph; pervade; offering, sacrifice (17.6).
The original meaning was "offering".
See 享 *xiang* **2552**: "offering, sacrifice".
亨 is one of the "Four Cardinal Virtues": *yuan heng li zhen:* **7707** 元 亨 **3867** 利 **0346** 貞.
See **9001**: *The Four Virtues.*

2107
Karlgren: 881d
PinYin: heng2
Rad./Strokes: 61+6

Duration, persistence, endurance, steadiness, continuity; for a long time.
Tag for the hexagram 32.

2109 Karlgren: 1f
PinYin: h4, he2
Rad./Strokes: 9+5

What? how? why? what is? for that reason, therefore.
Sometimes is replaced by 荷: "Bear, carry; receive" (21.6, 26.6).

 2111 Karlgren: 1g
PinYin: he2
Rad./Strokes: 85+5

River, stream, *He* (Yellow) river.

 2115 Karlgren: 8e
PinYin: he2
Rad./Strokes: 30+5

Harmony, concord, conciliation, peace, contented; respond; balance, rhythm.

 2119 Karlgren: 642n
PinYin: he2
Rad./Strokes: 108+5

United, joined, assemble, gather; why not?

2120 Karlgren: 642p
PinYin: ke4
Rad./Strokes: 30+10

Crunch, shut (the jaws), bite, chew; (to be) through.
Used as the second character in the hexagram 21 tag. The other character in the same hexagram has a similar meaning: **5764** 噬.

 2122 Karlgren: 313d
PinYin: he2
Rad./Strokes: 73+5

How? what? where? when? why? why not?

 2131 Karlgren: 1117b
PinYin: he4
Rad./Strokes: 196+10

Crane. This bird is the most favored of all Chinese bird symbols. It is an emblem of longevity, wisdom and nobility.

 2134 Karlgren: 1129x
PinYin: he4
Rad./Strokes: 30+10

To scold with severity (the doubled character in 37.3 intensifies its meaning), stern, severe.

 2135 Karlgren: 113a
PinYin: hou2
Rad./Strokes: 9+7

Feudal lord, (vassal) prince, marquis; officer, governor, chief; skilled archer.
From 亻 (**3097** 人), "person" who shoots **5784** 矢, "arrows" at a 工, "target".
"The shooting at a target was used in antiquity, for the election of feudatories and officials. The precision in shooting was supposed to represent the uprightness of the heart, and vice-versa. Hence the derived meaning, aristocracy." *(Wieger)*.
Ancient representations in oracular bones are illustrative:

 2143 Karlgren: 115a
PinYin: hou4
Rad./Strokes: 60+6

Later, behind, rear, afterward, come after; follow; descendants, successor.
From 彳, "footprints", 夂, "walk", and 幺, "silk thread": walking along, one behind other *(Karlgren)*.

2144
Karlgren: 112a
PinYin: hou4
Rad./Strokes: 30+3

Sovereign, lord, prince; empress; descendants, heirs.

2147
Karlgren: 114a
PinYin: hou4
Rad./Strokes: 27+7

Munificent, generous, liberal; ample, tolerant; substantial, thick, large.

乎

2154
Karlgren: 55a
PinYin: hu1
Rad./Strokes: 4+4

Exclamatory or interrogatory particle; preposition: in, at, on, over, beside.

虎

2161
Karlgren: 57b
PinYin: hu3
Rad./Strokes: 141+2

Tiger. Emblem of bravery and cruelty: strong, wild, extreme yang.
Ancient versions in oracular bones show the tiger shape:

戶

2180
Karlgren: 53a
PinYin: hu4
Rad./Strokes: 63+0

Door, inner door, the house entrance door; household, family.
See **4418** 門, which is the external door that connects the courtyard with the outside.
178

2184
Karlgren: 41h
PinYin: hu2
Rad./Strokes: 57+5

Bow (it is the only meaning used in the *YiJing*); bend, curved. It means the long wooden bow used for war and hunting. From 弓, "bow" and **3504** 瓜, phonetic.

2185
Karlgren: 41i
PinYin: hu2
Rad./Strokes: 94+5

Fox, foxes.
From 犭, "dog" and **3504** 瓜, phonetic.

2207
Karlgren: 784h
PinYin: huo4
Rad./Strokes: 115+14

Harvest, cut grain, reap.
From 禾, "grain" and 蒦, phonetic.

2217
Karlgren: 44a
PinYin: hua2
Rad./Strokes: 140+8

Flowers, blossom, elegance.
"Perhaps simply a picture of a luxuriant tree" *(Karlgren):*

2233
Karlgren: 600c
PinYin: huai2
Rad./Strokes: 61+16

Carry, hold; keep in the bosom; carry in the heart or breast; to cherish in the mind, be anxious about; to love, yearn, cling to.
From 忄 (**2735** 心, "heart") and 褱, "to carry in the bosom".

桓
2236
Karlgren: 164f
PinYin: huan2
Rad./Strokes: 75+6

Hesitation; around, surrounding, turn around, turn back.

It only appears in 3.1 along other character:

> **4904** 磐桓: "hindrance, large rock" and hesitation: turning around temporarily when facing an obstacle.

 患
2240
Karlgren: 159f
PinYin: huan4
Rad./Strokes: 61+7

Misfortune, calamity, disaster, tribulation; distress, grief, suffering.

From 串, phonetic and **2735** 心, "heart": related to the heart: suffering.

緩
2242
Karlgren: 255l
PinYin: huan3
Rad./Strokes: 120+9

Slow, delay; indulgent, lax; remiss, negligent; let things take their course.

From 糸, "silk" and 爰, "slow", phonetic.

 渙
2252
Karlgren: 167b
PinYin: huan4
Rad./Strokes: 85+9

Dispersion, dissolution, scattering; dispel misunderstandings, fantasies and fears; gush, splash; slack, relaxed.

Tag for the hexagram 59.

From 氵 (**5922** 水), "water", and 奐, phonetic.

荒
2271
Karlgren: 742e'
PinYin: huang1
Rad./Strokes: 140+6

Barren, dried-out, waste; wild, weed covered, uncultured, uncultivated, neglected; hollow.

From **7034** 亡, "devastation", 艹 (草), "grass, herbs", and **1439** 川, "flood": "devastation of plant life caused by floods".

隍
2295
Karlgren: 708j
PinYin: huang2
Rad./Strokes: 170+9

Dry moat around the city walls.

From 阝 (阜), "hill, mound", indicating the high city walls, and 皇, phonetic.

黃
2297
Karlgren: 707a
PinYin: huang2
Rad./Strokes: 201+0

Yellow, yellow-brown; color of the soil in central China. In the *YiJing* the yellow color is always favorable, it is the color of the middle and the moderation and it was the imperial color since the *Han* dynasty.

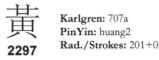 **悔**
2336
Karlgren: 947s
PinYin: hui3
Rad./Strokes: 61+7

Repent, regret, contrition; trouble.

This word indicates both an objective situation and a subjective reaction to such circumstance.

悔 appears 34 times. En 19 cases it is preceded by *wang* **7034** 亡, to indicate that regret/trouble will disappear.

179

Other words commonly used to indicate problems are:

4040 吝: Regret, distress.

3906 厲: Danger, threat.

1192 咎: Fault, blame, bad luck.

2808 凶: Misfortune, pitfall, ominous. This is the worse prognostic possible.

2337
Karlgren: 947t
PinYin: hui4
Rad./Strokes: 72+7

Dark, to get dark, obscure, twilight, shading; the last day of the lunar month; reticent.

2339
Karlgren: 533a
PinYin: hui4
Rad./Strokes: 61+8

Kindness, benevolence; favor, benefit; affectionate; gracious.
重, "attached" to the **2735** 心, "heart" *(Karlgren)*.

彙
2349
Karlgren: 524a
PinYin: hui4
Rad./Strokes: 58+10

Category, class; group, bunch; roots.

徽
2354
Karlgren: 584h
PinYin: hui1
Rad./Strokes: 60+11; 60+14

A three-fold (strong) cord. It is also used as loan for another character of similar pronunciation, meaning good, admirable, but this meaning is not used in the *YiJing*.

2356
Karlgren: 271
PinYin: hui1
Rad./Strokes: 64+12

Display, wave, fly a banner, signal; tear.

180

From 扌 (手), "hand" and **7059** 爲, "do, act": hand giving signals.

婚
2360
Karlgren: 457m
PinYin: hun1
Rad./Strokes: 38+8

Marriage, take a wife; bridegroom, ally. It always appears besides 媾:

婚媾 **3426**: (3.2, 3.4, 22.4, 38.6 y 51.6): to marry.

From **4776** 女, "woman" and 昏, phonetic

鴻
2386
Karlgren: 1172g'
PinYin: hong2
Rad./Strokes: 196+6

Wild goose or swan. It only appears (six times) in the hexagram 53.

The wild goose is an emblem of conjugal affection and fidelity because of the belief that they never take another mate after the death of the first.

From 江, "river", phonetic, and **4688** 鳥, "bird".

2395
Karlgren: 353a
PinYin: huo3
Rad./Strokes: 86+0

Fire, flame.

Fire and brightness are the symbols of the trigram ☲: The Adherent.

See **9000**: *The Eight Trigrams.*.

Ancient representations in oracle bones show a flame:

2402

Karlgren: 929a
PinYin: huo4
Rad./Strokes: 62+4

Perhaps, possibly, if, by chance; doubt-ful, uncertain; some, someone, some-thing, sometime.

或 was originally used for: 口, "terri-tory, state" protected by a 一, "wall" and 戈, "weapons" (now it is written **3738** 國); afterwards it was used as a loan for a word with the same sound, with the meaning that is used in the *Yi-Jing*.

2412

Karlgren: 784d
PinYin: huo4
Rad./Strokes: 94+14

Catch (in hunt), seize, get, obtain, hit the mark, find; succeed. What is caught, gotten or found may be a thing, a person, an opportunity, an idea or perception.

6362 田獲: (40.2): catch a prey in hunting.

From 犭 (犬) "dog" on the 艹 "grass", hunting, and 隻 phonetic.

2424

Karlgren: 876c
PinYin: xi4
Rad./Strokes: 9+7

Cling to, attach to, bind to, (en)tangled, involved, relation.

From 亻 (**3097** 人), "person" and 系, "connect": ties between persons.

喜

2434

Karlgren: 955a
PinYin: xi3
Rad./Strokes: 30+9

Pleasure, joy, happiness, gratification, delight.

From 壴, "drum" and **3434** 口, "mouth": play the drum and sing as an expression of happiness.

2436

Karlgren: 955e
PinYin: xi1
Rad./Strokes: 30+12

Laugh, giggle; merriment; an interjec-tion of joy.

If only appears in 37.3, duplicated, which indicates inordinate mirth.

From **3434** 口, "mouth" and **2434** 喜, "happiness".

2456

Karlgren: 413m
PinYin: die2
Rad./Strokes: 30+6

Bite, cleave, split, gnaw, damage.

From **3434** 口, "mouth" and **0982** 至, "reach".

繋

2458

Karlgren: 854d
PinYin: xi4
Rad./Strokes: 120+13

Tie, attach, bind, connect, tether, restrain; suspend, hang from a cord; keep in mind. From 毄, phonetic and 系, "silk thread".

西

2460

Karlgren: 594a
PinYin: xi1
Rad./Strokes: 146+0

West, western. Related to the autumn.

Older oracular bone representations show something like a bag tied at one end or a basket, suggesting the harvest in autumn:

2480 Karlgren: 787d
PinYin: xi4
Rad./Strokes: 141+12

Fear, fright, terror; sound of thunder.
The two times that it appears (only in
51.0 and 51.1) it is duplicated, and preceded by 震來.

0315 震**3768** 來虩虩: scared of
the thunder.

虩虩: Roaring or loud sound, fear
(intensified because the character
is duplicated).

2485 Karlgren: 796a
PinYin: xi4
Rad./Strokes: 36+0

Nightfall, evening, twilight, dark.
It shows the image of the crescent
moon, like **7696** 月; ancient representations in oracular bones show clearly
the moon:

2495 Karlgren: 925a
PinYin: xi1
Rad./Strokes: 61+6

Rest, pause; breathe, breathing-spell,
take breath, enjoy the rest, well-being,
prosper.
From **6960** 自, "nose" and **2735** 心,
"heart".

2499 Karlgren: 690a
PinYin: xi2
Rad./Strokes: 124+5

Double, duplicate; repeated, repeatedly;
practice, exercise, rehearsal, learning; to

practise flying (young birds learning to
fly flapping its wings).

7658 羽, "wings" above the **3124** 日
Sun : Young birds learning to fly.
Notice that the character has a stroke
above the Sun, but looking at ancient
representations in oracle bones, the
Sun is shown more clearly:

The Sun originally was drawn as a circle:

Used as the first character in the hexagram 29 tag.

2505 Karlgren: 850n
PinYin: xi1
Rad./Strokes: 167+8

Bestow (a reward), confer (honor, employment, rights or dignity), gift.
From 金 (**1057** 金), "metal" and **2952**
易, phonetic: metal (bronze, gold) was
used for coins and rank insignias.

2517 Karlgren: 33j
PinYin: xia2
Rad./Strokes: 162+9

Far, distant; disappear in the distance,
travel far away; remote in time.
From 叚, phonetic and 辶, "go, walk".

2520 Karlgren: 35a
PinYin: xia4
Rad./Strokes: 1+2

Below, down, descend.
Opposite of **5669** 上 *shang4*: above.

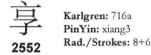 **享**

2552

Karlgren: 716a
PinYin: xiang3
Rad./Strokes: 8+6

Sacrifice, offering to a god or a superior; consecrate; treat.

A similar character, **2099** 亨 *heng1* is closely related with the *YiJing's* divinatory tradition. It comes from 享 *xiang3*, having just a stroke less. With time it took its own significance, but for the time when the *YiJing* was written, both of them had a similar meaning.

The *Zhouyi Zhezhong*, which was used by *Wilhelm* for his translation, uses 享 *xiang* en three places: 41.0, 42.2 and 59.X. *Kunst*, following the *Shisanjin zhushu* also uses *xiang* in 47.2, but 亨, *heng*, appears 47 times in both translations.

 巷

2553

Karlgren: 1182s
PinYin: xiang4
Rad./Strokes: 49+6

Narrow street, lane, alley.
From 共, "public", phonetic and **5590** 巳, abbreviation of **3037** 邑, "city": all people use the streets.

 嚮

2561

Karlgren: 714i
PinYin: xiang4
Rad./Strokes: 30+16

Getting towards, approach, face, near.
From 向, *xiang4*, "direction". Some representations of this character are very similar to 向:

相

2562

Karlgren: 731a
PinYin: xiang1
Rad./Strokes: 109+4

Each other, mutual, reciprocal, cooperative; look to, look at, assist, aid.

祥

2577

Karlgren: 732n
PinYin: xiang2
Rad./Strokes: 113+6

Omen of good luck, auspicious, good presage.
From 礻 (示, which might represent an altar with dripping sacrifices on it. 丅 is how it was written on oracle bones), and **7247** 羊, "sheep", phonetic.

小

2605

Karlgren: 1149a
PinYin: xiao3
Rad./Strokes: 42+0

Small, insignificant, common, humble, mediocre; diminish, belittle.

笑

2615

Karlgren: 1150a
PinYin: xiao4
Rad./Strokes: 118+4

Laugh, smile, merriment, good humor.

咸

2666

Karlgren: 671a
PinYin: xian2
Rad./Strokes: 30+6

Influence, wooing; joined, together, to unite, completely; reciprocity *(Lynn)*; feelings *(Shaughnessy)*; cut-off, chopping *(Kunst, Rutt)*.

Most translators take this character as a loan for different words, and hence assign different meanings to it. Usually it is translated as "influence".
Tag for the hexagram 31.

Karlgren: 368e
PinYin: xian2
Rad./Strokes: 154+8

2671

Virtuous and able, worthy, superior, wise, morally good.
It only appears in 53.X, along with another character: 賢德 **6162**, the meaning of both them along is: virtue and kindheartedness.
From 臤, phonetic and **5005** 貝, "cowries, money": good as money.

Karlgren: 192a
PinYin: xian2
Rad./Strokes: 169+4

2679

Defend, guard, protect, barricade, enclose; enclosure, stables, corral; discipline, train, restrain, forbid.
From **4418** 門, "door" and **4593** 木, "wood": the wood piece that crosses the door closing the entrance.

Karlgren: 241h
PinYin: xian4
Rad./Strokes: 140+7

2686

Weeds, edible greens of various sorts *Amarantus, Chenopodium, Portulaca oleracea,* spinach; mountain sheep. Many scholars (*Karlgren, Rutt, Whincup* and *Kerson Huang,* beween others) think that it is a variant character or an error for other character similar 莧, which means some kind of goat antelope (*Nemorhaedus* genus).

Karlgren: 613f
PinYin: xian3
Rad./Strokes: 170+13

2689

Danger, a narrow pass, precipice, a perilous defile, steep, dangerous and challenging obstacle that must be confronted.
From 阝 (阜, "mountain") and 僉, phonetic: a dangerous gorge.

Karlgren: 242a
PinYin: xian3
Rad./Strokes: 181+14

2692

Manifest, display, make clear; bright, clear, illustrious, conspicuous; girth.
From **3124** 日, "sun", shining over 絲, "silk threads"; at the side there is a 頁, "head".

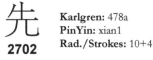

Karlgren: 416i
PinYin: xian4
Rad./Strokes: 170+6

2696

Hips, waist, loins, midsection; boundary (the waist is the boundary between the upper and the lower body parts); limit, frontier, dividing line.
From 阝 (阜, "hill") and **3327** 艮, "stop, limit", which is the character for ☶ *Ken,* Keeping Still one of the Eight Trigrams (see **9000**: *The Eight Trigrams*).

Karlgren: 478a
PinYin: xian1
Rad./Strokes: 10+4

2702

Before, first, foremost, in front, lead.
From 止, "foot" and 儿 (**3097** 人, "person"): following the steps of those who went first.

Karlgren: 663a
PinYin: xin1
Rad./Strokes: 61+0

2735

Heart; conscience, moral nature; soul; core; mind; source of feelings, intentions, will.

Some representations of this character suggest a heart:

信
Karlgren: 384a
PinYin: xin4
Rad./Strokes: 9+7
2748

Trust, believe, confidence, good faith; truthful, sincere, reliable.
From 亻 (**3097** 人), "person" and **7334** 言, "words": a person's word.

興
Karlgren: 889a
PinYin: xing1
Rad./Strokes: 134+8
2753

Rise up, be aroused; lift, raise, start, begin, prosper, flourish, be elated.
Hands () 舁, "lifting" **6615** 同, "together, with joint effort" (*Karlgren*).

行
Karlgren: 748a
PinYin: xing2
Rad./Strokes: 144+0
2754

Originally, in oracle bones from the *Shang* and *Zhou* dynasties early inscriptions, this character depicted a crossroad, as the three early representations below show:

The earlier meaning was road, mobilize. In the *YiJing* it usually means move, go, advance, act, do.

刑
Karlgren: 808b
PinYin: xing2
Rad./Strokes: 18+4
2755

Punishment, discipline, sanction.

7567 用刑: torture, apply corporal punishment.

形
Karlgren: 808d
PinYin: xing2
Rad./Strokes: 59+4
2759

Figure, shape, appearance.

休
Karlgren: 1070a
PinYin: xiu1
Rad./Strokes: 9+4
2786

Stop, rest, relax, quiet; happy, glad; resign, cease; good, fine; benefit, blessings, luck.
From 亻 (**3097** 人), "person" and **4593** 木, "tree": a person resting under a tree.

脩
Karlgren: 1077e
PinYin: xiu1
Rad./Strokes: 130+7
2795

This character means "dried meat", but in the *YiJing* is used as a loan for 修 and hence takes its meaning: cultivate, put in order, arrange, repair, elaborate.

羞
Karlgren: 1076h
PinYin: xiu1
Rad./Strokes: 123+5
2797

Shame, disgrace; inferior, unworthy; a prepared offering, prepared meat, sacrifice, offerings.
The original shape of this character was:

It depicted a **7247** 羊, "sheep" and a 彐 "hand": present a sheep with the hand, as an offering. Later, 丑 started to be used as a phonetic, replacing 彐.
The objective of presenting a sacrifice is purification, to become worthy. Therefore feelings of shame and unworthiness are related with a sacrificial offering.

2808

Karlgren: 1183a
PinYin: xiong1
Rad./Strokes: 17+2

Misfortune, pitfall, ominous, bad, un-
lucky, disastrous, trouble, accident.

This character is the worse prognostic
in the *YiJing*. It is the opposite of **0476**
吉: "good fortune".

From 凵, a pit full of bad stuff and 乂,
a person falling in the pit, hands first.

Other words used to depict trouble are:

4040 吝: Regret, distress.

3906 厲: Danger, threat.

1192 咎: Fault, blame, bad luck.

2336 悔: Repent, remorse, trouble.

盱

2819

Karlgren: 97u
PinYin: xu1
Rad./Strokes: 109+3

Look upward, stare, lift the eyes and regard, wide-eyed, amazed.

From **4596** 目, "eye, stare" and **7592**
于, phonetic.

2821

Karlgren: 78a
PinYin: xu1
Rad./Strokes: 141+6

Empty, vacant, hollow; hill, mound;
abandoned city, ruins, waste; unsub-
stantial, unreal.

2841

Karlgren: 82p
PinYin: xu2
Rad./Strokes: 60+7

Walk slowly, grave, slow, dignified; gen-
tly, quietly, leisurely; tardy, hesitant.

From 彳, "steps" and 余, phonetic.

需

2844

Karlgren: 134a
PinYin: xu1
Rad./Strokes: 173+6

Wait, serve; tarry, stop; get wet. Much
later after the *YiJing* was written the
meaning of "need, want, require" was
added.

From **7662** 雨, "rain" and **1756** 而,
phonetic: "stopped by rain, waiting it
out".

Tag for the hexagram 5.

2845

Karlgren: 134b
PinYin: xu1
Rad./Strokes: 120+14

Torn piece of silk; fine silk clothing,
jacket; silk torn in two pieces, one of
which was given as a token and the
other retained, to identify the bearers
when joined.

From 糸, "silk" and **2844** 需, phonetic.

2847

Karlgren: 133a
PinYin: xu1
Rad./Strokes: 181+3

Beard, whiskers; wait, expect, require.
Beard is the original meaning.

In 54.3 it is usually replaced by **8011**
嬬, "concubine, lover, slave, female
bondservant", following the *Mawangdui*
manuscript and other early texts, or by
6202 娣, "concubine, secondary wife,
younger sister".

Following the *Zhou* kings uses, when a
woman married, she was accompanied
by some bridesmaids, who become
secondary wives and concubines. They
were called younger sisters, 娣.

From 彡, "hair" and 頁, "head": "the
hair of the face" (*Karlgren*).

2851
Karlgren: 83h
PinYin: xu4
Rad./Strokes: 53+4

Order, sequence, sequential, put in order.

2862
Karlgren: 410e
PinYin: xu4
Rad./Strokes: 61+6

Worry, care about, fear, sorrow, pity.
From 忄 (**2735** 心), "heart" and **2901**
血, "blood", phonetic.

2881
Karlgren: 366a
PinYin: xuan2
Rad./Strokes: 95+0

Black, dark, blue-black; deep, profound. Originally meant a dyed thread of rope.

2886
Karlgren: 366e
PinYin: xuan4
Rad./Strokes: 167+5

Rings, carrying rings, ears or bar for carrying a three-legged bronze caldron (**6392** 鼎).
From **1057** 金, "metal" and **2881** 玄, phonetic.
Some representations show clearly a caldron:

2894
Karlgren: 236a
PinYin: xuan2
Rad./Strokes: 70+7

Return, revolve, move in orbit, spin, come full circle, make a circuit.
From 㫃, "banner" and 疋, "foot": walk around the banner.

2899
Karlgren: 409a
PinYin: xue2
Rad./Strokes: 116+0

Pit, cave, den, hole, underground dwellings.
From 宀, "roof, a house" with an entrance **3152** 入, "enter".

2901
Karlgren: 410a
PinYin: xue4
Rad./Strokes: 143+0

Blood, bleeding. The original representation showed a sacrificial vessel with content:

2906
Karlgren: 461a
PinYin: xun1
Rad./Strokes: 86+10

To smoke (meat), choke, suffocate; smoke out; fog, vapor, mist.
From 黑, "smoke" caused by burning 屮, "herbs" (*Karlgren*), as depicts the representation showed below:

2915
Karlgren: 392a
PinYin: xun2
Rad./Strokes: 72+2

Ten-day week; period of time.
From 勹, "wrap, bunch, cluster" and **3124** 日, "day": a group of days (*Karlgren*).
In ancient China the ten days weeks in use was based only on numeric considerations, without astronomic relation. The ten days were associated with the Ten Heavenly Stems.

The Ten Celestial or Heavenly Stems (*tian gan*, **6361** 天干 **3211**) are a Chinese system of cyclic numbers from the *Shang* dynasty.

Each day has the name of one of the Ten Heavenly Stems: *jia* (**0610**), *yi* (**3017**), *bing, ding, wu, ji* (**0429**), *geng* (**3339**), *xin, ren, gu* (癸).

The *Shang* people believed that there were ten suns, each of which appeared in order in a ten-day cycle 旬. The Heavenly Stems, were the names of the ten suns. They were found in the given names of the kings of the *Shang* in their Temple Names. These consisted of a relational term (Father, Mother, Grandfather, Grandmother) to which was added one of the ten stem names (e.g. Grandfather *Jia*). Some historians think the ruling class of the *Shang* had ten clans, but it is not clear whether their society reflected the myth or vice versa. The associations with *Yin-Yang* and the Five Elements developed later, after the collapse of the *Shang* dynasty.

Karlgren: 977a
PinYin: yi3
2930 **Rad./Strokes:** 49+0

Desist, stop, cease, completion, reach the culmination and stop.
It only appears in 26.1, where it replaces **5590** 巳.
See also **0429** 己, *ji3* and **5590** 巳, *si4*.

以
Karlgren: 976b
PinYin: yi3
2932 **Rad./Strokes:** 9+3

Thus, in that way, by means of, with, for; instrument, medium, method, use (of), way (to).

Karlgren: 956a
PinYin: yi2
2940 **Rad./Strokes:** 103+9

Doubt, mistrust, suspect, hesitate.
Ancient oracle bone representations show an old man with a cane and his mouth open as asking where to go (the mouth was drawn as a bird beak).

易
Karlgren: 850a
PinYin: yi4
2952 **Rad./Strokes:** 72+4

Change, versatility; ease, easy; name of a place (34.5, 56.6).
This is one of the characters that form the name *YiJing* 易經 **1123**.
Ancient oracle bone representations show different forms, as:

Some say that the character to the left is a depiction of the sun coming from behind a cloud. The right character may be a bird spreading its wings. *ShuoWen* (an old Chinese dictionary) says: "lizard, gecko, easy, change", between other meanings.

意
Karlgren: 957a
PinYin: yi4
2960 **Rad./Strokes:** 61+9

Think, thought, intention, will.
From **7418** 音, "sound, speech" and **2735** 心, "heart": speech in the heart.

2969
Karlgren: 960c
PinYin: yi2
Rad./Strokes: 181+7

The jaws, the chin, the cheeks; nourish, feed.

Tag for the hexagram 27.

From 臣, "chin" and 頁, "head".

 2982
Karlgren: 551a
PinYin: yi2
Rad./Strokes: 37+3

Hide, wound, suppress, kill, darkening; pacified, at ease, common, ordinary; barbarian tribes in the East; crying pheasant.

From **5943** 大, "big" and 弓, "bow": "barbarian, foreigner man with a bow" (*Karlgren*).

Gao says that 夷 is a transcription error and it should be replaced by **0968** 雉, "pheasant". Both characters had a similar pronunciation in the past. Many scholars now accept *Gao* view.

Used as the second character in the hexagram 36 tag

 2986
Karlgren: 551f
PinYin: yi2
Rad./Strokes: 85+6

Mucus from nose, to have a runny nose, snivel.

From 氵 (**5922** 水), "water" and **2982** 夷, phonetic.

衣 **2989**
Karlgren: 550a
PinYin: yi1
Rad./Strokes: 145+0

Clothes, garment, to wear.

 2990
Karlgren: 550f
PinYin: yi1
Rad./Strokes: 9+6

Depend on, lean upon; accord with, obey; trust.

From 亻 (**3097** 人), "person" and **2989** 衣, phonetic.

 2993
Karlgren: 21a
PinYin: yi2
Rad./Strokes: 40+5

Right, proper, sacrifice to the deity of the soil.

Early representations of this character, show "the sacred (phallic) pole of the *shê* altar to the soil, behung with slices of meat" (*Karlgren*):

宜 appears in several places, between them, in the hexagram 55 Judgment (*GuaCi*). *Marshall* interprets the hexagram 55 as the description of a solar eclipse in the city of *Feng* (see *feng*, **1897** 豐) and translates the Judgment as:

"Not mourning. *Yi* sacrifice at noon."

Marshall also quotes a passage from *La Chine Ancienne*, from *Henri Maspero*:

"If an eclipse of the sun occurred, it was necessary to go to the sun's assistance. The king went in haste to the mound of the God of the Soil and tied it with a red cord, which he wrapped three times around the tree of the god. Followed by his grand officers, he arranged them in battle formation, had the drum beaten, and himself loosed arrows with 'the bow

189

which aids the sun'. At the same time a victim was sacrificed to the God of the Soil, in the same way as was done whenever arms were taken up near him."

"So, it was not 'noon appropriate' at all; rather at noon the *yi* sacrifice was hastily performed by the king to allay the eclipse." (*Marshall*).

2995
Karlgren: 540m
PinYin: yi2
Rad./Strokes: 162+12

Leave behind, reject, abandon, neglect, lose through carelessness.
From 貴, "wealth" and 辶, "walk, go": lose something valuable.

2999
Karlgren: 395d
PinYin: yi4
Rad./Strokes: 61+18

Excellent, good, esteemed, admirable, beautiful, virtuous; restrain, concentrate, discipline, improve.

3003
Karlgren: 2u
PinYin: yi2
Rad./Strokes: 9+13

Ceremony, ritual, sacred dances; protocol, decorum, courtesy, proper behavior.
From 亻 (**3097** 人), "person" and 義, "righteousness".

3006
Karlgren: 2v
PinYin: yi4
Rad./Strokes: 149+13

Discuss, deliberate, negotiate, weight the options, plan for.
From **7334** 言, "words" and 義, "justice".

190

3008
Karlgren: 338a
PinYin: yi4
Rad./Strokes: 73+2

Drag, haul back; pull.
The shape of older representations of the character suggests two hands (⺕) dragging something (*Karlgren*).

3009
Karlgren: 954a
PinYin: yi4
Rad./Strokes: 102+6; 102+7

Different, unique, separate, strange, extraordinary; a foreigner, a stranger.
Ancient oracle bones representations show a person with a scary mask over the head (the head is like that of **3634** 鬼, "demon"), waving the hands in the air: strange, different.

3013
Karlgren: 537a
PinYin: yi4
Rad./Strokes: 18+14

Cut off nose (as punishment for serious crime).
From **5100** 鼻, "nose" and 刂 (刀), "knife".
See also **7697** 刖: "cut the feet".

3016
Karlgren: 394a
PinYin: yi1
Rad./Strokes: 1+0

One, number one.

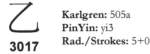

3017
Karlgren: 505a
PinYin: yi3
Rad./Strokes: 5+0

Name of the penultimate *Shang* Emperor; cyclic character: second stem. See also **2915** 旬: the ten days week.

3018
Karlgren: 918a
PinYin: yi4
Rad./Strokes: 56+0

Shoot with arrow and string attached. It was used to hunt birds and fishes to prevent the prey from bolting.
It only appears once, along 取:

弋取 **1615**: in 62.5: catch, seize.

亦
3021
Karlgren: 800a
PinYin: yi4
Rad./Strokes: 8+4

And, also, too, likewise, however.
From **5943** 大, "person", with 八 strokes indicating the sides: besides.
Ancient representations in oracle bones show more clearly a person:

邑
3037
Karlgren: 683a
PinYin: yi4
Rad./Strokes: 163+0

City, town; walled or fortified city, seat of the government for a district.
From 囗, that depicts the wall around the city and 巴 (卩), "seal", representing the authority of the government.

3042
Karlgren: 957e
PinYin: yi4
Rad./Strokes: 9+13

Hundred-thousand; many, great number; exclamation: alas, oh!; quiet, satisfied.

3051
Karlgren: 954d
PinYin: yi4
Rad./Strokes: 124+11

Wings(s) of a bird, flanks of an army; to assist, to protect.
From **7658** 羽, "wings" and **3009** 異, phonetic.

3052
Karlgren: 849a
PinYin: yi4
Rad./Strokes: 108+5

Increase, augment; more; benefit, profit, advantage.
Tag for the hexagram 42.
From **5922** 水, "water", turned sideways (its original shape was 𝄃) over 皿, "dish": "a vase so full of water that it overflows" (*Wieger*).
Notice that in the alternative form below, the upper component just looks like the ☵: *Kan* trigram, "water". See **9000**: *The Eight Trigrams*.

3072
Karlgren: 217a
PinYin: ran2
Rad./Strokes: 86+8

Thus, therefore, hence, in this way; yes, affirm, approve.
It only appears –preceded by 錯– in 30.1:

6793 錯然: cautious, circumspect, careful, polite.

Karlgren: 1164p
PinYin: nao2
3087 **Rad./Strokes:** 75+12

Sag, bend; bent wood; crooked; weak.
From **4593** 木, "tree" and 堯, phonetic.

人 **Karlgren:** 388a
PinYin: ren2
3097 **Rad./Strokes:** 9+0

Man, person(s); people; others; human
being, individual.
It depicts a person, showing his two
legs, with the rest of the body abbreviated. Ancient forms, as shown below,
depict the whole body seen from the
side:

In many cases it appears preceded by
大, "big":
   5943 大人: big, important, influ-
   ent, mature man; noble.

日 **Karlgren:** 404a
PinYin: ri4
3124 **Rad./Strokes:** 72+0

The Sun, day, daylight, daytime; daily.
See also **7696** 月, "the Moon".
Originally it was drawn as a circle:

若 **Karlgren:** 777a
PinYin: ruo4
3126 **Rad./Strokes:** 140+5

Like, just as, to be like; agree, conform
to; approve; concordant; compliant.

192

如 **Karlgren:** 94g
PinYin: ru2
3137 **Rad./Strokes:** 38+3

Thus, in this way, as, like, similar to, if
(conditional).

茹 **Karlgren:** 94r
PinYin: ru2
3139 **Rad./Strokes:** 140+6

Interlaced roots, shoots, roots.
From 草), "grass" and **3137** 如,
phonetic.

袽 **Karlgren:** 94p
PinYin: ru2
3140 **Rad./Strokes:** 145+6

Rags, tatters, caulking rags; silk thread.
From 衤 (**2989** 衣), "clothes" and
3137 如, phonetic.

濡 **Karlgren:** 134f
PinYin: ru2
3149 **Rad./Strokes:** 85+14

Moist, soak, immerse, wet.
From 氵 (**5922** 水), "water" and
2844 , phonetic.

入 **Karlgren:** 695a
PinYin: ru4
3152 **Rad./Strokes:** 11+0

Enter, go into (this is the meaning used
in the *YiJing*); to make to enter; put
into; bring in, present; encroach.
入 and **3097** 人, "person" are very
similar in their current forms.

肉 **Karlgren:** 1033a
PinYin: rou4
3153 **Rad./Strokes:** 130+0

Meat, flesh, fleshy, full.

3181
Karlgren: 1013a
PinYin: rong2
Rad./Strokes: 62+2

Weapons, arms; war chariot; violence, attack.
From 十, abbreviation of **0610** 甲, "armor" and 戈, "spear, battle axe" (*Karlgren*).

3196
Karlgren: 936a
PinYin: gai3
Rad./Strokes: 66+3

Change, reform, correct, amend.
From **0429** 己, phonetic, and 又, "hand": something done with the hand.

3204
Karlgren: 541a
PinYin: kai1
Rad./Strokes: 169+4

Open, establish, found, initiate, start.
From **4418** 門, "door"and 开 (ﾌﾟ), "two hands", stretching to lift the bolt from a door:

3211
Karlgren: 139a
PinYin: gan1
Rad./Strokes: 51+0

Shore, riverbank (this is the meaning used in the *YiJing*); invade, violate, oppose, offend against (it depicts a battering ram or pestle).

3223
Karlgren: 606a
PinYin: gan1
Rad./Strokes: 99+0

Sweet, pleasant, happy, enjoy.
Something sweet in the **3434** 口 "mouth".

3229
Karlgren: 607a
PinYin: gan3
Rad./Strokes: 66+8

Dare, venture, have the courage to try, bold, intrepid; rash, take offensive.
Ancient oracle bones versions show two hands (ﾌ) holding off an animal that can bite: courage:

3233
Karlgren: 140c
PinYin: gan1 quian2
Rad./Strokes: 5+10

This character has different meanings depending on its pronunciation:

> **quian2:** spirit power, creative, force, dynamic, strong, vigor, constant, heaven, heavenly generative principle (male), father, sovereign, power above the human, *yang* power, active, vigorous appearance (1.0, 1.3).
>
> It is the character of the trigram ☰: *The Creative*.
> See **9000**: *The Eight Trigrams*.
> Its duplication in 1.3 is usually interpreted as "diligent, vigorous", although some say it means "sad and fearful".
>
> **gan1:** dry, dried, sun dried, to make extremely dry, all gone, exhausted (21.4, 21.5).

Notice that both meanings are related, the Sun is the ultimate *yang*; it is both powerful and dynamic but also its rays have a drying effect.

幹

3235

Karlgren: 140d
PinYin: gan4
Rad./Strokes: 51+10

Manage, attend to business; correct, straighten, rectify; stem, framework, skeleton; the trunk of a tree or a body; substance, body.

The abbreviated form of this character means "stem". *The Ten Celestial* or *Heavenly Stems*, 天干, are a Chinese system of ordinals that first appeared during the *Shang* dynasty, as the names of the ten days of the week. They were also used in *Shang* period ritual as names for dead family members, who were offered sacrifices on the corresponding day of the *Shang* week.

This character only appears in the hexagram 18, *Decay*. *Wilhelm/Baynes* translate it as "to correct what as been spoiled by the father or mother".

Other character, *gu* **3475** 蠱, which also appears in several lines in the hexagram 18, and not in other place, also gives name to the same hexagram, has interesting meanings, not only "decay", but also "poison, evil magic, curse".

Both characters are related in the scope of the hexagram 18, hence the meaning of 幹 may mean not only to "straighten the corruption left the father", but also "rectify an ancestor's curse".

See also **2915** 旬: *The Ten Day Week, The Ten Heavenly Stems.*

坎

3245

Karlgren: 624d
PinYin: kan3
Rad./Strokes: 32+4

Abyss, pit, hole, chasm, gorge, precipice; snare, trap; dangerous position, critical time.

It is the character of the trigram ☵: *The Abysmal.* See **9000**: *The Eight Trigrams.*

Used as the second character in the hexagram 29 tag.

衎

3252

Karlgren: 139p
PinYin: kan4
Rad./Strokes: 144+3

Rejoice, to be pleased, to give pleasure; geese honking sounds, calls.

亢

3273

Karlgren: 698a
PinYin: kang4
Rad./Strokes: 8+2

Arrogant, haughty, overbearing, excessive, unbending; protect, defend, obstruct; gully (*Kunst*).

The character depicts a **5943** 大, "man" with exaggerated legs 几.

Ancient representations in bronze show a man standing firmly:

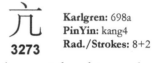

康

3278

Karlgren: 746h
PinYin: kang1
Rad./Strokes: 53+8

康, *Kang* was the title of one of the sons of the King Wen, the founder of the *Zhou* dynasty and, traditionally, the writer of the first part of the *YiJing*. It also means calm, peaceful, happy; prosperous; exalted; strong.

Kang Hou 康侯 **2135**, the Marquis of *Kang*, was the title of *Feng*, the ninth son of King *Wen*. 康 only appears in 35.0, and most possibly, by the time the text of the hexagram 35 was written,

Feng still was the Marquis of *Kang*. Afterwards he was bestowed the fief of *Wei* and since then he was know as the Marquis of *Wei*, and his previous title was forgotten from history.

Many *YiJing* versions, based on *Wilhelm/Baynes*, translate *Kang* as "vigorous", because in *Wilhelm* time it wasn't know that *kang hou* was the title of *Feng*.

Karlgren: 1039a
PinYin: gao4
3287   Rad./Strokes: 30+4

Inform, announce, report, proclaim.
From *niu*, **4737** 牛, "ox", over **3434** *kou*, 口, "mouth".
"To 牛 butt, attack with 口 the mouth" (*Wieger*).
In the *Mawangdui* manuscript and some *Han* stone tablets, it is drawn with an stroke less, as **0476** 吉, "good fortune, auspicious".

誥
Karlgren: 1039e
PinYin: gao4
3288   Rad./Strokes: 149+7

Command, order, decree, imperial mandate, notification, proclamation.
From **7334** 言, "words" and **3287** 告, "announce, proclaim".

高
Karlgren: 1129a
PinYin: gao1
3290   Rad./Strokes: 189+0

High, elevated, exalted, eminent, lofty, illustrious, higher.
高尚 **5670**: noble, lofty, integrity (18.6).
高大 **5943**: great, eminent; lofty (46.X).
See **6896** 宗.

The character depicts a tall building. Earlier representations show it clearly:

膏
Karlgren: 1129i
PinYin: gao1
3296   Rad./Strokes: 130+10

Fat, grease, far meat; richness, favors, dispensing favors.
From **3290** 高, "tall" and 月 (**3153** 肉), "meat".
Note: The component 月 can be taken from **7696** 月, "moon", 肉, "meat", or, in a few cases from 舟, "boat".

考
Karlgren: 1041d
PinYin: kao3
3299   Rad./Strokes: 125+0; 125+2

Examine, inspect; deceased ancestor or father, old.
From 耂 (**3833** 老), "old" and 丂, phonetic
Long time ago 考 meant "old", later "deceased father", and finally to give students examinations and inspect their work, since that is what the old man did.

革
Karlgren: 931a
PinYin: ge2
3314   Rad./Strokes: 177+0

Change, change seasons; revolution, overthrow; skin or hide, rawhide, hide without the hair, flay, peel off; ancient representations depict an animal hide spread out:

The meaning "revolution" may indicate how the deposed leader was deprived from his leadership as the hide is peeled off from a sheep.
Tag for the hexagram 49.

 3320
Karlgren: 903a
PinYin: ke4
Rad./Strokes: 10+5

Can, able, carry, sustain; conquest, dominate, prevail.

 3324
Karlgren: 766d'
PinYin: ke4
Rad./Strokes: 40+6

Guest, visitor; stranger, traveler, traveler from afar.
From 宀, "roof" and **3368** 各, "different", phonetic: one who stays in your house: guest.

3327
Karlgren: 416a
PinYin: gen4
Rad./Strokes: 138+0

Keeping still, limit, check, restrain, stop, enclose; obstinate, opposed; obstacle.
The character, in its ancient form, depicts a man with a (big) staring eye:

Tag for the hexagram 52.
It is the character of the trigram ☶: *The Mountain*.
See **9000**: *The Eight Trigrams*.

3339
Karlgren: 746a
PinYin: geng1
Rad./Strokes: 53+5

7th heavenly stem (i.e. a date in the Chinese calendar), cyclical character. An-

196

cient representations show a tool for threshing grain, two hands are shown holding a pestle:

It points to autumn and the harvest; related words are reward, bestow.
See **2915** 旬: The Ten Days Week.

 3343
Karlgren: 808a
PinYin: geng1
Rad./Strokes: 127+4

Plow, cultivate, till.
From 耒: "plow" and **1143** 井: "well": "a well' was also the term for a certain area of arable land belonging to one village" (*Karlgren*). Combined, it gives the idea of cultivation.

 3364
Karlgren: 1q
PinYin: ge1
Rad./Strokes: 76+10

Sing, song, sad or mournful songs.
From 哥: "brother" and 欠: "mouth wide open": sing.

 3377
Karlgren: 313i
PinYin: ge2
Rad./Strokes: 140+9

Climbing plant, creeping edible bean, *Pueraria Lobata (Dolichos, Pachyrhizus)*.
Its common name is kudzu, it is a vine that grows everywhere. It can be found in the woods of China, in Japan, India and the South of USA, where was introduced from Japan.
From 艹 (草), "grass" and **2122** 曷, phonetic.
It only appears in 47.6, along with 藟:
 4235: fast growing climbing plant.

Karlgren: 1a
PinYin: ke3
3381 **Rad./Strokes:** 30+2

Can, able, may; permit, allow; satisfactory, proper, suitable.
From **3434** 口, "mouth" and 丁 (丂), "exclamation": approve.

Karlgren: 112e
PinYin: gou4
3422 **Rad./Strokes:** 38+6

Couple, mate, meet, interlock, locking; coming to meet; good.
In 44.6 姤 stands for a homonym meaning interlocking of horns by two animals fighting one another (*Karlgren*) (the sixth hexagram line is often associated with horns or the head).
From **4776** 女, "woman" and **2144** 后, phonetic
Tag for the hexagram 44.

婧

Karlgren: 109e
PinYin: gou4
3426 **Rad./Strokes:** 38+10

Marriage, a second marriage, mating, match, families united by marriage; suitor, groom; allying, friendship, favor.
From **4776** 女, "woman" and 冓, "to meet, people interlocking".

Karlgren: 110a
PinYin: kou3
3434 **Rad./Strokes:** 30+0

Mouth, an opening, a hole. Ancient representations are more graphic:

寇

Karlgren: 111a
PinYin: kou4
3444 **Rad./Strokes:** 40+8

Bandit, invader, enemy, robber, violent people, outcasts, plunderers.
To 攴 break into a 完 house (*Karlgren*).

Karlgren: 49i
PinYin: gu4
3455 **Rad./Strokes:** 66+5

Cause, reason; because of, come before as a cause; purpose.

Karlgren: 51a
PinYin: gu3
3467 **Rad./Strokes:** 130+4

Thigh/s, haunches, rump, loins.
From 月 (**3153** 肉), "flesh" and 殳, "beat": "Thigh, rump, part of the flesh which is beaten" (*Karlgren*).

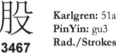

Karlgren: 41c
PinYin: gu1
3470 **Rad./Strokes:** 39+5

Isolated, solitary, alone; fatherless, orphan, without a protector.
From **6939** 子, "child" and **3504** 瓜, phonetic: a child without parents.

蠱

Karlgren: 52a
PinYin: gu3
3475 **Rad./Strokes:** 142+17

Decay, corruption, poisonous worms in the food or the stomach, poison, evil influence, seduction, madness, insanity, curse, spell.
Ancient representations of this character show a vessel with worms or insects:

Tag for the hexagram 18.
See **3235** 幹 for more details about the meaning of this character in the hexagram 18.

Karlgren: 50a
PinYin: gu3
3479 **Rad./Strokes:** 207+0

Drum, drumbeating.
From 壴 "drum" (no longer in use) and 支, "stick": a hand with a drumstick..

Karlgren: 1202a
PinYin: gu3
3483 **Rad./Strokes:** 150+0

Valley, hollow, ditch, gully, river bed, a river separating hills.
Ancient versions depict a valley and its mouth or (in other interpretation) a riverbed separating the hills on either side.

Karlgren: 1039k
PinYin: gu4
3484 **Rad./Strokes:** 75+7

Handcuffs (wooden), shackles, manacles.
An ancient version on oracular bone shows a man in profile with his hands shackled:

Some characters with similar meaning are: **0706** 校 and **0993** 桎.

198

Karlgren: 49t
PinYin: ku1
3492 **Rad./Strokes:** 75+5

Withered, dry wood, decayed, rotten.
From **4593** 木: "tree" and 古, "old", phonetic.

Karlgren: 49u
PinYin: ku3
3493 **Rad./Strokes:** 140+5

Bitter, galling, suffering; *Sonchus* (a wild herb), *Lactuca* (lettuce).
From ⺿ (**6739** 草) "herbs" and 古, phonetic.

Karlgren: 41a
PinYin: gua1
3504 **Rad./Strokes:** 97+0

Melon, gourd, cucumber.
The outer strokes are vines, and the inner part 厶 is a melon. Ancient versions on bronze show it clearly:

Karlgren: 42a
PinYin: gua3
3517 **Rad./Strokes:** 40+11

Little, few; alone, solitary, friendless, single standing, widow; unique; resourceless, inadequate.
From 宀, "roof", 百, "head" and 分, "divide, separate": one who lives in a house whose head is dead: widow.

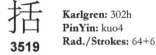

Karlgren: 302h
PinYin: kuo4
3519 **Rad./Strokes:** 64+6

Tie, tied up, closed; bring together; include, embrace.

From 扌 (手), "hand" and **5705** 舌, phonetic: something done with the hand.

3535 Karlgren: 312a
PinYin: guai4
Rad./Strokes: 37+1

Breakthrough, make a breach, split, cut off, pull off; resolute, decisive.
Tag for the hexagram 43.

3547 Karlgren: 312k
PinYin: kuai4
Rad./Strokes: 61+4

Glad, pleased, cheerful, satisfied.
From 忄 (**2735** 心), "heart" and **3535** 夬, phonetic.

官

3552 Karlgren: 157a
PinYin: guan1
Rad./Strokes: 40+5

Office, official, officer, public servant, official's residence, public charge.
From 宀, "roof" and 㠯, "mound": a house with many rooms.

貫

3566 Karlgren: 159a
PinYin: guan4
Rad./Strokes: 154+4

String, string together, pass a string through, thread tightly together.
The graph shows a string passed through cowries (coins, see **5005** 貝):

盥

3569 Karlgren: 161a
PinYin: guan4
Rad./Strokes: 108+10; 108+11

Ablution, hand washing, cleansing before a sacred ceremony.

Clean the 臼 "hands" in a 皿 "bowl" with **5922** 水 water.

Ancient representations show hands (the fingers) over a bowl:

關

3571 Karlgren: 187b
PinYin: guan1
Rad./Strokes: 169+11

Passage, frontier pass; barrier, pass gates.
From **4418** 門, "gate" and unidentifiable strokes inside it.
It only appears in 24.X, besides other character:

5092 閉關: close the border, close the door to visitors.

觀

3575 Karlgren: 158i
PinYin: guan1
Rad./Strokes: 147+18

Contempla/te/tion, look at, observe, watch; regard, examine, evaluate; scenery, sight, aspect.
From 雚, phonetic **0860** 見, "see, observe".
Tag for the hexagram 20.

光

3583 Karlgren: 706a
PinYin: guang1
Rad./Strokes: 10+4

Light, illumination, brilliance, glory, honor.
From **2395** 火, "fire" and 儿, "person" (**3097** 人).
Ancient representations in oracle bone show fire over a person seen on profile.

3598

Karlgren: 739v
PinYin: kuang1
Rad./Strokes: 118+6

Open, square basket woven with strips of bamboo.
From 竹, "bamboo" and 匡, "rectify, square basket".

 3609

Karlgren: 879a
PinYin: gui1
Rad./Strokes: 32+3

Jade tablet or baton as token of rank; seal of office, official seal, jade pointed at top. It was conferred by the king in official ceremonies and its size and shape varied with the rank.
From 土, "earth, clay, land", duplicated: "The token used in conferring fiefs (doubled)" (*Karlgren*).

歸 **3617**

Karlgren: 570a
PinYin: gui1
Rad./Strokes: 77+14

Send in marriage, marriage of a woman, go as a bride to the new home; return to, revert to, to send back.
This character, from the bridegroom viewpoint, means "return", because the bridegroom went for his bride to take her back to his own home.
From 帚, "broom" (wife), 止, "foot, go" and 㠯, "wall": the new bride goes to her new home.
Used as the first character in the hexagram 54 tag.

龜 **3621**

Karlgren: 985a
PinYin: gui1
Rad./Strokes: 213+0

Turtle, symbol of longevity.

200

Ancient representation on oracle bones:

During the *Shang* and *Zhou* dynasties, ox shoulder blades and turtle's shells were used to divine. With time, the *Zhou* dynasty replaced that method by the yarrow stalks (*Achillea millefolium*) procedure to query the *YiJing*. The image on the left shows a turtle shell used for oracular consultation during the *Shang* dynasty.

Most turtle shells were from aquatic species and it was the ventral part of the carapace which was used, the plastron. The plastron was polished on one side and perforated with rows of small holes on the other side. The oracular query was inscribed as a pair of sentences, one positive and other negative on the polished side. Intense heat was applied to the hollows to produce cracks in the polished surface. According to the cracks that appeared it was decided if the positive or negative sentence was the answer from the oracle and finally the interpretation was inscribed on the polished side.

 3633

Karlgren: 986a
PinYin: gui3
Rad./Strokes: 118+11

Bowl, square basket of bamboo, tureen of rice, small or plain rice basket; a kind of vessel or basked used at sacrifices.
From 竹, "bamboo", **3327** 皀 and 皿, "dish".

鬼
3634

Karlgren: 569a
PinYin: gui3
Rad./Strokes: 194+0

Gui tribe (enemies of the *Zhou*), barbarians; ghosts, foreign devils, demons, disembodied spirits, goblins, ghouls.
From 儿, "body", 田, "monstrous head" and ∠, "tail".

Ancient representation on oracular bone:

See **3009** 異, "strange".

刲
3642

Karlgren: 879h
PinYin: kui1
Rad./Strokes: 18+6

Stab, cut, to cut open and clean (as fish), prepare for sacrifice (disembowel).
From 刂, "knife" and **3609** 圭, "jade pointed at top"

闚
3649

Karlgren: 875d
PinYin: kui1
Rad./Strokes: 169+11

Peek, observe furtively; to pry, spy.
From **4418** 門, "door", **1908** 夫, "man" and **0860** 見, "see": peep through a door crack.

虧
3650

Karlgren: 28a
PinYin: kui1
Rad./Strokes: 141+11

Wane, diminish, lessen; failure, loss, deficiency; danger.

睽
3660

Karlgren: 605i
PinYin: kui2
Rad./Strokes: 109+9

Diverging, extraordinary; squint (eyes not aligned); opposition, polarization, estrangement.
It is the hexagram 38 tag, and appears there four times.
From **4596** 目, "eye" and 癸, "the last of the 10 Heavenly Stems" (see **2915** 旬: *The Ten Days Week*): "strange to see".
In the *Mawangdui* manuscript it is replaced by 乖: perverse.

饋
3669

Karlgren: 5401
PinYin: kui4
Rad./Strokes: 184+12

Present food, offer food to a superior, to make a present; meal, food.
From **5810** 食, "meal" and 貴, "highly valued".

坤
3684

Karlgren: 421a
PinYin: kun1
Rad./Strokes: 32+5

Earth, receptive; compliance; matter, field; feminine, mother.
Tag for the hexagram 2. Also It is the character of the trigram ☷: *Earth: The Receptive*. See **9000**: *The Eight Trigrams*.
It is the opposite to "Heaven" **6361** 天, *tian1*.
Both the *Mawangdui* manuscript and the stone *Han* tables use the character 川 *chuan*, "river" as replacement for the hexagram 2 tag. Notice that 堃 "compliance, obedience, female" is also routinely glossed as 順 *shun* "in the flow, obey, submit to". *Shaughnessy* suggests that "water flowing smoothly within a channel" leads to the original sense of this name.
Rutt points out that an archaic form of *kun* is written with three parallel chevrons 巛 (a variant of 川) pointing to

the left, resembling early forms of *chuan*, and is also a variant for the three broken lines used do draw the earth trigram in oracle bones. This graph may well be the left part of *shun*, instead of *chuan*.

3688

Karlgren: 420a
PinYin: kun4
Rad./Strokes: 31+4

Oppression, obstruction; besieged, surrounded; entangled; distress, exhaustion, anxiety.
From **4593** 木, "tree"and 囗, "an enclosure".
Tag for the hexagram 47.

3698

Karlgren: 1172d
PinYin: gong1
Rad./Strokes: 19+3

Deeds, accomplishments, merits, good result, praiseworthy.
From 工, "work" and 力, "power; strength; ability": work well done.
Compare with 攻 **3699**.

3699

Karlgren: 1172e
PinYin: gong1
Rad./Strokes: 66+3

Attack, assault, take the offensive; criticize; work at.
Combines 工, "work" with 攵, "beat".
Compare with 功 **3698**.

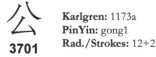

3701

Karlgren: 1173a
PinYin: gong1
Rad./Strokes: 12+2

Prince, feudal lord, duke, noble of rank (the nobiliary titles, from high to low, were: duke, marquis, count, viscount, baron); public, impartial, with justice, fair.
There are several etymological interpretations:

- The correct **4845** 八, "division" of 厶, "private" things (*Karlgren*). This points to the prince public business and duties.
- The speaking from the **3434** 口, "mouth" that is released and made **4845** 八 "public"; that means proclamations from the authorities. Ancient representations in oracle bones support this interpretation:

3704

Karlgren: 1006f
PinYin: gong1
Rad./Strokes: 158+3

Oneself, (own) body, person.
From **5718** 身, "body, person, oneself" and 弓, phonetic.

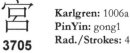

3705

Karlgren: 1006a
PinYin: gong1
Rad./Strokes: 40+7

House, palace, dwelling place, chambers, mansion, temple.
The character shows two 口 rooms and a **3434** 宀 roof, or (in another interpretation), a door and a window under the roof, as some ancient representations in bronze and oracle bones show:

3706

Karlgren: 887f
PinYin: gong1
Rad./Strokes: 130+4

Arm, esp. the upper arm, from elbow to shoulder.

Originally was written as 厶, "a bent arm", but both ⺕ (now 𠂇), "a hand" and 月 (**3153** 肉), "flesh" were added to it.

恭

3711

Karlgren: 1182l
PinYin: gong1
Rad./Strokes: 61+6

Respect, reverence, courtesy.
From共, phonetic, and 小 (**2735** 心), "heart".

鞏

3718

Karlgren: 1172c'
PinYin: gong3
Rad./Strokes: 177+6

Bind, bind with thongs; strengthen, secure, guard.

From 工, "work", phonetic, **3314** 革, "leather" (that didn't appear in earlier forms), to reinforce the meaning of binding and (on top right), what seems to be a person reaching out with both hands (now it is seen as 凡).

The images below show the evolution of this character:

恐

3721

Karlgren: 1172d'
PinYin: kong3
Rad./Strokes: 61+6

Fear, apprehensive, anxious, worried.
From 巩, phonetic, and **2735** 心, "heart".

恐 only appears in 51.X, along with 懼:

恐懼 **1560**: fear, dread, to be afraid of.

過

3730

Karlgren: 0018e
PinYin: guo4
Rad./Strokes: 162+9

Pass, pass through, go across, go beyond, excess, beyond the ordinary or proper limit; ; transgression, fault.

From 咼, phonetic, and 辶 (辵), "walk, go".

It appears besides 涉 at 28.6:

過涉 **5707**: transition; transference; to cross a ferry.

果

3732

Karlgren: 351a
PinYin: guo3
Rad./Strokes: 75+4

Fruit (of a plant), come to fruition, realization, result, effect; bring to result, reach the conclusion; determined, courageous, go to the bitter end.

The more ancient representations of this graph show a plant with its fruit:

國

3738

Karlgren: 0929o
PinYin: guo2
Rad./Strokes: 31+8

State, country, nation, kingdom, a dynasty; capital city.

Formerly **2402** 或 represented a **3434** 口 territory protected by **3016** 一 a wall and 戈 weapons. Then 或 was surrounded by 囗, depicting the borders of a country, producing the full form 國. (或 was borrowed for the similar sounding word *huò* "or").

Karlgren: 798g
PinYin: xi1
3763 **Rad./Strokes:** 130+8

Seasoned, dried and/or salted meat.
It only appears in 21.3 along with other
related character:

腦肉 **3153**, "meat, flesh": seasoned meat (using salt, smoke,
etc.) prepared for a journey.

From 月 (**3153** 肉), "meat, flesh" and
昔, "dried meat".

 Karlgren: 0944a
PinYin: lai2
3768 **Rad./Strokes:** 9+6

Come, arrive, return, bring.

 Karlgren: 1135a
PinYin: lao2
3826 **Rad./Strokes:** 19+10

Toil, diligent work; deeds, achievements, merits.
From 炊, (**2395** 火, "fire" duplicated)
over 冖, "roof" and 力, "strength":
"To toil at the lamp's light, during
night" (*Wieger*).

老 **Karlgren:** 1055a
PinYin: lao3
3833 **Rad./Strokes:** 125+0

Old, aged.
From 耂 (**3299** 考), "an old man",
leaning on a **5076** 匕, "cane" (匕 is a
spoon, but the original graph is similar
to a cane):

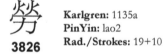

里 **Karlgren:** 978a
PinYin: li3
3857 **Rad./Strokes:** 166+0

Unit of distance, about 500 m or 1800
feet; a village with 25-50 families; place
of residence.
From 土, "soil, earth, land" and **6362**
田, "field": a measure of land and
fields.

 Karlgren: 519a
PinYin: li4
3867 **Rad./Strokes:** 18+5

Favorable, lucky, advantageous, profit-
able, beneficial, furthering, harvesting;
sharp, sharp witted.
From 禾, "grain" and 刂 (刀),
"knife": harvesting grain with a knife:
benefit, profit.
In *Shang* oracle bones, 利 was used as
adjective, meaning "sharp".
Kunst proposes the following semantic
development for this character: "sharp
> trenchant, incisive > incisive deter-
mination > advantageous determination > advantageous in general".
It is one of the "Four (Heavenly)
Virtues" (so called by the Confucian
school): *yuan heng li zhen:* **7707** 元 **2099**
亨 利 **0346** 貞.
See **9001**: *The Four Virtues.*

藜 **Karlgren:** 519l
PinYin: li2
3877 **Rad./Strokes:** 140+15

Tribulus terrestris, it is a flowering plant
in the family *Zygophyllaceae,* its thorns
are sharp enough to puncture bicycle
tires and to cause painful injury to bare
feet; thistles, brambles.

3886
Karlgren: 597d
PinYin: li3
Rad./Strokes: 113+13

Social manners, politeness, propriety; ceremony, rituals.

The simplified form in use for at least 2500 years is 礼, and its genesis helps to understand the meaning of this graph:

礼 comes from 示 (示, *shi*), "altar" and ㇄ (simplified from 曲 over 豆), "a vase full of flowers, offered as a sacrifice to the gods". The bronze graph shown below depicts clearly its origins:

In ancient China, social manners and ritual were intimately related. In Confucianism, the acts of everyday life are considered rituals and should be performed in the proper way, following the established patterns.

 3893
Karlgren: 562a
PinYin: lu3
Rad./Strokes: 44+12

Step on, treading, track, walk or follow a trail or way; footwear, shoes; conduct, behavior; ceremonies.
Tag for the hexagram 10.

離 **3902**
Karlgren: 23f
PinYin: li2
Rad./Strokes: 172+11

Brightness, radiance, attach, cling; name of a bird. The modern meaning is leave, separate.
From 离, "demon", phonetic and 隹, "bird": an ominous bird, perhaps an Owl or Oriole. *Rutt* says it is the Black-naped oriole, *Oriolus chinensis*. In the *Shi Jing* odes the oriole song is frequently related to tragedy, sadness and sorrow. That suggest that orioles could be birds of sad omen.

Tag for the hexagram 30, also it is the character of the trigram ☲: *The Clinging, Fire.*

See **9000** *The Eight Trigrams.*

厲 **3906**
Karlgren: 340a
PinYin: li4
Rad./Strokes: 27+13

Danger, threat; oppressive, cruel, wicked, brutal, harsh; sickness, malevolent devil; grind, polish, sharpen; discipline.
From **7030** 萬, "scorpion" and 厂, "cliff, cave": cruel, dangerous.
Other characters commonly used to indicate trouble are:

4040 吝: Regret, distress.

1192 咎: Fault, blame, bad luck.

2336 悔: Repent, remorse, trouble.

2808 凶: Misfortune, pitfall, ominous. This is the worse prognostic possible.

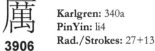 **3912**
Karlgren: 520a
PinYin: li4
Rad./Strokes: 85+7

Treat; command, overlook, manage; come and inspect
From 氵 (**5922** 水), "water" and **7116** 位, "position": the water flows everywhere.

3914

Karlgren: 878a
PinYin: li4
Rad./Strokes: 198+8

Attached, interconnected, tied, interdependent, depend on; congregate; couple, pair.

The character shows a deer with its antlers. In some bronze graphs the deer is clearly depicted but in others, only the antlers are visible:

The meaning of pair and congregate are related with the image of deer joined in a herd.

3921

Karlgren: 694a
PinYin: li4
Rad./Strokes: 117+0

Stand up or erect; set up, establish; raise, ascend; keep the position or the course, resist, endure.

Ancient versions on oracle bone show a man standing on the ground, legs spread.

3930

Karlgren: 858h
PinYin: li4
Rad./Strokes: 72+12

Calculate; calculate the course of stars or astronomical events, ephemeris; the calendar, seasons.

From 禾, "grain", duplicated, under 厂, "works" and **3124** 日, "Sun, a day": regulation of agricultural work along the seasons: the calendar.

The next character, **3931** 歷, has a similar meaning.

206

3931

Karlgren: 858e
PinYin: li4
Rad./Strokes: 77+12

Calendar, calculate; number; successively, a sequence; classification; history, era, age, past; experience.

From 禾, "grain", duplicated, under 厂, "works" and 止, "foot, throughout": regulation of agricultural works through time: the calendar.

Some *YiJing* translations replace this character with **3930** 曆, which is very similar, in 49.X.

3941

Karlgren: 735a
PinYin: liang2
Rad./Strokes: 138+1

Good, fine, gorgeous, excellent; virtuous; natural.

3953

Karlgren: 736a
PinYin: liang3
Rad./Strokes: 11+6

Two, twice, two times, duplicated, double, again; pair, couple.

It can be seen as a yoke for two oxen or a scale with a weight in each of the two arms. The two graphs shown below are ancient representations in bronze:

3984

Karlgren: 291a
PinYin: lie4
Rad./Strokes: 18+4

Rend, tear, divide; sort, distribute, arrange in order, classify, organize.

From 歹, "a piece of a broken bone" and 刀, "knife".

3987

Karlgren: 291c
PinYin: lie4
Rad./Strokes: 85+6

Clear, limpid, pure.
From 氵 (**5922** 水), "water" and 列, phonetic: clear as water.

連
4009

Karlgren: 213a
PinYin: lian2
Rad./Strokes: 162+7

Union, alliance, connection; a kind of carriage, travel or carry on a carriage; toilsome, difficult, slow.
From **0280** 車, "carriage" and 辶, "go": cars travelling in a row (*Karlgren*).

4012

Karlgren: 213b
PinYin: lian2
Rad./Strokes: 85+10; 85+11

Flowing water, ripples raised on water by wind, in streams, dripping (as tears). See the previous character: **4009** 連.
This character adds 氵 (**5922** 水), "water" to the left of the previous character, giving so the idea of running water, dripping, flowing, spreading on.

林
4022

Karlgren: 655a
PinYin: lin2
Rad./Strokes: 75+4

Woods, forest, grove, copse.
Many **4593** 木 trees.

臨
4027

Karlgren: 669e
PinYin: lin2
Rad./Strokes: 131+11

Approach, oversee, inspect, supervise (a sacrifice), ceremonial wailing.
Tag for the hexagram 19.

From **0327** 臣, "minister, officer" and **5281** 品, "kind, variety": supervise things.

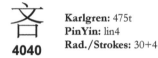
4033

Karlgren: 387i
PinYin: lin2
Rad./Strokes: 163+12

Neighbor, neighborhood, extended family, associate, assistant.
From 粦, phonetic, and 阝 (**3037** 邑), "place, city".

吝
4040

Karlgren: 475t
PinYin: lin4
Rad./Strokes: 30+4

Humiliation, regret, shame, distress, grief, sorrow; miserly, niggardly.
吝 is a warning of trouble. Its meaning covers both an external objective situation as the subjective feelings involved with it.
It typically appears at the end of a text line (in 16 out of 20 occurrences). It is modified by *xiao* **2605** 小, "small", in 21.3 and 45.3. It follows *lin* **0346** 貞, "perseverance" in 11.6, 32.3, 35.6 and 40.3.
Other characters commonly used to indicate trouble are:

> **3906** 厲: Danger, threat.
>
> **1192** 咎: Fault, blame, bad luck.
>
> **2336** 悔: Repent, remorse, trouble.
>
> **2808** 凶: Misfortune, pitfall, ominous. This is the worse prognostic possible.

4067

Karlgren: 898c
PinYin: ling2
Rad./Strokes: 170+8

Hill, mound, tumulus, barrow; ascend a hill, ascend; transgress, overstep the limits, invade, encroach upon, usurp. In the *YiJing* it seems to mean only a hill. Originally it was written 㚄, from 先, "mound" over 夂, "walk slowly". 阝 (阜), "hill", was added later.

4071
Karlgren: 836i
PinYin: ling2
Rad./Strokes: 173+16

Supernatural, numinous, spiritual, magic; sorcerer, diviner.
From 霝, "raindrops" and **7164** 巫, "sorcerer": sorceresses dance to invoke the spirits to make rain.

4083
Karlgren: 1114p
PinYin: liu2
Rad./Strokes: 102+5

Detain, protract, delay, tarry, a long time.

4129
Karlgren: 1125a
PinYin: le4
Rad./Strokes: 75+11

Music, joyous, happy.
Probably the graph shows a stringed instrument made of wood **4593** 木 and string 幺.

4152
Karlgren: 120a
PinYin: lou4
Rad./Strokes: 85+11

Leak, drip.
From 氵 (**5922** 水), "water", 尸 (**7212** 屋, "roof, room, house") and **7662** 雨, "rain": rain water dripping through the roof.

4158
Karlgren: 69q
PinYin: lu2
Rad./Strokes: 53+16

Hut, hovel, shack, a thatched cottage; a rustic place to pass the night.
From 广, "hut" and 盧, phonetic.

4191
Karlgren: 1032f
PinYin: lu4
Rad./Strokes: 170+8

Highland, plateau, heights, dry land.
From 先, phonetic, over 土, "soil, earth"; later 阝 (阜), "hill" was added to the left.

4196
Karlgren: 1208h
PinYin: lu4
Rad./Strokes: 113+8

Prosperity, revenue, salary, favors, official recognition, blessings.
From 礻 (示), "altar" y 录, phonetic. The simplified form (禄) can be found carved in good luck charms.

4203
Karlgren: 1209a
PinYin: lu4
Rad./Strokes: 198+0

Deer (mature male with antlers). Earlier graphs show the animal shape:

4220
Karlgren: 180c
PinYin: luan4
Rad./Strokes: 5+12

Disorder, confusion, rebellion, anarchy, chaos, a mess, confused and tangled situation.

The original meaning was "a mess or tangle of threads", but its actual meaning is similar to the one used in the *YiJing*.

 4235

Karlgren: 577g
PinYin: lei3
Rad./Strokes: 140+15

Vines, climbing plant, creeper.
From 艹, "herb" and 畾, phonetic.
See **3377** 葛, with a similar meaning.

 4236

Karlgren: 577o
PinYin: lei2
Rad./Strokes: 173+5

Thunder, shock, terrifying, arousing power surging from the earth.
From **7662** 雨: "rain" and **6362** 田, "field". Ancient representations shown several fields with a lightning bolt moving between them.

It is a simplified form for 靁.
See **0315** 震, "thunder": ☳ and also **6358** 電: "lightning".

 4240

Karlgren: 14c
PinYin: lei2
Rad./Strokes: 123+13

Bound, entangled, tethered; break, damage; weak, lean, emaciated.

4244

Karlgren: 529a
PinYin: lei4
Rad./Strokes: 181+10

Class, category, group, kind; discriminate, categorize.

"Categories: 米 rice, exemplifying the vegetable kingdom, 犬 dog, the animal kingdom, and 頁 head, the human world" (*Karlgren*).

 4252

Karlgren: 470e
PinYin: lun2
Rad./Strokes: 120+8

Woof, silk threads, to twist or bend silk; classify, coordinate, adjust.
From 糸 (糸), "silk thread" and 侖, phonetic.

4254

Karlgren: 470f
PinYin: lun2
Rad./Strokes: 159+8

Wheel/s.
From **0280** 車, "carriage" and 侖, phonetic.

4255

Karlgren: 1015f
PinYin: long2
Rad./Strokes: 170+9

Bulge upward, rise above all others, high, ample, surpassing, plentiful, eminent, prosperous.

4258

Karlgren: 1193a
PinYin: long2
Rad./Strokes: 212+0

Dragon, powerful force that surges from the waters, associated with rain, floods, heaven, the trigram ☰ and the hexagram 1.
Ancient representations of this characters are more graphic than the actual sign:

The Chinese dragon is a legendary animal which is long in body, has a big mouth and has many horns. It also has supernatural godly power. It is connected with heaven and spiritual energy. It is at home either under the waters or flying in heaven. Also it is related with the supreme authority (the emperor). Different from the western dragon, it is not evil, but beneficial.

The dragon occupies an important place in the Chinese mythology and appears in arts, literature, songs and legends. The origin of the Chinese dragon (as symbol) is not known, but precedes the written history.

4286
Karlgren: 77a
PinYin: lu3
Rad./Strokes: 70+6

Wanderer, traveler; stranger; stay away from home; guest, to lodge; multitude, troops.
From 㫃, "banner" and **6919** 从, "follow" (it also means "two men" **3097** 人): two men camping under a banner or following a banner. Ancient representations in bronze and oracle bones show this meaning clearly:

Tag for the hexagram 56.

4297
Karlgren: 502c
PinYin: lu4
Rad./Strokes: 60+6

Law, rule, discipline, follow a model; ranks; standard bamboo tuning pitch pipes.
From 彳, "step" and 聿, "writing on paper" (⺻ hand holding pen): written regulations for the march.

4300 攣
Karlgren: 178n
PinYin: luan2
Rad./Strokes: 64+19

Attach, link, bind, tie together; connect, continue.
From 䜌, "confusion" and 手, "hand": intertwine 糸 silk threads with the hand.

4310 馬
Karlgren: 40a
PinYin: ma3
Rad./Strokes: 187+0

Horse. The evolution of this character can be seen below:

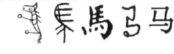

4354 莽
Karlgren: 709a
PinYin: mang3
Rad./Strokes: 140+8

Thicket, weeds, underbrush, luxuriant grass.
From ⺿ (草), "grass", 犬, "dog" and 廾, "more grass": the grass has grown enough to hide a dog..

4364 茅
Karlgren: 1109c
PinYin: mao2
Rad./Strokes: 140+5

Reeds, cogongrass, white grass, *mao*, used for wrapping offerings.

From 艹 (*cao* 草), "grass" and *máo* 矛, phonetic.

繆
4387
Karlgren: 904f
PinYin: mo4
Rad./Strokes: 120+15

Rope, stranded black cord.
From 糸 "silk threads" and 墨, "black ink".

妹
4410
Karlgren: 531k
PinYin: mei4
Rad./Strokes: 38+5

Younger sister, maiden, daughter, daughter of a secondary wife; virgin.
From **4776** 女, "woman" and **7114** 未, "not yet": girl not yet nubile.
Used as the second character in the hexagram 54 tag.

沬
4412
Karlgren: 531p
PinYin: mei4
Rad./Strokes: 85+5

Mei star; small stars, a faint light.
It only appears in the hexagram 55. It is not clear if it is the name of a star or to which star is related.
In some translations it is replaced by mo **4549** 沫: "saliva, froth, star mo".
Kunst and *Whincup* replace it with 昧: "dark spot, hidden, obscure".
In the *Mawangdui* manuscript it is replaced by 茉: "white jasmine"
See **6472** 斗: The Big Dipper, which also appears in the hexagram 55.

門
4418
Karlgren: 441a
PinYin: men2
Rad./Strokes: 169+0

Gate, door.

This is the external door, separating courtyard and street, compare with **2180** 戶, "inner door, the house entrance door".
The graph shows a double swinging door.

> 門庭 **6405**: front entrance and courtyard (36.4, 60.2).

悶
4420
Karlgren: 441d
PinYin: men4
Rad./Strokes: 61+8

Sad, depressed, sorrowful, melancholy.
From **4418** 門, "outer door", phonetic and **2735** 心, "heart": a confined heart.

蒙
4437
Karlgren: 1181a
PinYin: meng2
Rad./Strokes: 140+10

Ignorant, immaturity, inexpert, youthful folly; go with covered eyes against; cover, hidden, in darkness, deception, conceal, cheat.
Sometimes it is translated as "dodder", any of various leafless, annual parasitic herbs of the genus *Cuscuta* that lack chlorophyll and have slender, twining, yellow or reddish stems and small whitish flowers.
Tag for the hexagram 4.

迷
4450
Karlgren: 598e
PinYin: mi2
Rad./Strokes: 162+6

Lose way, go astray; miss, error; delude, infatuation.
From 辵, "go" and 米, phonetic

Karlgren: 17h
PinYin: mi2
Rad./Strokes: 175+11

4455

Share, empty, consume, scatter, to waste.

Karlgren: 312d
PinYin: mei4
Rad./Strokes: 145+4

4456

Sleeves, sleeve of a robe, embroidered garments, gown.
From **2989** 衤, "clothes" and **3535** 夬, phonetic.

Karlgren: 405p
PinYin: mi4
Rad./Strokes: 40+8

4464

Dense, thick, intimate, confidential; hidden, secret; silent.
From 宓, "quiet, still", phonetic, and **5630** 山, "mountain": hidden in the mountains.

Karlgren: 1160a
PinYin: miao4
Rad./Strokes: 53+12

4473

(Ancestral) temple, a shrine, used to honor gods and ancestors.
From *zhao* **0233** 朝, "morning" and *guang* 广, "roof": the house for the morning rites.

Karlgren: 1158a
PinYin: miao3
Rad./Strokes: 109+4

4476

Weak-sighted, one-eyed, having one eye smaller than the other.
From *mu* **4596** 目, "eye" and *shao* 少, "small".

Karlgren: 294b
PinYin: mie4
Rad./Strokes: 85+10

4483

Submerge, destroy, extinguish, exterminate.
From 氵(水), "water, 灭, "extinguish, kill" and 戉, "a halberd or battle axe": destroys like a flood.

Karlgren: 311a
PinYin: mie4
Rad./Strokes: 140+11

4485

Destroy, extinguish; throw away, disregard, ignore, contempt, minute, worthless; not have, nothing.
From 苜, "squint" (ancient meaning, no longer used), phonetic and 戍, "defend".

Karlgren: 223a
PinYin: mian4
Rad./Strokes: 176+0

4497

Face, countenance; reputation, facade.
From 百, "head, face" and **4596** 目, "eye": an eye in the middle of the face. Some ancient graphs are more representative:

Karlgren: 457a
PinYin: min2
Rad./Strokes: 83+1

4508

People, the masses, citizenry, the common people, crowd.
It is similar to 氏, "clan, family", but its etymology is uncertain.

4528

Karlgren: 841a
PinYin: ming2
Rad./Strokes: 14+8

Dark, darkness, obscured, benighted, confused, ignorant, blind; the underworld.

From **3124** 日, "Sun", ⼍, "covered" and 六, "six": the Sun covered in the six directions (four cardinal points plus above and below), the hours when the Sun is covered, the night.

4534

Karlgren: 760a
PinYin: ming2
Rad./Strokes: 72+4

Light, brightness, clarity, clear; enlightenment, discernment; seeing, perception; agreement, contract.

From **3124** 日, "Sun" and **7696** 月, "Moon".

鳴

4535

Karlgren: 827a
PinYin: ming2
Rad./Strokes: 30+11

Cry of a bird or animal, a sound, to make sounds, distinctive sound, voice, express, proclaim.

From **3434** 口, "mouth" and **4688** 鳥, "bird".

命

4537

Karlgren: 762a
PinYin: ming4
Rad./Strokes: 30+5

Heaven's will; command(s), fate, destiny; will; investiture; birth and death as limits of life.

6361 天命: *tian ming*: mandate of heaven; destiny; fate.

0984 致命: fatal; deadly; sacrifice one's life (47.X).

From , "order, command", the lower part comes from ⼌, a person kneeling and the top part may indicate a roof and **3434** 口, "mouth".

In the oracular bones representation shown below, the kneeling person can be seen clearly:

沫

4549

Karlgren: 0277b
PinYin: mo4
Rad./Strokes: 85+5

Foam, froth, saliva, tiny bubbles; explained in various commentaries as referring to the small stars behind the handle of the celestial Dipper.

In some translations this character replaces *mei* **4412** 沬, which is very similar but has a different pronunciation.

From 氵 (**5922** 水), "water" and 末, "small, the highest branches of a tree", phonetic.

莫

4557

Karlgren: 802a
PinYin: mo4
Rad./Strokes: 140+7

Nobody, nothing, none, no, not one, not at all, there is not, an absolute negative; evening, late.

From **3124** 日, "Sun", 艹, "plants", and **5943** 大, "big" (originally 大 was 艹): the setting Sun fading away in the grass at the horizon.

Ancient representations in bronze and oracle bones are shown below:

213

4559
Karlgren: 802o
PinYin: mu4
Rad./Strokes: 140+10

Cover, covering, curtain, screen, tent, canopy, baldachin.
From **4557** 莫, phonetic, and 巾, "piece of cloth".

 4578
Karlgren: 948f
PinYin: mou2
Rad./Strokes: 149+9

Plan, scheme; consult, appraise, deliberate.
From **7334** 言, "words" and 某, phonetic

 4580
Karlgren: 1231f
PinYin: mao4
Rad./Strokes: 140+5

Flourishing, luxuriant; vigorous, healthy; beautiful, excellent.
From 艹 (草), "herbs" and 戊, phonetic.

 4582
Karlgren: 947a
PinYin: mu3
Rad./Strokes: 80+1

Mother.
The character shows a woman with her breasts. Representations in bronze and oracle bones are more graphic:

7037 王母 (35.2): grandmother; Queen Mother of the West (leading Daoist goddess), this meaning is posterior to the time when the *YiJing* was written.

See **5082** 妣: ancestress, dead mother or grandmother.

214

 4584
Karlgren: 947g
PinYin: mu3
Rad./Strokes: 64+5

Big toe or thumb; in the first line it means big toe, since the first line is related with the feet, but in the upper trigram it means big thumb.
From 扌 (手), "hand" and **4582** 母, phonetic.

 4593
Karlgren: 1212a
PinYin: mu4
Rad./Strokes: 75+0

Tree, wood, timber, wooden.
Shows a tree with its branches over the ground and its roots down in the earth, as the representation shown below depicts:

目 **4596**
Karlgren: 1036a
PinYin: mu4
Rad./Strokes: 109+0

Eye/s, look, see.
The character shape seems to be an eye rotated 90 degrees. Ancient versions are more graphic:

納 **4607**
Karlgren: 695h
PinYin: na4
Rad./Strokes: 120+4

Bring in, convey to, hand to, present; take, receive, let in.
納婦**1963**: take a wife (4.2).

乃
4612
Karlgren: 945a
PinYin: nai3
Rad./Strokes: 4+1

Then, and, also, thereupon, as it turned out, namely, after all, only then; really, indeed.

南
4620
Karlgren: 650a
PinYin: nan2
Rad./Strokes: 24+7

The South. The region associated with Summer, fire, work in community and vegetation.

難
4625
Karlgren: 152d
PinYin: nan2
Rad./Strokes: 172+11

Difficult, arduous, trouble, hardship, calamity, complication.
From 莫, "distress" and 隹, "bird".
"The state in which are the 隹 birds, when the earth is 莫 dried and barren; famine, misery, difficulty of living" (*Wieger*).

囊
4627
Karlgren: 730l
PinYin: nang2
Rad./Strokes: 30+19

Sack, bag, pouch.
Some older versions show clearly a sack with stuff inside it:

能
4648
Karlgren: 885a
PinYin: neng2
Rad./Strokes: 130+6

Able, can, power, talent, ability, expertise.

Formerly it meant a bear, which suggests strength and agility, as can be seen in the ancient characters shown below:

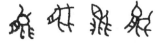

梔
4659
Karlgren: 563c
PinYin: ni3
Rad./Strokes: 75+5

Brake, chock for stopping a car; spindle.
From **4593** 木, "wood" and 尼, phonetic: some made with wood.

泥
4660
Karlgren: 563d
PinYin: ni2
Rad./Strokes: 85+5

Mud, sludge; mire, an area of wet, soggy ground, to be mired; to paste, to plaster; impeded, obstructed.
From 氵 (**5922** 水), "water" and 尼, phonetic.

鳥
4688
Karlgren: 1116a
PinYin: niao3
Rad./Strokes: 196+0

Bird.
Ancient representations in bronze and oracle bones show a bird:

臲
4700
Karlgren: 285d
PinYin: nie4
Rad./Strokes: 132+10

Unstable, unsteady, jittery, on edge, worried.
From 臬, phonetic, and 危, "danger, high, precipitous".

年
Karlgren: 364a
PinYin: nian3
4711 **Rad./Strokes:** 51+3

Year(s), season(s), harvest(s).
From 禾, "grain" over **3097** 人, "person", as older big seal, bronze and oracle bones versions show:

With the pass of time 千 replaced 人, in the lower part.

寧
Karlgren: 837a
PinYin: ning2
4725 **Rad./Strokes:** 40+11

Peace, peaceful, rest, serenity, at ease, body and mind at ease.
From **2735** 心, "heart", 宀, "roof", 皿, "dish"; the addition below is not 丁 in the seal but 丂, "take breath, rest" (*Karlgren*).
The character shown below depicts a roof over the heart, food and rest:

凝
Karlgren: 956h
PinYin: ning2
4732 **Rad./Strokes:** 15+14

Consolidate, secure, fix; concentrate, achieve; congeal, coagulate, harden, solidify.
From 冫, "ice" and 疑, "doubt": freeze; from there come the other meanings.

牛
Karlgren: 998a
PinYin: niu2
4737 **Rad./Strokes:** 93+0

Cow, bull, ox(en).

Older representations are very graphic:

內
Karlgren: 695e
PinYin: nei4
4766 **Rad./Strokes:** 11+2

Inside, inner, interior; to bring in, enter.
Enter **3152** 入 in a 冂 empty space, in the interior.

女
Karlgren: 94a
PinYin: nu3
4776 **Rad./Strokes:** 38+0

Maiden, woman, lady, girl, feminine.
The following oracle bones image, shows a woman on profile.

Compare with **4582** 母, "mother" and **3097** 人, "person".

我
Karlgren: 2a
PinYin: wo3
4778 **Rad./Strokes:** 62+3

We, us, I, my, mine, our.

惡
Karlgren: 805h
PinYin: e4
4809 **Rad./Strokes:** 61+8

Evil, bad; ugly; wrong, fault, bad; hate.
From 亞, "inferior", phonetic, over **2735** 心, "heart".

遏
Karlgren: 313l
PinYin: e4
4812 **Rad./Strokes:** 162+9

Curb, repress, check, stop, suppress; cease.
From **2122** 曷, phonetic, and 辶, "go".

罷
4841
Karlgren: 26a
PinYin: ba4
Rad./Strokes: 122+10

Stop, cease, leave off, give up; finish; weary, exhausted.
From 罒 (网), "net" over **4648** 能, "bear": a bear caught in a net.

八
4845
Karlgren: 281a
PinYin: ba1
Rad./Strokes: 12+0

Eight, eighth, eight times.

拔
4848
Karlgren: 276h
PinYin: ba2
Rad./Strokes: 64+5

Pull up, pull out, uproot, pluck up.
From 扌 (手), "hand" and 犮, "to pull up", phonetic.

敗
4866
Karlgren: 320f
PinYin: bai4
Rad./Strokes: 66+7

Defeat, destruction, ruin, spoil.
From **5005** 貝, phonetic, and 攵 (攴), "beat".

班
4889
Karlgren: 190a
PinYin: ban1
Rad./Strokes: 96+6

Divide, scatter, distribute, classify, arrayed, ordered, dispose according to rank.
From 王(玉), **7666**, "jade", duplicated, on both sides, and 刂 (刀), "knife": "To cut up pieces of jade and bestow the half as rank insignia upon feudatory chiefs" (*Karlgren*).

磐
4904
Karlgren: 182g
PinYin: pan2
Rad./Strokes: 112+10

Boulder, large rock; stable, immovable, hindrance.
From 般, phonetic, and **5813** 石, "rock".

包
4937
Karlgren: 1113a
PinYin: bao1
Rad./Strokes: 20+3

Bundle, wrap, reed mat for wrapping; kitchen, butchering room; contain, support, take responsibility over.
From 勹, "wrap" and **5590** 巳, "fetus": a fetus in the **4937** 勹 womb (*Wieger*).

苞
4941
Karlgren: 1113c
PinYin: bao1
Rad./Strokes: 140+5

Dense, massive, luxuriant, thick-leafed, shrubbery, bushy.
From 艹 (草), "plant" and **4937** 包, phonetic.

保
4946
Karlgren: 1057a
PinYin: bao3
Rad./Strokes: 9+7

Preserve, protect, maintain, care for.
"On the oracle bones and bronzes, in some cases we see the child safe in the adult's arms, and other times the child is carried on the back, just as children are carried in China today" (*Lindqvist*):

Karlgren: 1244k
PinYin: bao4
4954 **Rad./Strokes:** 153+3

Panther, leopard.
It only appears in 49.6 besides other character:

豸變 **5245**: the leopard's versatility, from rags to riches.

Ancient representations on oracle bones show an animal rotated 90 degrees:

北

Karlgren: 909a
PinYin: bei3
4974 **Rad./Strokes:** 21+3

North. The character depicts two persons standing, back to back, as the following oracle bones graph shows:

In China, the north has traditionally been considered the "back side". Maps shown the south on top and compasses pointed south.

6605 (*East*) 東北: the northeast, it means advance, frontier, boundary, finalization, limit between two cycles. Mountain: dark and cold winter night.

白

Karlgren: 782a
PinYin: bai2
4975 **Rad./Strokes:** 106+0

White, simple, easy to understand, bare, pure; color of death an mourning.
This is a modification of **3124** 日, "Sun, day", adding an stroke on top.

218

Karlgren: 781a
PinYin: bai3
4976 **Rad./Strokes:** 106+1

Hundred, hundredth, a hundred times, numerous, many.

Karlgren: 782f
PinYin: bo2
4979 **Rad./Strokes:** 50+5

Silk, undyed silk.
From **4975** 白, phonetic, over 巾, "piece of cloth, napkin".

Karlgren: 909e
PinYin: bei4
4989 **Rad./Strokes:** 130+5

Back, spine, back side, behind.
The back side traditionally is related with the North **4974** 北.
From **4974** 北, "North" and **3153** 肉, "flesh".

貝

Karlgren: 320a
PinYin: bei4
5005 **Rad./Strokes:** 154+0

Coins, cowry shells, formerly used in China for currency.
Cowry is the common name for a group of small to large sea snails, marine gastropod molluscs in the family *Cypraeidae*. The shells were used as coins in Ancient China; as the thunder, they were symbol of fertility (because its similarity to the vulva).
Cowries were not indigenous around the Yellow River, but were imported from coastal areas or might come through Central Asia. After the Spring-Autumn Period (770–476 BC), cowries

gradually began to be replaced for iron an copper coins.
See **5054** 朋: two strings of cowries.
Older versions of this character show the image of a shell:

5019
Karlgren: 514a
PinYin: pei4
Rad./Strokes: 164+3

Match, equal, pair, colleague, consort; worthy, to be qualified.
From 酉, "wine" and **0429** 己, "oneself".

5020
Karlgren: 501f
PinYin: pei4
Rad./Strokes: 85+4

Covering, veil, darkened, abundant, copious or/and sudden rain.
From **5922** 氵(水), "water" and 市, phonetic.

5027
Karlgren: 437a
PinYin: bi4
Rad./Strokes: 154+5

Ornate, elegant, motley, brilliant; embellish, adorn.
From 艸 (three 屮 plants) on top with **5005** 貝, a cowry shell, used as decoration on the bottom.
Tag for the hexagram 22.

奔
5028
Karlgren: 438a
PinYin: ben1
Rad./Strokes: 37+6; 37+5;

Hurry, hasten, rush toward, run away.

Shows a man **5943** 大(人) **3097** running through **2326** 艸 high grass.
Ancient representations show the running man more clearly:

朋
5054
Karlgren: 886a
PinYin: peng2
Rad./Strokes: 74+4

Friend, companion, pair, equal, comrade; a string of cowries (used as coins in ancient China, see **5005** 貝: cowry shells). It may have represented two strings of cash, now written like **7696** 月, doubled. For two thousand years it was believed that the character depicted the feathers of the gigantic *peng* 鵬 bird, but the archeological evidence doesn't support that theory.

彭
5060
Karlgren: 750a
PinYin: peng2
Rad./Strokes: 59+9

Forceful, overbearing, fullness, plenitude, an overwhelming sound. It only appears in 14.4, where *Kunst* replaces it for other character with similar sound (*beng*), that means "sacrifice in the ancestral temple door".

匕
5076
Karlgren: 565a
PinYin: bi3
Rad./Strokes: 21+0

Sacrificial spoon, used to pour libations in the sacrifices, ladle.

5077
Karlgren: 566g
PinYin: bi3
Rad./Strokes: 81+0

Union, go together with, assemble, associate with, combine, ally with, pair; compare.

It shows two 比 (**3097** 人 inverted man) men, one besides the other, as the following early version shows clearly:

Tag for the hexagram 8, which is the only place where this character appears.

5082
Karlgren: 566n
PinYin: bi3
Rad./Strokes: 38+4

Ancestress, foremother, deceased mother or grandmother.
From **4776** 女, "woman" and **5077** 比, phonetic.
See **4582** 母: mother.

5092
Karlgren: 412a
PinYin: bi4
Rad./Strokes: 169+3

Close, shut, close the door.
From **4418** 門, "door" and 才, "talent".
Karlgren says that 才 doesn't mean talent but it is a picture of the bolt of a door. The bronze graph shown below depicts clearly two hands (⺕) below a door bolt.

5093
Karlgren: 25g
PinYin: bi3
Rad./Strokes: 60+5

That one, that, there, those, other, another.

5100
Karlgren: 521c
PinYin: bi2
Rad./Strokes: 209+0

Nose.
Oracular bones inscriptions show the shape of a nose:

5101
Karlgren: 341a
PinYin: bi4
Rad./Strokes: 66+8

Broken, worn out, shabby, tattered, ruin; damage; unworthy, poor, vile.
巾 cloth 攵 broken as to be **4845** 八 (divided:) torn (doubled) into rags" (*Karlgren*).

5109
Karlgren: 405a
PinYin: bi4
Rad./Strokes: 61+1

Must, necessarily, certainly, unavoidability.

5170
Karlgren: 408a
PinYin: pi3
Rad./Strokes: 23+2

Companion, one of a team or yoke, peer, mate, match.
It only appears in 61.4:
4310 馬匹: horses.

辟
5172
Karlgren: 853a
PinYin: bi4
Rad./Strokes: 160+6

Escape, avoid, go away from; ward off; keep away. It also means expel, punish and apply the laws.
From 尸 (卩), "seal" (symbol of authority, a magistrate), **3434** 口, "mouth" and 辛, "criminal": "A (seal-holder) magistrate pronouncing a sentence over a criminal" (*Karlgren*).

 辨
5240
Karlgren: 219b
PinYin: bian4
Rad./Strokes: 160+9

Discriminate, distinguish, discern, identify; divide, distribute; frame that divides a bed from its stand.
Some translations replace it by **5242** 辯 in 10.X.

 辯
5242
Karlgren: 219e
PinYin: bian4
Rad./Strokes: 160+14

Discriminate, distinguish, dispute, argue; scrutinize, regulate.
Some translations use this character instead **5240** 辨 in 10.X.
From **7334** 言, "words" and 辛, "bitter, pungent", duplicated on both sides.

 變
5245
Karlgren: 178o
PinYin: bian4
Rad./Strokes: 149+16; 29+6

Change, transform, metamorphose, alter.
From **7334** 言, "words", two 糸 "silk threads" to the sides and 攵 (攴), "beat" on the bottom.

In the two places where it appears (49.5 and 49.6) the change is either described as changing as a tiger or changing as a panther or leopard.

2161 虎變: change as a tiger: innovate, adapt to new circumstances.

4954 豹變: the leopard's versatility, from rags to riches.

 翩
5249
Karlgren: 246k
PinYin: pian1
Rad./Strokes: 124+9

Flutter, fly to and from, flap the wings. It only appears in 11.4, where the doubled character intensifies its quality.
From 扁, "phonetic" and **7658** 羽, "feathers, wings".

 賓
5259
Karlgren: 389a
PinYin: bin1
Rad./Strokes: 154+7

Guest, visitor.
Its original shape, engraved on oracle bones, shows a person under a roof:

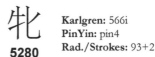 **頻**
5275
Karlgren: 390a
PinYin: pin2
Rad./Strokes: 181+7

Repeated, incessant, urgent, pressing; on the brink of.

牝
5280
Karlgren: 566i
PinYin: pin4
Rad./Strokes: 93+2

Female (used for farm animals and birds), female sexual organs, cow.
From **4737** 牛, "cow" and 匕, phonetic.

5281

Karlgren: 669a
PinYin: pin3
Rad./Strokes: 30+6

Kind, variety, classes, categories.

It only appears in 57.4 as reference to three kinds of game caught in the hunt. Traditionally, animals caught in real hunts were divided in three categories:

1. Dried meat for the *dou* sacrificial vessel (*gandou*).
2. Meat for honored guests (*binke*).
3. Provisions for the sovereign's kitchens (*chongjun zhi pao*).

That is the reason three kinds of game are mentioned in 57.4.

 5283

Karlgren: 899b
PinYin: bing1
Rad./Strokes: 15+4

Ice.

From **5283** 冫, "ice" (originally this character only had this component) and **5922** 水, "water".

 5292

Karlgren: 840b
PinYin: bing4
Rad./Strokes: 1+7

In common, together, both, side by side; all, many.

It is said that this character is the corrupt form of 立立. Also it is related to 并. The character is a variation of a graph showing two men side by side. The oracle bones version of this character is shown below:

 5301

Karlgren: 824j
PinYin: ping2
Rad./Strokes: 98+6

Earthen jar, jug, base, bottle.

From **5292** 并, phonetic, and 瓦, "earthenware".

 5303

Karlgren: 825a
PinYin: ping2
Rad./Strokes: 51+2

A plain, level, equal, even; equalize, harmonize, regulate, pacify; peace.

平施 **5768**: distribute or confer impartially (15.X).

 5317

Karlgren: 25m
PinYin: bo3
Rad./Strokes: 157+5

Lame, limping, crippled.

From 𧾷 "foot" y 皮, phonetic.

 5337

Karlgren: 1228a
PinYin: bo1
Rad./Strokes: 18+8

Flay, strip, peel; pluck, lay bare, strip (as clothes or badges of office); split, slice, crack.

From 录, "carve" (this is the older meaning, now it means record) and 刂 (刀), "knife".

Tag for the hexagram 23.

 5345

Karlgren: 25i
PinYin: pi2
Rad./Strokes: 170+5

Slope, incline, slanting; river bank, embankment, dyke.

From 阝 (阜), "hill" and 皮, phonetic.

5351
Karlgren: 195r
PinYin: po2
Rad./Strokes: 106+12

White, silver, gray; white or silver haired; old, aged.
From **4975** 白, "white" and 番, phonetic.

5373
Karlgren: 102d'
PinYin: bu1
Rad./Strokes: 162+7

Flee, escape, run away.
From 甫, phonetic, and 辵, "go".

5379
Karlgren: 999a
PinYin: bu4
Rad./Strokes: 1+3

No, not, negative prefix; without, none, nothing, will not, need not, will not be.

5401
Karlgren: 1211b
PinYin: pu2
Rad./Strokes: 9+12

Servant, slave, follower, retainer, vassal; a charioteer.
From 亻(**3097** 人), "person" and 菐, "bush", phonetic.

5415
Karlgren: 648a
PinYin: san1
Rad./Strokes: 1+2

Three, thrice, third time or place.

5424
Karlgren: 704a
PinYin: sang1
Rad./Strokes: 75+6

Mulberry tree. Tree from the *Moraceae* family. Its leaves are the food source of the silkworm which produces the silk.

It only appears once in the hexagram 12. The same two characters that appear in 12.5 (**4941** 苞桑) are used as well in the ode 162 of the *ShiJing*; were they are translated as "bushy mulberry trees". "The rhyme here in Hexagram 12 appears to hope that some danger will disappear; and may advise tying a talisman on a tree, an ancient prophylactic still used in Siberia and Korea" (*Rutt*).
From **4593** 木, "tree" and, over it, several hands (picking mulberry leaves from the tree for the silk worms). The hands () can be seen more clearly in some versions of this character:

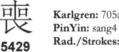

5429
Karlgren: 705a
PinYin: sang4
Rad./Strokes: 30+9

Lose, let drop, disappear, destroy, perish, mourning, burial.
Originally comes from 哭, "weep" over **7034** 亡, "death": weep over a dead person. Its actual form has changed a lot, but its ancient shape was:

5446
Karlgren: 908a
PinYin: se4
Rad./Strokes: 32+10

To stop up, block, hinder, impede, seal, close; a (frontier) pass, strait.

5459

Karlgren: 770a
PinYin: suo3
Rad./Strokes: 120+4

This character has many different meanings: rope; demand, ask; search, think deeply; exhausted, scattered; **disquieted, apprehensive, tremble, fear.** The meanings marked in bold are the ones that are used in the *YiJing*.

It only appears in 51.6, duplicated and preceded by another character, related with the thunder, meaning the fear caused by the sound of thunder, which is intensified because 索 is repeated:

> **0315** 震索索: startled and agitated.

所

5465

Karlgren: 91a
PinYin: suo3
Rad./Strokes: 63+4

That which, place, location, residence, dwelling; reason, a cause, whereby; function, position, role; habitual focus or object.

From 户, "door" and 斤, "axe": To build a living place (*Karlgren*).

瑣

5466

Karlgren: 13b
PinYin: suo3
Rad./Strokes: 96+10

Trivial, small, petty, annoying, touchy, fussy, contemptible; in tiny pieces. In only appears in 56.1, duplicated, which intensifies its meaning.

5488

Karlgren: 67c
PinYin: su1
Rad./Strokes: 140+16

Distraught; tremble, fear; sound of thunder, rumbling sound; revive, awakens, enlivens, stimulate, excite. It only

224

appears in 51.3, doubled, which intensifies its quality.

The *Mawangdui* manuscript replaces this character by 朔, "first day of the lunar month, new moon, a new beginning", which coincides with "revive", one of the meanings of 蘇.

According to *Jingdian shiwen* it should be replaced by **5494** 愬, "afraid", which also is a match with another of the meanings of 蘇.

The modernist school takes it as a phonetic representation of the "sound of thunder".

From 穌, "revive" under 艹 (草), "herb".

素

5490

Karlgren: 68a
PinYin: su4
Rad./Strokes: 120+4

Simple, plain, unadorned; white, white silk.

From 糸, "silk" and 主, on top, representing mulberry branches (see **5424** 桑).

愬

5494

Karlgren: 769b
PinYin: su4
Rad./Strokes: 61+10

Fear, caution, panicky appearance; appeal, plead, accuse, complain.

It only appears in 10.4, where the doubled character intensifies its meaning.

From 朔, phonetic, and **2735** 心, "heart".

俗

5497

Karlgren: 1220a
PinYin: su2
Rad./Strokes: 9+7

Mores, popular usage; common, vulgar, unrefined, current.

From 亻 (**3097** 人, "man") and **3483** 谷, "valley".

5502

Karlgren: 1030a
PinYin: su4
Rad./Strokes: 36+3

Early, soon, eager; early in the morning, after dawn.

5505

Karlgren: 1222i
PinYin: su4
Rad./Strokes: 162+7

Invitation, invite; rapid, quick, urge on, hurried.
From **5891** 束, phonetic, and 辶, "go": indicator of motion.

5506

Karlgren: 1222k
PinYin: su4
Rad./Strokes: 184+7

Stew of meat and vegetables, meal, rice stew.
From **5810** 食, "eat, food" and **5891** 束, phonetic.

5519

Karlgren: 575v
PinYin: sui1
Rad./Strokes: 172+9

Although, even if, still, though it be, supposing.
From 虫, "reptile" with a big **3434** 口 head and 隹, "bird", as phonetic. It was borrowed for a homophone meaning 'although'.

5523

Karlgren: 11g
PinYin: sui2
Rad./Strokes: 170+13

Follow, pursue; conform to, respond, follow a way or religion; subsequently, in the course of time; listen to, submit; marrow, flesh.
Gao proposes replacing it by 髓, "marrow" in 31.3 and 52.2.
From 隋, phonetic, and 辶, "go".
Tag for the hexagram 17.

5530

Karlgren: 526d
PinYin: sui4
Rad./Strokes: 162+9

Advance; push through, go forward; proceed, prolong; follow along, pursuit, comply with; consequently, then, next.

5538

Karlgren: 346a
PinYin: sui4
Rad./Strokes: 77+9

Years, seasons, harvests.
Two foot steps 止小, passing the scythe 戌, over the crops: the yearly harvest.

5548

Karlgren: 435a
PinYin: sun
Rad./Strokes: 64+10

Decrease, diminish, lessen; damage, injure.
From 扌 (手),"hand"and 員,"member".
The original shape was:

From ○ round and **5005** 貝, "cowry shell, coin": a round coin.
The image above shows a shell and two strings because the cowries were inserted in strings. That explains the meaning "decrease", since 損 means to take coins with the hand, diminishing the number of cowries.
Tag for the hexagram 41

5550

Karlgren: 433a
PinYin: xun4
Rad./Strokes: 49+9

Humble, yield, compliant, obedient, mild, bland, insinuating. *Kunst* and *Rutt* say it is the abbreviated form of *zhuan* 饌, "food" and means "food offering".

It is the character of the trigram ☴: *The Gentle, Wind.* See **9000**: *The Eight Trigrams.* Also is the tag for the hexagram 57.

Two kneeling persons 巳 (卩 in front of a table 丌: "submission".

Old representations of this character show this idea clearly:

訟

5558

Karlgren: 1190b
PinYin: song4
Rad./Strokes: 149+4

Conflict, litigation, dispute, to demand justice, accusation.

From **7334** 言, "words" and **3701** 公, "public": public dispute.

Tag for the hexagram 6.

斯

5574

Karlgren: 869a
PinYin: si1
Rad./Strokes: 69+8

Then, this, thereupon, so, thus; cleave, tear apart.

From **0525** 其, "basket" and 斤,"axe": To split wood, fuel, and put into a basket (*Karlgren*). A bronze representation can be seen below:

思

5580

Karlgren: 973a
PinYin: si1
Rad./Strokes: 61+5

Think, consider, ponder; brood, reflect, plan.

Interaction of the head 田 (although 田 means field) and the **2735** 心, heart. An older form is shown below:

死

5589

Karlgren: 558a
PinYin: si3
Rad./Strokes: 78+2

Die, death, doomed.

From 歹, "bad, vicious" and 匕 (**3097** 人), "man".

巳

5590

Karlgren: 967a
PinYin: si4
Rad./Strokes: 49+0

6th earthly branch. The period from 9.00 a.m. to 11.00 a.m. Usually it is replaced with other characters:

- In 26.1 and 41.1 may be replaced by **2930** 已 *yi*: Stop.
- *Wilhelm* replaces it with **0429** 己 *ji3* in 41.1 and 49.0: Self.
- Usually 巳 *yi3* is kept in 49.0 and 49.2, but *Kunst* replaces it with **5592** 祀 *si4*: Sacrifice.

Its shape is the image of a fetus, the germ of human life:

See **4937** 包, "wrap".

5592 祀
Karlgren: 967d
PinYin: si4
Rad./Strokes: 113+3

Sacrifice, autumnal sacrifice after harvest, libation, offering to the gods or the dead ancestors.
From 礻 (示) *shi4*, altar and **5590** 巳, *si4*, phonetic.

5598 四
Karlgren: 518a
PinYin: si4
Rad./Strokes: 31+2

Four, four times, quadruple.
It only appears in 30.X and 44.X, always alongside 方:
四方 **1802**: four directions; the limits of the earth, everywhere.

5606 沙
Karlgren: 16a
PinYin: sha1
Rad./Strokes: 85+4

Sand, gravel, sandbank, beach.
From 氵 (**5922** 水), "water" and 少, "small".

5615 殺
Karlgren: 319d
PinYin: sha1
Rad./Strokes: 79+6

Kill, slaughter, slay; diminish, reduce.
From 乂, "Kill, slaughter, slay; diminish, reduce. **4593** 木, "tree" y 殳, "kill".

5630 山
Karlgren: 193a
PinYin: shan1
Rad./Strokes: 46+0

Mountain, hill, peak.
Ancient representations show a mountain range (three mountains):

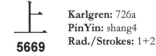

5657 善
Karlgren: 205a
PinYin: shan4
Rad./Strokes: 30+9

Good, virtuous; perfect, improve.
From **7247** 羊, "sheep" over **7334** 言, "words". 羊 means "good" here.

5669 上
Karlgren: 726a
PinYin: shang4
Rad./Strokes: 1+2

Up, above, on, over, upwards, top, rise; higher, superior; first, best.
It is the opposite to **2520** 下, below.

5670 尚
Karlgren: 725a
PinYin: shang4
Rad./Strokes: 42+5

High, ascend, admirable, superior, surpass, respected, esteemed, reward; still, yet an besides, in addition to.
Karlgren says that it is identical or is related etymologically to **5669** 上: over, top.
See **5672** 賞 reward.

5671 裳
Karlgren: 725d
PinYin: chang2
Rad./Strokes: 145+8

Lower garment, skirt, clothing, garment used from the waist down worn by both men and women; ceremonial garment.
From **5670** 尚, phonetic, and **2989** 衣, "clothes".

5672

Karlgren: 725n
PinYin: shang3
Rad./Strokes: 154+8

Reward, award, gifts, tributes.
From **5670** 尚, phonetic, and **5005** 貝, "money".

5673

Karlgren: 734a
PinYin: shang1
Rad./Strokes: 30+8

Bargain, discuss, deliberate, negotiate, calculate; merchant, trader.

商兌 **6560**: consult and consider; discuss and deliberate (58.4).

Kunst and *Rutt* replace it with **5672** 賞 *shang4*: reward, en 58.4.

5699

Karlgren: 48a
PinYin: she3
Rad./Strokes: 135+2

Quit, abandon, let go, leave, put down, set aside, put away, store; stop, rest in, halt, resting place, encampment.

5702

Karlgren: 793d
PinYin: she4
Rad./Strokes: 155+4

Forgive, pardon, liberate, let go.

5703

Karlgren: 807a
PinYin: she4
Rad./Strokes: 41+7

Shoot with a bow; aim and hit the target.
Ancient representations in oracle bones show clearly a bow and arrow.

5705

Karlgren: 288a
PinYin: she2
Rad./Strokes: 135+0

The tongue.
Shows the image of a 千 tongue sticking out of a **3434** 口 mouth.

5707

Karlgren: 634a
PinYin: she4
Rad./Strokes: 85+7

Cross, wade across (a river, stream), ford, pass through or over.
From **5922** 氵(水), "water" and 步, "step".

5711

Karlgren: 290a
PinYin: she4
Rad./Strokes: 149+4

Found, establish, arrange, set up.
From **7334** 言, "words, speech" and 殳, "beat, weapon": To command and beat (*Karlgren*).

5712

Karlgren: 385a
PinYin: shen1
Rad./Strokes: 102+0

Spread, extend, prolong, stretch; repeat, again, further; exhibit; explain, express; the 9th of the Twelve Earthly Branches. 3-5 p.m.
The original form of the character showed two hands 𦥑 stretching something long 丨.

5718

Karlgren: 386a
PinYin: shen1
Rad./Strokes: 158+0

Body, trunk, torso, person, psyche, oneself, lifespan; pregnant woman, womb (*Kunst*, 52.4).

Ancient forms of this character show a person walking on profile, with a protruding belly:

 慎

5734

| Karlgren: 375i |
| PinYin: shen4 |
| Rad./Strokes: 61+10 |

Careful, cautious, circumspect.

From **2735** 忄 (必), *xin1*, "heart" and 真 (眞), "true".

 生

5738

| Karlgren: 812a |
| PinYin: sheng1 |
| Rad./Strokes: 100+0 |

Live, give birth to, to be born living being; produce; sacrificial animal, victim.

It is the image of a growing plant. Ancient representations show it clearly:

See **5739** 牲.

牲

5739

| Karlgren: 812e |
| PinYin: sheng1 |
| Rad./Strokes: 93+5 |

Offering, sacrificial victim.

The six sacrificial animals were: horse, ox, lamb, cock, dog and pig.

From **4737** 牛, *niu*, "ox" and **5738** 生, phonetic.

眚

5741

| Karlgren: 812i |
| PinYin: sheng3 |
| Rad./Strokes: 109+5 |

Disaster, calamity, serious mistake; offence by mishap or fault; cloudy eyes,

disease of the eye, new moon, eclipse, meanings that indicate blindness or lack of light, a mistake due to ignorance or an error of judgment.

From **5738** 生, phonetic, and **4596** 目, "eye".

In 24.6 y 62.6 it appears alongside 栽:

> **6652** 栽眚: disaster due to external causes and a serious error; ruin, failure, collapse.

省

5744

| Karlgren: 812l |
| PinYin: xing3 |
| Rad./Strokes: 109+4 |

Visit, inspect, study, go and visit, inspection visit; examine oneself; frugal, to save, to reduce.

It only appears in 20.X, 24.x and 51.X; in the two first places appears alongside 方:

> 省方, *fang1*, **1802**: take a tour of inspection on all sides.

From 少, "few, small" and **4596** 目, "eye": to watch carefully the smallest details and costs.

升

5745

| Karlgren: 897a |
| PinYin: sheng1 |
| Rad./Strokes: 24+2 |

Climb, push upwards, rise, go up, arise.

Tag for the hexagram 46.

Ancient representations show a ladle with a hand holding it:

Lately, the character 升 was borrowed for the word *sheng1*, "rise", which has the same sound.

Karlgren: 893p
PinYin: sheng4
5754 **Rad./Strokes:** 19+10

Defeat, subdue, vanquish, overcome; excel, surpass, be better than; victory, triumph, success.

From 朕, phonetic, and 力, "strength".

Karlgren: 561a
PinYin: shi1
5756 **Rad./Strokes:** 44+0

Corpse; one who impersonates the death (usually a child) at a sacrifice.

The original form, as seen on bronze inscriptions, show a person, seated, on profile:

It only appears two times, in 7.3 and 7.5, in both cases alongside **7618** 轝, "carriage, cart". Carrying corpses in a carriage may indicate clearing the field after the battle, but this expression (轝尸) also may indicate either carrying King *Wen* corpse, or his spirit tablet, to the battle, since the same expression appears in *Chuci* (poems written in he fourth century BC) where it is said that at the battle of *Mu*, where the *Zhou* army finally defeated the *Shang*, the corpse of King *Wen* was carried into battle (*Rutt*).

師

Karlgren: 559a
PinYin: shi1
5760 **Rad./Strokes:** 50+7

Army, troops, militias; multitude; master, leader; take as a master, imitate, follow a role model or norm.

The garrison 帀 all around the 𠂤 wall of the city (*Karlgren*).

Tag for the hexagram 7.

Karlgren: 336a
PinYin: shi4
5763 **Rad./Strokes:** 118+7

Divination by yarrow (*Achillea millefolium*) stalks, consult the oracle. The *Achillea* can be seen in pastures and on roadsides throughout the northern hemisphere. It forms an upright stem, fluffy, 30 to 90 cm tall, finely divided leaves and small flower clusters. It provides the stalks traditionally used for divination with the *YiJing*.

From 竹, "bamboo" and **7164** 巫, "diviner, wizard".

Karlgren: 336c
PinYin: shi4
5764 **Rad./Strokes:** 30+13

Bite, gnaw, snap at, chew.

From **3434** 口, "mouth" and **5763** 筮, phonetic.

Used as the first character in the hexagram 21 tag.

豕

Karlgren: 1238f
PinYin: shi3
5766 **Rad./Strokes:** 152+0

Pig, boar, swine. Symbol of wealth and luck.

豕 is not a common word in modern Chinese, but it is used as a component in several characters. The modern word for pig is 豬.

Ancient versions on oracle bones show an animal rotated 90 degrees:

施
5768
Karlgren: 4l'
PinYin: shi1
Rad./Strokes: 70+5

Expand, spread out, dispense, distribute, give, bestow.
5303 平施: 15.X: distribute or confer evenly, impartially.

史
5769
Karlgren: 975a
PinYin: shi3
Rad./Strokes: 30+2

Scribe, historian, chronicles, annals; diviner; invoker (of spirits) (*Kunst*).
From 又 (⺕), "hand", holding an instrument (**1504** 中). The hand can be seen more clearly in bronze representations:

使
5770
Karlgren: 975n
PinYin: shi3
Rad./Strokes: 9+6

Send on a mission, order, cause, envoy, messenger, ambassador, agent.
From 亻 (**3097** 人), "person" and 吏, "government official", phonetic.

始
5772
Karlgren: 976e'
PinYin: shi3
Rad./Strokes: 38+5

Begin, beginning, start, first.
From **4776** 女, "woman" and 台, phonetic: we all start in the womb.

士
5776
Karlgren: 970a
PinYin: shi4
Rad./Strokes: 33+0

Young man, bachelor, man, gentleman, warrior, soldier, officer.

From **5807** 十, "ten" over **3016** 一, "one" (*Shuowen*).
Some scholars think that 士 originally was a phallic symbol. In Japanese, 士 is the character for "samurai".
士夫 **1908**: 28.5: young husband (for an older wife).

時
5780
Karlgren: 961z
PinYin: shi2
Rad./Strokes: 72+6

Time, season, epoch, period, opportune moment.
From **3124** 日, "day" and 寺, "temple", phonetic.

矢
5784
Karlgren: 560a
PinYin: shi3
Rad./Strokes: 111+0

Arrow. Ancient forms are more representative:

事
5787
Karlgren: 971a
PinYin: shi4
Rad./Strokes: 6+7

Serve, service; affairs, business, matters. The character shows a ⺕ hand, holding some type of instrument.

視
5789
Karlgren: 553h
PinYin: shi4
Rad./Strokes: 147+4

See, look, inspect, observe, regard.
From 礻, phonetic, and **0860** 見, "see".

5790
Karlgren: 339a
PinYin: shi4
Rad./Strokes: 1+4

Generation, epoch, age; world, worldly, society, vulgar.

It is related with 卅, *sa4*, "thirty"; originally composed of **5807** 十, *shi2*, "ten", triplicate: 30 years, a generation (the average life span in the past).

5794
Karlgren: 866a
PinYin: shi4
Rad./Strokes: 72+5

This, that; this is, is; to be right; indeed, correctly; preceding statement.

From **3124** 日, "Sun", and the lower part is a different form of **0351** 正, "true".

5799
Karlgren: 330l
PinYin: shi4
Rad./Strokes: 19+11

Power, capacity, potency, force, authority, influence; aspect, circumstances, condition.

From 埶, "plant, cultivate, art, talent" and 力, "strength": force combined with skill.

5806
Karlgren: 402a
PinYin: shi1
Rad./Strokes: 37+2

Lose, let go, neglect, an omission; fail, err; lose control.

From 手, *shou3*, "hand" and something dropping from it.

十

5807
Karlgren: 686a
PinYin: shi2
Rad./Strokes: 24+0

Ten; complete, perfect, whole.

5810
Karlgren: 921a
PinYin: shi2
Rad./Strokes: 184+0

Eat, feed, ingest; food, give food to; nourishment; salary of an officer, livelihood; eclipse (eating of Sun or Moon).

The character can be seen as a food container **3941** 皀 with a lid, or as a person mouth over a food container. Notice that some of the ancient representations shown below look like a mouth **3434** 口 (凵) pointing below:

It appears four times, in three cases (5.X, 27.X and 53.2) is preceded by 飲:

> **7454** 飲食: eat and drink, eating together.

5813
Karlgren: 795a
PinYin: shi2
Rad./Strokes: 112+0

Rock, pebble, stone, shingle.

"A 口 piece of rock fallen down or taken down from a 厂 cliff". Note the alteration of 厂 in the modern writing" (*Wieger*).

碩

5815
Karlgren: 795e
PinYin: shu4
Rad./Strokes: 112+9

Large, great, stately, eminent, ripe, full grown, maturity.

From **5813** 石, phonetic, and 頁, "head".

5816
Karlgren: 795h
PinYin: shi2
Rad./Strokes: 208+5

Some kind of rodent with long tail:

squirrel, long tailed marmot, field mouse.

It only appears in 35.4:

 5871: a squirrel, rodents that destroy the harvests.

 5821
Karlgren: 398a
PinYin: shi2
Rad./Strokes: 40+11

Contents, substance; actual, real; full, fill; solid, truthful, honest; fruit.

From **3566** 貫, a string of cowries (coins), under a 宀, *mian2*, "roof": real wealth.

識 **5825**
Karlgren: 920k
PinYin: shi2
Rad./Strokes: 149+12

Record, remember, archive, annals; commemorate; know, learn, recognize, be acquainted with.

From **7334** 言, "words" and 戠, phonetic.

收 **5837**
Karlgren: 1103a
PinYin: shou1
Rad./Strokes: 66+2

Take, gather together, collect, catch, receive, take and remove; harvest.

From 丩, "hook, to join or connect the vines" and 又 (ㅋ), "hand".

首 **5839**
Karlgren: 1102a
PinYin: shou3
Rad./Strokes: 185+0

Head; foremost, first; leader, chief.

Shows 百 head with ∨∕ hair over it

 5840
Karlgren: 1085a
PinYin: shou4
Rad./Strokes: 29+6

Receive, accept, consent, agree; endure, suffer; compliant, tranquil.

Shows a ∨∕ (ㅋ) hand reaching down, giving, and other 又 (ㅋ) hand reaching up, receiving a 冖 thing:

狩 **5845**
Karlgren: 1099c
PinYin: shou4
Rad./Strokes: 94+6

Hunt, great winter hunt, inspection tour.

From 犭, "dog" and 守, phonetic: hunting with dogs.

It only appears in 36.3:

4620 南狩: "southern hunt". *Rutt* says that "the southern hunt may have been a ceremonial hunt after a battle or a sobriquet for the battle itself".

數 **5865**
Karlgren: 123r
PinYin: shu3
Rad./Strokes: 66+11

Number, count, calculate; method, norm, rule; degree.

From 攵 (攴), "beat" and 婁 (屢), "repeatedly": clapping with a finger to help the counting.

鼠 **5871**
Karlgren: 92a
PinYin: shu3
Rad./Strokes: 208+0

Rat, mouse, rodent. It only appears in 35.4:

5816 : a squirrel, rodents that destroy the harvests.

5874
Karlgren: 804a
PinYin: shu4
Rad./Strokes: 53+8

Numerous, many, multitude, the masses; ample, abundant; many chances for.

1798 蕃庶: numerous (35.0).

束 **5891**
Karlgren: 1222a
PinYin: shu4
Rad./Strokes: 75+3

Roll, bundle; tie together, gather into a bundle; bind, restrain, control.

Some bronze representations look like a bag tied at the two ends:

 5908
Karlgren: 355a
PinYin: shuai1
Rad./Strokes: 145+4

Reduce, decrease, lessen; weaken, decline.

帥 **5909**
Karlgren: 499a
PinYin: shuai4
Rad./Strokes: 50+6

Lead (an army), commander, leader, officer; direct, arrange, govern; follow the lead, obey, imitate.

霜 **5919**
Karlgren: 731g
PinYin: shuang1
Rad./Strokes: 173+9

Frost, hoarfrost.
It only appears in 2.1, preceded by other character, **3893** 履霜, they may mean:

- The coming winter; signs of decay.

- An approaching marriage. Two *ShiJing* odes use the same characters with that meaning.
- Ceremonial walking on hoarfrost for the autumnal sacrifices.

水 **5922**
Karlgren: 576a
PinYin: shui3
Rad./Strokes: 85+0

Water, river, stream, flood, liquid, fluid. Ancient versions of this character show running water:

Compare with **1439** 川, river, flowing water.

順 **5935**
Karlgren: 462c
PinYin: shun4
Rad./Strokes: 181+3

Follow, obey, yield, agree, submissive, docile.
From **1439** 川, *chuan1*: "river, flowing water", phonetic, and 頁, *ye4*, "head".

說 **5939**
Karlgren: 324q
PinYin: tuo1 shuo1
Rad./Strokes: 149+7

It has different meanings depending on its pronunciation:
- Remove, take off, come off, let loose (*tuo1*): 4.1, 9.3, 26.2, 33.2, 38.6.
  According to some translators it should be replaced with **6468** 脫: "remove".
- Pleasure, joy, satisfaction; talk, persuade, stimulate, say, explain, exhort (*shuo1*): 47.5.

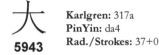

Karlgren: 317a
PinYin: da4
Rad./Strokes: 37+0

5943

Big, great, tall; excessive, arrogant; spread out and reach everywhere.

It shows a **3097** 人 "man" with arms and legs spread, to indicate "big"

Used as the first character in the tags of the hexagrams 14, 26, 28 and 34.

In ancient oracle bones representations it has the shape of a person:

In many cases (1.2, 1.5, 6.0, 12.2, 12.5, 30.X, 39.0, 39.6, 45.0, 46.0, 47.0, 49.5, 57.0) it appears besides 人, "man":

大人 **3097**: great man, mature man, man of great virtue, important, noble, with influence.

In other places (5.0, 6.0, 13.0, 15.1, 18.0, 26.0, 27.5, 27.6, 42.0, 59.0, 61.0, 64.3) it appears alongside other two characters:

5707 涉大川 **1439**: cross (ford) the big river (to start an important endeavor).

他

Karlgren: 4c'
PinYin: ta1
Rad./Strokes: 9+3

5961

Harm, obstacle, calamity; other.

From 亻 (**3097** 人), "person" and 也, "also". 也 may have been a phonetic.

See **6439** 它, tuo1, which has a similar meaning.

帶

Karlgren: 315a
PinYin: dai4
Rad./Strokes: 50+8

6005

Belt, large belt; band or ribbon worn about the waist that serves as a purse; girdle.

"Great belts were emblems of rank and authority that remained in use until the twentieth century" (*Rutt*).

Karlgren: 316a
PinYin: tai4
Rad./Strokes: 85+5

6023

Great, extensive, exalted, superior, prosperous, successful; liberal; extreme, excessive, arrogant; influential, spread out and reach everywhere, permeate, pervade; peace, quiet.

Tag for the hexagram 11, which is the only place where it appears, two times.

眈

Karlgren: 656j
PinYin: dan1
Rad./Strokes: 109+4

6028

Glare, stare; look downwards; glare intensely; the glare of a tiger. It only appears in 27.4, where it appears duplicated:

眈眈: eyeing gloatingly; looking at greedily.

From **4596** 目, "eye" and 尤, "doubtful": look and hesitate.

坦

Karlgren: 149d
PinYin: tan3
Rad./Strokes: 32+5

6057

Level, smooth, flat; smooth appearance, a ease, in peace, satisfied. It only appears in 10.2, duplicated, which in-

235

tensifies its meaning and also means "flat and extended".
From 土, "soil, earth" and 旦, "dawn".

道 **6136**
Karlgren: 1048a
PinYin: dao4
Rad./Strokes: 162+9

Road, course, path, way, method; show the way, lead, explain.
From **5839** 首, "head" and 辶, "go". In the older part of the *YiJing* (Judgment (*gua ci*) and lines), that are the ones attributed to King *Wen*, 道, *dao*, only means a literal road or path, and as a metaphor, a way to do things; but with the passage of time, *dao* become the basis a system of beliefs called *Daoism* (previously spelled *Tao* and *Taoism*). *Daoism* is a religious/philosophical tradition that emphasizes living in harmony with the *Dao*. In *Daoism*, *Dao* not only means "way, road", but also indicates something that is both the source and the driving force behind everything that exists. Following the *Dao* becomes a way of life and is the way to happiness and a long life. Each Art and Science is called a *dao*, but the source off all art and science is called the *Dao*, or the Way.

咷 **6152**
Karlgren: 1145t
PinYin: tao2
Rad./Strokes: 30+6

Wail, weep, cry loudly, lament, moaning.
From **3434** 口, "mouth" and 兆, phonetic.
It only appears in 13.5 and 56.6, in both cases preceded by 號:

> **2064** 號咷: cry loudly; screams and groans, weeping and groans.

得 **6161**
Karlgren: 905d
PinYin: de2
Rad./Strokes: 60+8

Get, obtain, gain; reach, achieve; can; attain the desired thing.
From **5005** 貝, *bei4*, money, over 寸, *cun4*, "hand": get some money.

德 **6162**
Karlgren: 919k
PinYin: de2
Rad./Strokes: 60+12

Virtue, spiritual power, moral integrity; quality, nature, aptitude, ability, character.
From 彳, "steps", **1006** 直, "straight" and (added later) **2735** 心, "heart": to walk a straight (virtuous) road, following your heart.

> 德行 **2754**: morality and conduct, virtue (29.X, 60.X).

登 **6167**
Karlgren: 883e
PinYin: deng1
Rad./Strokes: 105+7

Rise, ascend, climb, mount, step up; ripen; raise.
From 癶, "legs" (two 止 feet) and 豆, "beams" (it was taken as a loan, but here it means "pedestal"): To ascend upon a pedestal, firstly with one foot, then with the other (*Wieger*).

羝 **6195**
Karlgren: 590h
PinYin: di1
Rad./Strokes: 123+5

Goat, ram, he-goat.
From **7247** 羊, "sheep, goat" and 氐, phonetic
It appears in two places, 34.3 and 34.6, always besides to another character:

> 羝羊 **7247**: three years old male goat, fully grown.

6198

Karlgren: 4b'
PinYin: di4
Rad./Strokes: 32+3

Earth, soil, ground.
From 土, "earth" and 也, *ye3*, "also", phonetic. The pronunciation have changed, the current pronunciation is *di4*.

6201

Karlgren: 591a
PinYin: di4
Rad./Strokes: 57+4

Younger brother, junior, respectful towards elder brothers.

6202

Karlgren: 591d
PinYin: di4
Rad./Strokes: 38+7

Younger secondary wife, under the authority of the first wife; concubine.
From **4776** 女, *nu3*, "wife" and **6201** 弟, *di4*, "younger brother".

6204

Karlgren: 877a
PinYin: di4
Rad./Strokes: 50+6

Sovereign, emperor, god.

帝乙 **3017** (*di yi*) was the name of the penultimate *Shang* emperor. In 11.5 and 54.5 *di yi* indicates that emperor.

In 16.X, 42.2 and 59.X it means *Di*, the supreme god of the *Shang*, which also was revered by the *Zhou*.

6221

Karlgren: 877q
PinYin: di2
Rad./Strokes: 66+11

Enemy, opponent that is an equal; an equal, comrade, a match, mate.

From 商, phonetic, and 攵 (攴), "beat".

靚
6230

Karlgren: 1023e
PinYin: di2
Rad./Strokes: 147+15

See face to face; to be admitted to an audience; encounter; to be visible.
From 賣, phonetic, and **0860** 見, "see".

涕
6250

Karlgren: 591m
PinYin: ti4
Rad./Strokes: 85+7

Tears, weep, snivel, mucus.
From 氵 (**5922** 水), "water" and **6201** 弟, phonetic.

稊
6252

Karlgren: 591g
PinYin: ti2
Rad./Strokes: 115+7

Shoot, sprout, newly sprouted leaf, a new shoot from a dried stem.
From 禾, "grain" and **6201** 弟, phonetic

惕
6263

Karlgren: 850i
PinYin: ti4
Rad./Strokes: 61+8

Wary, cautious, alert, alarmed; fear, respect, to stand in awe of.
From 忄 (**2735** 心), "heart" and **2952** 易, phonetic

逖
6265

Karlgren: 856f
PinYin: ti4
Rad./Strokes: 162+7

Far, distant; removed, remove, send away, keep at distance.

6314
Karlgren: 413r
PinYin: die2
Rad./Strokes: 125+6

Old age (70 or more years), aged, old, infirm.
From **3833** 老, "old" and **0982** 至, "utmost", phonetic.

6318
Karlgren: 339l
PinYin: xie4
Rad./Strokes: 85+9

Clear, filter, purify (these are the preferred meaning for 48.3, the only place where this character appears); ooze, seep, leak; turbid, muddy, unsettled.
From 氵(**5922** 水), "water" and 枼, phonetic.

6337
Karlgren: 375m
PinYin: dian1
Rad./Strokes: 181+10

Summit, peak, top, top of head; invert, upturn, topple, fall on the head; overthrow.

6358
Karlgren: 385m
PinYin: dian4
Rad./Strokes: 173+5

Lightning, sudden illumination, complete clarity.
From **7662** 雨, "rain" and 电, "lightning".

6361
Karlgren: 361a
PinYin: tian1
Rad./Strokes: 37+1

Heaven, firmament, the sky, cosmos; celestial, divine, power above the human; tattoo on forehead, head shaved (38.3).

Heaven

There is another character (**3233** 乾, *quian2*) related with heaven, because it is the character for the trigram ☰, *The Creative, The heaven*.
See **9000**: *The Eight Trigrams*.
The concept of *heaven* covers not only the physical heavens, the starry sky, but also involves heavenly providence. The celestial will governs human affairs; the Heaven is a sacred space, but does not include the connotations of a personal deity, as the God of the religions of the West.
Heaven covers, Earth (**3684** 坤) *supports*: this is the traditional formula that determines the roles of these two complementary principles, and defines their situations symbolically, being at the top and the bottom respectively, in relation to the beings located between Heaven and the Earth, as the people.
The important role of humanity is to be a mediator between these two principles. Human beings are not only animals or spirits, but have a bit of Heaven and a little of Earth inside them.
天 is combined with other characters to form some important concepts, not included in the *YiJing*, but present in later exegesis of it:

> **6198** 地天: *Heaven and Earth*: the dynamic relationship between the primary powers generates nature and the human world.

> 天命 **4537**: *tian ming: The Mandate of Heaven*. The "Mandate of Heaven" is an ancient Chinese philosophical concept, which originated during the *Zhou* dynasty. The Mandate determines

whether an emperor of China is sufficiently virtuous to rule; if he does not fulfill his obligations as emperor, then he loses the Mandate and thus the right to be emperor.

Older versions of this character on oracle bones show the image of a person with a large head, which later became a line. It is an anthropomorphic image of the power of Heaven.

See **5943** 大, "big, great" and **3097** 人, "person".

Brand on the forehead;
to shave off the head

This character has a completely different meaning in 38.3, which is: to brand on the forehead, head shaved.

According to *Wilhelm*, *Legge* and *Sherril-Chu* it means to cut off the hair or the top knot.

This knot was a symbol of status, so it means that the subject status is diminished or its pride is injured.

The *Kangxi zidian*, explains *tian* as *kun* 髡 **5057** 'shaving the hair' as a form of punishment.

Ritsema-Karcher replaces *tian* 天 with *yao*, 夭: "stricken".

According to *Karlgren* (#1141a) *yao* means: bend (*Tso*); break, cut off (*Chuang*); premature death (*Shu*); kill, destroy (*Shi*); delicate, slender, young and beautiful (*Shi*).

Nevertheless most traditional Chinese commentators agree with the mean-

ings: to brand on the forehead or to shave off the head.

Han epoch commentators explain *tian* as "to tattoo the forehead". Also other Chinese scholars sustain that *tian* is a loan for the word 顛 in the sense of "branding or tattooing the forehead", coincidently with *Han* time commentators interpretation.

6362 Karlgren: 362a
PinYin: tian2
Rad./Strokes: 102+0

Field, cultivated land; hunt. The character is the picture of a cultivated field, divided in four sectors.

6390 Karlgren: 833e
PinYin: ding3
Rad./Strokes: 181+2

Top of the head, crown.
From 丁, phonetic, and 頁, "head".

6392 Karlgren: 834a
PinYin: ding3
Rad./Strokes: 206+0

Caldron; three-legged bronze caldron with two ears.

Bronze vessels were used during the *Shang* and *Zhou* dynasties as sacred objects in the rituals. It was believed that the ancestors could intercede for the living if they were honored and respected. There were several types of containers, but the one used for sacrifices to ancestors was 鼎, *ding3*.

All representations in bronze and oracle bones of this character show a caldron:

It was also considered a symbol of imperial power. Legend has it that *Yu the Great* had made nine caldrons symbolizing the nine states of China. The nine caldrons became the "Mandate of Heaven", indicating the supremacy of imperial power and the unification and prosperity. *Yu the Great* honored the nine caldrons as "Treasures Protecting the Country," and when subjects came to court, they offered worship to the nine caldrons. Since then the nine caldrons became the most important ritual objects.

In the *YiJing* 鼎 symbolizes a ritual of transformation.

Tag for the hexagram 50.

定
6393

Karlgren: 833z
PinYin: ding4
Rad./Strokes: 40+5

Settle, establish, put in place, make certain, fix, resolve, decide; settled, certain; quiet.
From 宀, "roof" and **0351** 正, phonetic.

庭
6405

Karlgren: 835h
PinYin: ting2
Rad./Strokes: 53+7

Courtyard (of palace), court, audience chamber; hall, courtyard, chambers; family.
From 广, "house" and 廷, "royal court".

多
6416

Karlgren: 3a
PinYin: duo1
Rad./Strokes: 36+3

Too much, many, numerous; excessive; often.
From **2485** 夕 duplicated (image of the moon, like **7696** 月), "dusk": two moons = many.

朵
6419

Karlgren: 10a
PinYin: duo3
Rad./Strokes: 75+2

Hang, hanging open, move (specifically the jaw in chewing). It only appears in 27.1 along other character:

朵頤 **2969**: the movement of the jaw in chewing.

The character shows a **4593** 木 with drooping top branches depicted (*Karlgren*).

它
6439

Karlgren: 4a
PinYin: tuo1
Rad./Strokes: 40+2

Another, other; danger, calamity, obstacle.
See **5961** 牠, *ta1*, which has a similar meaning.

沱
6442

Karlgren: 4k
PinYin: tuo2
Rad./Strokes: 85+5

Flowing, flow; water diverting into streams, running or streaming water; tears or rain falling heavily.
From **5922** 氵, "water" (水), and 它, phonetic.

6468

Karlgren: 344m
PinYin: tuo1
Rad./Strokes: 130+7

Remove.

This character is not present in traditional *YiJing* versions, but *Kunst* and others use it as a replacement for 說 **5939**, *shuo1*, in the places where the meaning "remove" is used.

From 月 (**3153** 肉), "flesh" and **6560** 兑, phonetic

斗

6472

Karlgren: 116a
PinYin: dou3
Rad./Strokes: 68+0

Big dipper (a cluster of seven stars in the constellation *Ursa Major*, four forming the bowl and three the handle of a dipper-shaped configuration, also called *Plow* or *Plough*); dipper; a unit of measure for grain.

It only appears in 55.2 and 55.4 where it means *Big Dipper*.

Ancient representations in bronze and oracle bones show the shape of a ladle because in China the *Big Dipper* is called the *Northern Ladle*:

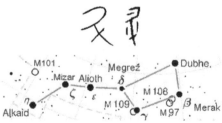

Also, a reference to a star can be found in 55.3, **4412** 沬, the *Mei* star.

度

6504

Karlgren: 801a
PinYin: du4
Rad./Strokes: 53+6

Measure (of length); law, rule; limits,

regulate; calculate; consider; interval in music.

From 广, "house, 廿, "twenty" and 又, "hand": "To have in one's hand (twenty:) all the inhabitants of the house: rule, regulate" (*Karlgren*).

毒

6509

Karlgren: 1016a
PinYin: du2
Rad./Strokes: 80+4

Poison, venom; hate, cruel, evil, hurtful, kill with poison, narcotics.

From **5738** 生, "life" (picture of a plant) and **4582** 母 (毋, "do not"): "forbidden herbs" (*Karlgren*).

獨

6512

Karlgren: 1224i
PinYin: du2
Rad./Strokes: 94+13

Alone, single, solitary, only; isolated; meditative.

From 犭, "dog" and 蜀, phonetic: lone sheep dog guarding a herd of sheep (*Shuowen*).

瀆

6515

Karlgren: 1023j
PinYin: du2
Rad./Strokes: 15+15

Importune, harass, insult, molest, abuse, annoy, disrespect; canal, ditch, drain.

塗

6525

Karlgren: 82d'
PinYin: tu2
Rad./Strokes: 32+10

Dirt, mud; mire, plaster, smear.

From **5922** 氵, "water" (水), 余, phonetic, and 土, "earth, soil".

Karlgren: 62e
PinYin: tu2
6536 **Rad./Strokes:** 60+7

Walk, go on foot; foot soldier; follower, adherent; servant; common people, multitude.
From 彳, "step" and 走, "walk".

 Karlgren: 489a
PinYin: tu1
6540 **Rad./Strokes:** 116+4

Suddenly, abruptly; break through, bursting forth, abrupt attack.
From **2899** 穴, "cave, hole" and 犬, "dog": like a dog coming out/in a cave (catching a prey?): sudden.

 Karlgren: 324a
PinYin: dui4
6560 **Rad./Strokes:** 10+5

Joyousness, happiness; cheerful talk, openness, interaction, exchange, mouth; barter.
"Good words that dispel grief and rejoice the hearer; hence the two meanings, to speak, to rejoice." (*Wieger*).
Tag for the hexagram 58, which is the only place where this character appears. It is the character of the trigram ☱: *The Joyous, Lake*. See **9000**: *The Eight Trigrams*.
It is related with **0277** 澤: lake.

Karlgren: 511a
PinYin: dui4
6562 **Rad./Strokes:** 41+11

Harmony, correspond to, suitable, agreeing with; right, correct, proper.

 Karlgren: 512a
PinYin: tui4
6568 **Rad./Strokes:** 162+6

Retreat, withdraw, back up, retire; decline, refuse.

 Karlgren: 464p
PinYin: dun1
6571 **Rad./Strokes:** 66+8

Earnest, generous, authentic, honest, sincere; staunch, strong, thick, solid.

 Karlgren: 428d
PinYin: dun4
6586 **Rad./Strokes:** 162+11

Retreat, escape, evade, withdraw; hide away, skulk; young pig, piglet.
The modernist school sees this character as a loan: "In the received text the tag character is *dun* 'withdraw'. This is taken to be a loan for *tun* 豚, 'young pig'. The precise meaning of *tun* is hard to discover. It probably means a pig in its prime, rather than a piglet" (*Rutt*).
Tag for the hexagram 33.
From **6600** 豚, "piglet, small pig", phonetic, and 辶, "go".

Karlgren: 427a
PinYin: zhun1
6592 **Rad./Strokes:** 45+1

Difficult; to sprout, begin to grow; assemble, accumulate, hoard; a camp, to garrison soldiers, a village, massed, bunched.
It depicts a germinating plant coming to light through the surface of the earth. The plant must go through obstacles and establish a presence in a place full of potential dangers, hence the idea of initial difficulty.

The oldest character representations clearly show a plant budding through the surface of the earth:

Tag for the hexagram 3.

6600
Karlgren: 428a
PinYin: tun2
Rad./Strokes: 152+4

A small, suckling pig. *Shuowen* says "pig meat".
From 月 (**3153** 肉), "meat, flesh" and **5766** 豕, "pig".
See **6586** 遯.

6602
Karlgren: 429c
PinYin: tun2
Rad./Strokes: 130+13

Buttocks, rump.
From 殿, *dian4*, "the rear" and 月 (**3153** 肉, *rou4*), "flesh".

東

6605
Karlgren: 1175a
PinYin: dong1
Rad./Strokes: 75+4

East.
"The **3124** 日 Sun appearing at the horizon. To show that it is on a level with the horizon, it is represented shining under the top of the 木 trees that are at the horizon. By extension, the East whence light rises" (*Wieger*).

棟

6607
Karlgren: 1175f
PinYin: dong4
Rad./Strokes: 75+8

Ridgepole, main beam supporting house, ridge of a roof.

From **4593** 木, "wood" and **6605** 東, phonetic

6611
Karlgren: 1188m
PinYin: dong4
Rad./Strokes: 19+9

Move, stir, take action, excite, arouse.
From 重, "heavy", phonetic, and 力, "strength": move heavy stuff.

6615
Karlgren: 1176a
PinYin: tong2
Rad./Strokes: 30+3

Gather people, assemble, join, partake in; identical, together, fellowship; in agreement, identical, identified.
Used as the first character in the hexagram 13 tag.

童

6626
Karlgren: 1188o
PinYin: tong2
Rad./Strokes: 117+7

Youth, boy, young person (boy or girl); page, pupil; servant; a virgin, pure, undefiled; young animal without horns (esp. calf or lamb).

6652
Karlgren: 940a
PinYin: zai1
Rad./Strokes: 86+3

Calamity, disaster, injury; misfortune from without (undeserved); calamities from Heaven, as floods, famines, pestilence, etc.
From **2395** 火, *huo3*, "fire", and **1439** 川 (巛), *chuan1*, "river". "Calamity, divine Judgment. Floods and fire make up the character which stands for divine judgment; as these are regarded as calamities sent from Heaven" (*Wilder*).

243

6653

Karlgren: 943a'
PinYin: zai4
Rad./Strokes: 159+6

Transport, carry, load, bear; contain, sustain; load a vessel or cart, conveyance.

From **0280** 車, "wagon, cart" and 𢦏, phonetic.

6657

Karlgren: 943i
PinYin: zai4
Rad./Strokes: 32+3

Be at, at, in, on, within, be present; to lie in, depend upon, involved with; be living, dwell, located in.

From 土, "land" and 才, phonetic: at this place.

Similar to *yu2* 于 **7592**.

再

6658

Karlgren: 941a
PinYin: zai4
Rad./Strokes: 13+4

Twice, second, again, repeated.

6679

Karlgren: 660g
PinYin: zan1
Rad./Strokes: 118+12

Hairpin, hair clasp, wear in the hair; skewer; loan for *zhen*, quick, rapid.

臧

6704

Karlgren: 727f'
PinYin: zang1
Rad./Strokes: 131+8

Good, right; generous; command.

From **0673** 戕, phonetic, and **0327** 臣, "minister".

6746

Karlgren: 906a
PinYin: ze2
Rad./Strokes: 18+7

Then, thus, accordingly, consequently, and so, in that case; law, rule, pattern; follow a law.

6755

Karlgren: 924f
PinYin: ze4
Rad./Strokes: 72+4

Sun setting in the afternoon, the afternoon; to decline.

From **3124** 日, "Sun" and 仄, "leaning to one side": The Sun aslant in the West.

6758

Karlgren: 906e
PinYin: ce4
Rad./Strokes: 61+9

Sorrow, grief, sadness, deeply pained; to pity, sympathize.

From 忄 (**2735** 心), "heart" and **6746** 則, phonetic.

左

6774

Karlgren: 5a
PinYin: zuo3
Rad./Strokes: 48+2

Left side, to the left; the left bank of a river, the East; help, assist, support.

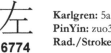 **6980**: 7.4: withdraw to the barracks (the army).

左右: 11.X: help, assist, support; control; influence.

Derived from ⺕, the left hand.
See **7541** 右: the right side.

作

6780

Karlgren: 806l
PinYin: zuo4
Rad./Strokes: 9+5

Act, do, make, work, perform; rise,

stand up, get to work; project, under-taking, ceremony, to sacrifice.

作事 **5787**: 6.X: handle matters or business.

5943 大作: 42.1: important event; masterpiece; great project or ex-hibition.

From 亻 (**3097** 人), "person" and 乍, phonetic: action of a person.

錯
6793
Karlgren: 798s
PinYin: cuo4
Rad./Strokes: 167+8

Cautious, hesitant, scared; whetstone, grindstone, to polish; crisscrossed, crossed; confused, complicated; wrong, mistaken. The initial uncertainty leads to caution and gradual improvement. It only appears in one place:

錯然 **3072**: 30.1: Cautious, thoughtful and diligent. (*HanYu-CiDian*)

祖
6815
Karlgren: 46b'
PinYin: zu3
Rad./Strokes: 113+5

Ancestor, grandfather.
From 礻, "altar" (示) and **0803** 且, phonetic. The 示 altar is used for mak-ing sacrifices to the ancestors.

足
6824
Karlgren: 1219a
PinYin: zu2
Rad./Strokes: 157+0

Leg, foot, base, support.
Some ancient representations on oracle bones show a foot:

族
6830
Karlgren: 1206a
PinYin: zu2
Rad./Strokes: 70+7

Clan, kin, extended family; group of families; tribe.
From 㫃, "banner" and **5784** 矢, "ar-row": military unit, clan (*Karlgren*).

罪
6860
Karlgren: 513a
PinYin: zui4
Rad./Strokes: 122+8

Crime, offense, misdeed, wrongdoing, sin.
From 罒 (网), "net", over **1819** 非, "bad, wrong".
A net 网 to capture the 非 wrongdoer.

摧
6866
Karlgren: 575l'
PinYin: cui1
Rad./Strokes: 64+11

Draw back; chop, destroy, break; re-press, to cause to cease, to extinguish.
From 扌, "hand" and 崔, phonetic: something done with the hand.

萃
6880
Karlgren: 490m
PinYin: cui4
Rad./Strokes: 140+8

Collect, assemble, gather together, massing; bunched, thick, dense; crowd, collection, group.
Tag for the hexagram 45.

245

6886

Karlgren: 430i
PinYin: zun1
Rad./Strokes: 75+12

Goblet, jug, wine-cup, flask, cup.

6896

Karlgren: 1003a
PinYin: zong1
Rad./Strokes: 40+5

Clan, kin, sect, faction, school; ancestor; ancestral temple; ancestral hall.
From 宀, "roof" and 示, "altar": ancestral temple, where the ancestors are revered.

3290 高宗: 63.3: *Gao Zong*: Eminent Ancestor: Dynastic title of the *Shang* king *WuDing*.

6919

Karlgren: 1191d
PinYin: cong2
Rad./Strokes: 60+8

Follow (somebody or a way or doctrine), adhere, obey, pursue; follower attendant; attend to business; from, by, since, whence, through.
From 彳, "footprint", to the left, 止, "foot", on the bottom and **3097** 人, "two persons": one who follows another person.
Older versions only show two persons: 从.

6921

Karlgren: 1178a
PinYin: cong2
Rad./Strokes: 29+16

Thicket, thickly-growing, a clump of threes, hedge, grove; dense, crowded together.
From 丵, "bush", over **1615** 取, "take".
It only appears in 29.6:

246

叢棘 **0486**: a place of detention (a pit, in 29.6).

6923

Karlgren: 555e
PinYin: zi1
Rad./Strokes: 30+6

Sigh, lament, sob.

6927

Karlgren: 555h
PinYin: zi1
Rad./Strokes: 154+5

Property, wealth, goods, provisions, materials; means of living, rely on, depend on.
From **6980** 次, phonetic, and **5005** 貝, "money".

6932

Karlgren: 969d
PinYin: zi1
Rad./Strokes: 140+8

Clearing, breaking new ground for cultivation; land that has been under cultivation for one year, recently broken field.
From 艹 (草), "grass" and 甾, "incult or new-broken ground"

6935

Karlgren: 966b
PinYin: zi1
Rad./Strokes: 140+6

This (loan); coarse straw mat.
From 艹 (草), "grass, straw" and 幺, "silk threads": some kind of fabric.

6939

Karlgren: 964a
PinYin: zi3
Rad./Strokes: 39+0

Child, son, daughter, offspring; suffix; bride, wife; gentleman, officer, master, prince; young lady; the first of the *Earthly Branches*.

This character appears 87 times, most of the times besides 君 (73 times), forming the word *JunZi*, whose original meaning was "son of a prince or ruler". See **1715** 君 for more details.

Ancient representations in bronze show clearly the head, arms and torso of a baby, the legs are not shown because they are wrap in swaddling clothes:

字
6942

Karlgren: 964n
PinYin: zi4
Rad./Strokes: 40+3

Conceive, pregnant; pledge, betrothal; breed; nurture, nourish, suckle.
From **6939** 子, "child", under a 宀 "roof": "To bear and nurse; to have children in one's house" (*Wieger*).

胏
6950

Karlgren: 554g
PinYin: zi3
Rad./Strokes: 130+5

Slice of dried meat with bone.
From 月 (**3153** 肉), "meat, flesh" and 朿, phonetic.

自
6960

Karlgren: 1237m
PinYin: zi4
Rad./Strokes: 132+0

From, origin, source, cause, reason; oneself, yourself.
ShuoWen says: "nose, snout". Indeed ancient representations show a nose:

In China, one points to the own nose to signal oneself. Breathing and the human spirit are traditionally associated.

次
6980

Karlgren: 555a
PinYin: ci4
Rad./Strokes: 15+4

Camp, take a position, to stop at a place, halt; lodge, hostel, lodging place, hut; hard-going; put in order, order, sequel, next in order, second, second rate.

外
7001

Karlgren: 322a
PinYin: wai4
Rad./Strokes: 36+2

Outside, beyond, external, foreign, unfamiliar, extraordinary, barbarian.
From **2485** 夕, "nightfall" (shows a crescent moon, as **7696** 月) and 卜, "predict, divine" (using a turtle shell): "divination by the moon: outdoors" (*Karlgren*).

萬
7030

Karlgren: 267a
PinYin: wan4
Rad./Strokes: 140+9

Literally: ten thousands, e.g. many, countless. *ShuoWen* says "an insect". Ancient representations on bronze and oracle bones show an scorpion (the original meaning):

亡
7034

Karlgren: 742a
PinYin: wang2
Rad./Strokes: 8+1

Go away, disappear, exile; fail; destroy, perish, not have, not exist.

Its original shape was 凵, which combines **3152** 入, "enter" and 凵, "a corner": "To enter a nook, a hiding place" (*Karlgren*). Afterwards 入 got flattened into 宀.

妄
7035
Karlgren: 742g
PinYin: wang4
Rad./Strokes: 38+3

Expect, look forward, hope (loan, see note below), presume, pretense; extravagant, foolish, absurd, wild, disorderly, lawless, reckless, rude; false, errancy.

Basically this character means "reckless, disorderly", but some translators take it as a loan character for **7043** 望 "expect".

It only appears both in the lines and as the tag of the hexagram 25, always preceded by **7173** 无, which means "no, not":

无妄: its literal meaning is "no error", although if we take 妄 as a loan for 望, it would mean "no expectancy". In both cases the meaning of 无妄 is "truth, innocence, somebody who acts in accordance with the situation intuitively, attuned to the exigencies of the moment".

From **7034** 亡, phonetic, and **4776** 女, "woman".

王
7037
Karlgren: 739a
PinYin: wang2
Rad./Strokes: 96+0

King, prince, sovereign, ruler.
From **5415** 三, three strokes representing heaven, earth and mankind (according to the traditional Chinese conception, man is located between heaven and earth to form the great triad), joined together by a vertical stroke ｜ representing the king.

望
7043
Karlgren: 742m
PinYin: wang4
Rad./Strokes: 74+7

Full Moon; the 15th day of the lunar calendar; hope; expect; look forward to. It only appears in 9.6, 54.5 and 61.4, always preceded by the same character:

0409 幾望: The moon is nearly full.

From **7034** 亡, phonetic, **7696** 月, "Moon" and **7037** 王, "king". 王 was drawn as in seal characters and it may mean a person standing on the 土 earth, to watch the Moon.

罒
7045
Karlgren: 742l
PinYin: wang3
Rad./Strokes: 122+3

Not, no, negative, absence; a net (empty spaces between the threads), entangle, confusion.

往
7050
Karlgren: 739k
PinYin: wang3
Rad./Strokes: 60+5

Go, to go to, go forward, go towards; depart, bygone, former.
It appears 51 times, in 21 cases is preceded by **7519** 攸: goal:

攸往: place to go; have a goal.

From 彳, "walk" and **7037** 王, phonetic.

威
7051
Karlgren: 574a
PinYin: wei1
Rad./Strokes: 38+6

Dignity, respect; awesome, majestic;

248

impress, terrify; the mother of one's husband.

From 戍, "destroy, weapon" and **4776** 女, "woman": wife's mother in law, an imposing figure.

7059
Karlgren: 27a
PinYin: wei2
Rad./Strokes: 87+8

Act, do, accomplish, make, to be; act for, stand for, support, help; become.

The more ancient depictions of this character seem to show a hand guiding or feeding an elephant.

"It has been suggested that an obsolete area word for elephant had once served as phonetic" (*Schuessler*).

7066
Karlgren: 575n
PinYin: wei2
Rad./Strokes: 61+8

Think; namely, it is; only; alone. Initial particle, many times cannot be translated. From 忄 (**2735** 心), "heart" and 隹, phonetic.

7067
Karlgren: 575o
PinYin: wei2
Rad./Strokes: 120+8

Tie up, bound, bind together; guiding rope of a net; guiding principle, rule; but only.

From 糸, "silk thread" and 隹, phonetic.

謂
7079
Karlgren: 523d
PinYin: wei4
Rad./Strokes: 149+9

Say, tell; call; mean; name.

It only appears in 62.6 besides other character:

5794 是謂: this is what is called...

From **7334** 言, "words" and 胃, phonetic.

7089
Karlgren: 342a
PinYin: wei4
Rad./Strokes: 144+9; 144+1

Protect, guard, defend; good.

From 韋, phonetic, placed inside 2754 行, "walk".

Older versions in bronze show four feet around a circle or square, possibly indicating the walled area guarded by the sentinel (*Karlgren*):

7093
Karlgren: 571d
PinYin: wei2
Rad./Strokes: 162+9

Oppose, go against; disobey, disregard, refuse; go away, leave; deviate from; error; perverse.

From 韋, phonetic, and 辶, "go".

尾
7109
Karlgren: 583a
PinYin: wei3
Rad./Strokes: 44+4

Tail, rear, back, behind, the end; last.
From **5756** 尸, "body" and 毛, "hair".

未
7114
Karlgren: 531a
PinYin: wei4
Rad./Strokes: 75+1

Not yet, before. The eight of the twelve Earthly Branches. 1-3 p.m.

The oracle bones representation shown below depicts the image of a tree with its branches:

Used as the first character in the hexagram 64 tag.

Karlgren: 539a
PinYin: wei4
7116 **Rad./Strokes:** 9+5

Position, location; category, rank, status; situation.
From 亻 (**3097** 人), "person" and **3921** 立, "stand up or erect".

Karlgren: 475a
PinYin: wen2
7129 **Rad./Strokes:** 67+0

Elegant, refined, ornate, stylish; civil, polite, urbane; literary, artistic, cultural pursuits.
Ancient representations on bronze show a man with a tattooing on the breast:

問
Karlgren: 441g
PinYin: wen4
7141 **Rad./Strokes:** 30+8

Ask, make inquiries, interrogate, question.
From **4418** 門, "door" and **3434** 口, "mouth": words spoken outside the door, go outside and ask.

250

聞
Karlgren: 441f
PinYin: wen2
7142 **Rad./Strokes:** 128+8

Hear; to be heard; make known, fame; smell.
From **4418** 門, "door", and **1744** 耳, "ear".

Karlgren: 1184p
PinYin: weng4
7151 **Rad./Strokes:** 98+13

Earthen vessel, jug.
From 雍, phonetic, and 瓦, "tile, earthenware".

Karlgren: 1204f
PinYin: wo4
7161 **Rad./Strokes:** 64+9

Grasp, squeeze; restrain; handful.
From 扌 (手), "hand", and **7212** 屋, *wu*, phonetic.

Karlgren: 1204g
PinYin: wo4
7162 **Rad./Strokes:** 85+9

Soak, smear, moisten, stain.
From **5922** 氵 (水), "water" and **7212** 屋, *wu*, phonetic.

巫
Karlgren: 105a
PinYin: wu1
7164 **Rad./Strokes:** 48+4

Magician, sorcerer, shaman, wizard, witch.

无
Karlgren: 106a
PinYin: wu2
7173 **Rad./Strokes:** 71+0

No, not, negative; without, does not possess, not have.

Ancient representations on bronze show a dancer with fancy sleeves or some ornament in his arms/hands. The character was borrowed for sound:

See **7208** 勿, do not, no, must not. Used as the first character in the hexagram 25 tag.

7188

Karlgren: 58f
PinYin: wu2
Rad./Strokes: 30+4

I, my, we, our. First person pronoun. From 五, phonetic, and **3434** 口, "mouth".

7195

Karlgren: 104a
PinYin: wu3
Rad./Strokes: 77+4

Martial, military; warlike, warrior. From 戈, "weapon, halberd, spear, battle axe" and 止, "stop": a weapon to stop aggressions.

7208

Karlgren: 503a
PinYin: wu4
Rad./Strokes: 20+2

Do not, no. Negative imperative. See **7173** 无, which has a similar meaning.

7209

Karlgren: 503h
PinYin: wu4
Rad./Strokes: 93+4

Thing/s, being/s, creature/s; substance, the physical world, all living things; others.

From **4737** 牛, "ox" and **7208** 勿, phonetic

厃

7211

Karlgren: 487e
PinYin: wu4
Rad./Strokes: 26+7

Unsafe, unsteady, uncertain, uncomfortable, to limp; stump, stake. It only appears in 47.6, preceded by 臲:

4700 臲厃: jittery; worried; anxious.

From 兀, phonetic, and 危, "danger".

屋

7212

Karlgren: 1204a
PinYin: wu1
Rad./Strokes: 44+6

Roof, canopy, shelter, room, house. From **5756** 尸, "lie as a corpse, sit motionless" and **0982** 至, "arrive; reach": "Place where a man being arrived takes rest" (*Wieger*).

牙

7214

Karlgren: 37a
PinYin: ya2
Rad./Strokes: 92+0

Tusks, fangs, teeth. The bronze character shown below is a graphic representation of a tooth:

啞

7226

Karlgren: 805f
PinYin: e4
Rad./Strokes: 30+8

Laugh, sound of laughter. When duplicated it also means: the raucous sounds of crows; the sound of a baby learning to speak; babble.

It only appears in 51.0 and 51.1, duplicated in each case, which intensifies its meaning.
From **3434** 口, "mouth" and 亞, phonetic.

| **7247** | **Karlgren:** 732a
PinYin: yang2
Rad./Strokes: 123+0 |

Sheep, ram, goat.
Ancient representations in bronze show the horns, ears and legs of the animal:

It two of the five places where it appears (34.3 and 34.6), it is located besides other character, which makes more specific its meaning:

6195 羝羊: three years old male goat, fully grown.

| **7259** | **Karlgren:** 720j
PinYin: yang2
Rad./Strokes: 64+9 |

Display, make known, announce, extol; scatter, spread; lift, raise; stir.
From 扌 (手), "hand" and 昜, phonetic.

| **7261** | **Karlgren:** 720q
PinYin: yang2
Rad./Strokes: 75+9 |

Poplar, willow, aspen.
From **4593** 木, "tree" and 昜, phonetic.
See **0547** 杞: willow.

| **7314** | **Karlgren:** 831
PinYin: ye3
Rad./Strokes: 166+4 |

Meadow, open country, countryside, fields, wilderness.
From **3857** 里, "village" (composed by 土, "land" and **6362** 田, "field") and 予, phonetic.

| **7315** | **Karlgren:** 800j
PinYin: ye4
Rad./Strokes: 36+5 |

Night, darkness.
It may come from **3021** 亦, phonetic, and **2485** 夕, "night, the Moon", as the bronze character shown below depicts:

| **7334** | **Karlgren:** 251a
PinYin: yan2
Rad./Strokes: 149+0 |

Talk, speech, words, sayings, big flute.
The bronze version shown below depicts a **3434** 廿 mouth with a flute (*Lindqvist, Karlgren*).

| **7347** | **Karlgren:** 607h
PinYin: yan2
Rad./Strokes: 30+17 |

Stern, strict, severe, rigorous; solemnity, dignity, gravity, majestic.

| **7364** | **Karlgren:** 253b
PinYin: yan4
Rad./Strokes: 40+7 |

Rest, repose; feast, banquet; leisure, pleasure. It only appears in two places:

宴樂 **4129**: 5.X: peace and happiness; to feast.

宴息 **2495**: 17.X: rest and leisure.

It is related with **0026** 安: quiet, at peace.

燕
7399
Karlgren: 243a
PinYin: yan4
Rad./Strokes: 86+12

At peace, calm, soothed, rest; swallow. Ancient versions on oracle bones show a swallow:

音
7418
Karlgren: 653a
PinYin: yin1
Rad./Strokes: 180+0

Sound, tone, pronunciation of words, message, noise.

It shows a 曰 (**3434** 口) mouth with something inside it and a tongue sticking out, representing the sound flowing off. The top part may have represented a flute in the past. Ancient depictions of this character are more graphic than the actual one:

殷
7423
Karlgren: 448a
PinYin: yin1
Rad./Strokes: 79+6

Great, ample, exalted, flourishing, abundant; a kind of sacrifice. It only appears in 16.X:

殷薦 **0872**: exalted, superlative worship; glorify, praise and feelings of awe intensified.

奟
7427
Karlgren: 450h
PinYin: yin2
Rad./Strokes: 36+11

Sacrum, lumbar area, small of the back, lower back, loins; spinal meat.

引
7429
Karlgren: 371a
PinYin: yin3
Rad./Strokes: 57+1

Guide, lead, pull, attract, stretch, draw the bow.

From 弓, "bow" and │, the bow string: draw the bow.

陰
7444
Karlgren: 651y
PinYin: yin1
Rad./Strokes: 170+8

Shade, darkness; northern slope of a height; cloudy; dark cosmogenic principle. This character represents the *Yin* principle in the *Yin-Yang* philosophy, whose symbol (also called *Tai-Chi*) is shown below.

In the *YiJing*, with his philosophy of change and transformation of opposites, there is the germ of the ideas that lead to the *Yin-Yang* doctrine, several centuries later.

Note that only *Yin* 陰 appears in the text of the *YiJing, Yang* 陽 doesn't appear in the earlier layers of the *YiJing* text.

From , phonetic (今, "now", phonetic, 云, "cloud") and 阝 (阜), "hill", which was added later to describe the shaded side of a hill.

253

Karlgren: 654a
PinYin: yin3
Rad./Strokes: 184+4

7454

Drink; swallow; give to drink.
It appears four times, in 3 cases (5.X, 27.X and 53.2) followed by 食:

食食 **5810**: drink and eat; eating together.

Karlgren: 815a
PinYin: ying2
Rad./Strokes: 108+4

7474

Fill, full, satisfied; overfill, overflowing. From 皿, "vessel", suggesting to fill a vessel. The other component is obscure. Ancient representations show clearly a cup below:

Karlgren: 1120m
PinYin: yue1
Rad./Strokes: 120+3

7493

Bind, lump together; cord, rope; restrain, restrict; bond, contract, covenant, an agreement.
From 糸, "silk thread" and 勺, "spoon", phonetic.

糩

Karlgren: 1119g
PinYin: yue4
Rad./Strokes: 113+17

7498

Yue summer sacrifice to all the ancestors entitled to special sacrifices, when food is sparse; small offering, a sacrifice offered with few resources.
From 礻 (示), "altar" and 龠, "ancient small measure", phonetic.

Karlgren: 1125p
PinYin: yao4
Rad./Strokes: 140+15

7501

Medicinal plant, medicine, healing herbs; to take medicine, treat; peony.
From 艹 (**6739** 草), "herb" and 樂, *yao4*, phonetic.

Karlgren: 1124f
PinYin: yue4
Rad./Strokes: 157+14

7504

Leap, jump; shamanic dance of flight, a rite of passage.
From 𤴓 (**6824** 足), "foot" and 翟, pheasant feathers used in dances.

幽

Karlgren: 1115c
PinYin: you1
Rad./Strokes: 52+6

7505

Dark, obscure; solitary, secluded, hidden from view; secret, difficult to understand.
From **5630** 山, "mountain" and 幺, "small", phonetic: a small, quiet, hidden retreat in the mountains.

牖

Karlgren: 1082a
PinYin: you3
Rad./Strokes: 91+11

7507

Window, opening in wall or roof to let the light enter; to enlighten, to lead.

憂

Karlgren: 1071a
PinYin: you1
Rad./Strokes: 61+11

7508

Grieved, sad, mournful; grief, melancholy.
From 頁, "person with a big head", 夂, "walk slowly" and **2735** 心,

"heart": a person walking slowly with the heart showing: sad.

由
Karlgren: 1079a
PinYin: you2
Rad./Strokes: 102+0
7513

Source, cause, reason; proceed from.
"It represents the germination of a fruit-stone, or a large grain; **6362** 田 represents the grain, on the top of which the germ is coming up... By extension, beginning, principle, origin, starting point, cause, to produce, etc." (*Wieger*).

Karlgren: 1077a
PinYin: you1
Rad./Strokes: 66+3
7519

Goal, direction, destination, objective; distant, far away; a place; that which, whereby, thereby, for which; mark of the passive voice.
"A ford; place; the place where; that which, the one who, corresponding in the oldest texts to the **5465** 所, "place", of later ages -- [**3097** 人 a man walking and 攴 punching with a | stick: wade, ford..." (*Karlgren*).

有
Karlgren: 995o
PinYin: you3
Rad./Strokes: 74+2
7533

Have, possession, there be, there is.
Used as the second character in the hexagram 14 tag.
The ancient form of this character:

Shows a hand to the right (the image of the possession), over **7696** 月,

"the Moon", rotated 90 degrees, which is seen more clearly in the actual form (without rotation). Originally 彐 meant "to have in the hand, to have", but later 月, was added. Some scholars think that the character used was not the moon but **3153** 肉, "flesh, meat", whose ancient representation was 仈. Following this idea, the original meaning may be "a hand holding meat, in possession of".

宥
Karlgren: 995r
PinYin: you4
Rad./Strokes: 40+6
7536

Pardon, lenient, indulgent, to forgive; to be large minded.
From , "roof" and **7533** 有, "have": to let back in the house: forgive.

友
Karlgren: 995e
PinYin: you3
Rad./Strokes: 29+2
7540

Companion, friend, associate, partner, couple, boy/girl friend.
It shows two hands, 𠂇 and 又, joined in friendship.
In the past the character had other form:

Which repeated twice 彐, "hand", whose actual representation is 又.

右
Karlgren: 995i
PinYin: you4
Rad./Strokes: 30+2
7541

Right, the right hand, on the right, make things right.
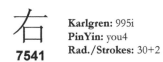 左右: (11.X): help, assist, support; control; influence.

Originally it was the image of a right hand ⺋.

See **6774** 左: the left side.

Karlgren: 995l
PinYin: you4
7543 **Rad./Strokes:** 113+5

Divine help, help, aid, protection, blessing.

It only appears in 14.6:

> **6361** 天祐: protection or help from heaven..

From 礻 (示), "show, proclaim, altar" and **7541** 右, "right".

Karlgren: 1187a
PinYin: rong2
7560 **Rad./Strokes:** 40+7

Generosity, tolerance; contain, hold, embrace, admit; support, endure.

> 容民**4508**: 7.X: contain or tolerate people.
> 容 **4946** 保民: 19.X: tolerate and protect people.

From 宀, "roof" and **3483** 谷, "valley": "a hollow, cavity with cover" (*Karlgren*).

Karlgren: 1185a
PinYin: yong4
7567 **Rad./Strokes:** 101+0

Use, apply, put to use, apply the oracle to real world situations, act; use in sacrifice (only 45.0); hereby, thereby, herewith (*Shaugnessy*), like "hereby offer sacrifice".

"This character primitively represented the bronze ex-voto offered to the Ancestors, placed in the temple as a memorial for their offspring. Afterwards it was given the shape of a bronze tripod. The vessel was used for the offerings to the Manes, hence *chuang-chu* to use, usage. The offerings brought blessing, hence *chuan-chu* aptitude, efficacy, utility, etc." (*Wieger*).

Ancient representations show it as a cauldron:

See **6392** 鼎, "cauldron".

Karlgren: 1185z
PinYin: yong1
7578 **Rad./Strokes:** 32+11

Wall, a fortified wall, defensive wall.
From 土, "soil, earth" and 庸, phonetic.

Karlgren: 843d
PinYin: rong2
7582 **Rad./Strokes:** 75+10

Honor, glory; flourish, luxuriant, prosper.

Karlgren: 764a
PinYin: yong3
7589 **Rad./Strokes:** 85+1

For a long time, constant, permanent, everlasting; prolong; distant, far reaching.

Ancient representations show "the unceasing flow of **5922** 水 water veins in the earth" (*Wieger*):

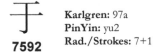 **7592**
Karlgren: 97a
PinYin: yu2
Rad./Strokes: 7+1

At, to, in, into, on, from, by, go, go to, move towards, proceed, be.
Similar meaning to *yu2* **7643** 於 and *zai4* **6657** 在.

豫 **7603**
Karlgren: 83e
PinYin: yu4
Rad./Strokes: 152+9

Think beforehand, take precautions, anticipate, hesitate; joy, happy, amusement, recreating, enthusiasm, contentment, at ease; elephant (*Kunst, Rutt*).
ShuoWen says this character means "elephant", but "There is probably no such word. There is no early text in which this word means 'elephant'" (*Schuessler*).
From 予, phonetic, and 象, "elephant".
Tag for the hexagram 16.

 7606
Karlgren: 82f
PinYin: yu2
Rad./Strokes: 102+7

Field in the 2nd or 3rd year of cultivation, plowed for such a length of time.
It only appears in 25.2:
6932 菑畬: farming; husbandry.
From *yu* 余, phonetic, over **6362** 田, "field"

 7615
Karlgren: 89b
PinYin: yu3
Rad./Strokes: 134+8

With, and; associate with, together with, participate in, be present at; help; give.
From 舁, "two pairs of hands, lift", around 与, "participate in".

譽 **7617**
Karlgren: 89i
PinYin: yu4
Rad./Strokes: 149+14

Fame, renown, reputation, honor, honored, praised.
From **7615** 與, phonetic, and **7334** 言, "words".

輿 **7618**
Karlgren: 89j
PinYin: yu2
Rad./Strokes: 159+10

Wagon, cart, chariot, carriage; carrier, transport, transportation; carry on the shoulders; contain, hold.
From 舁, "two pairs of hands, lift", around **0280** 車, "carriage": cart hauled by men; palanquin (a covered litter carried on poles on the shoulders of four or more bearers).

遇 **7625**
Karlgren: 124h
PinYin: yu4
Rad./Strokes: 162+9

Meet, encounter, come across, happen.
From 禺, phonetic, and 辶, "go, walk".

渝 **7635**
Karlgren: 125h
PinYin: yu2
Rad./Strokes: 85+9

Change, to change one's mind or attitude, retract, amend; fail, change for worse.

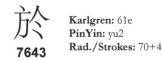 **7643**
Karlgren: 61e
PinYin: yu2
Rad./Strokes: 70+4

On, in, at, by, from; with reference to; interjection.

It was formerly used as a variant of the proposition **7592** 于, which has a similar meaning

Karlgren: 59h
PinYin: yu2
7648 **Rad./Strokes:** 141+7

Take precautions, to provide against; foresee; anxious, not at ease; forester, gamekeeper (3.3). It only appears in three places, 3.3, 45.X and 61.1.

5379 不虞: 45.X: eventuality; contingency.

From 虍 (**2161** 虎), "tiger" and 吴, phonetic.

語

Karlgren: 58t
PinYin: yu3
7651 **Rad./Strokes:** 149+7

Speak, to tell, conversation, discourse, words. It only appears one time:

7334 言語: 27.X: spoken language; speech.

From **7334** 言, "words" and **7188** 吾, phonetic.

羽

Karlgren: 98a
PinYin: yu3
7658 **Rad./Strokes:** 124+0

Feathers, wings, plums.
Some representations are very graphic:

雨

Karlgren: 100a
PinYin: yu3
7662 **Rad./Strokes:** 173+0

Rain, shower, sudden downpour.

258

Ancient representations on oracle bones show raindrops falling tipped by the wind:

禦

Karlgren: 60p
PinYin: yu4
7665 **Rad./Strokes:** 113+11

Defend against, fight off, resist, withstand, hold out against, hinder.
From 御, "control, manage", phonetic, over 示, "indicate, altar". There are different interpretations about the meaning of the components of this character:

- Pray to prevent danger.
- Establish ethical or religious boundaries.
- Establish precautionary measures.

玉

Karlgren: 1216a
PinYin: yu4
7666 **Rad./Strokes:** 96+1

Jade, a precious stone, a gem; precious. It represents three threaded pieces of jade (probably rings), the 丶 dot was added to distinguish it from **7037** 王 *wang2*, "king". Originally it didn't have a dot, as the oracle bones version below shows:

裕

Karlgren: 1202h
PinYin: yu4
7667 **Rad./Strokes:** 145+7

Tolerating, indulgent, forgiving, liberal; ample, abundant, opulent.
Kunst takes it as a loan for 浴, "bathe" in 18.4. It only appears in 18.4 and 35.1

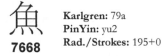

7668
Karlgren: 79a
PinYin: yu2
Rad./Strokes: 195+0

Fish, symbol of abundance.

3566 貫魚 23.5: strung fish. "*Gao* says this symbolizes the organizing of palace women, who were called to the king in prescribed order" (*Rutt*).

Ancient bronze representations show an actual fish:

7671
Karlgren: 1202d
PinYin: yu4
Rad./Strokes: 76+7

Desire, wish, expectation, longing; lust, passion.
From **3483** 谷, phonetic, and 欠, "short of breath, panting, yawning".

7685
Karlgren: 1215a
PinYin: yu4
Rad./Strokes: 94+10

Justice, litigation, lawsuit, criminal cases; prison, jail.
From 犭 (犬), "dog", **7334** 言, "words" and 犬, another dog: dogs yelling at each other: lawsuit: prison.
See **0355** 政: civil law.

7687
Karlgren: 1020a
PinYin: yu4
Rad./Strokes: 130+4

Give birth; rear, breed, raise, nurture, nourish, bring up, educate.
From 云, "newborn baby", over 月 (from **3153** 肉, "meat, flesh, fleshy"):

"To satisfy, to feed a child (or an animal), so that it becomes fleshy, strong, fat" (*Wieger*).

7694
Karlgren: 304a
PinYin: yue1
Rad./Strokes: 73+0

To say, says, said, tell, calling, called, appointed, speaking, say. It is a verbal prefix.
It shows a mouth **3434** 口 with something inside it. Some older bronze representations are more graphic:

There are two interpretations for *yue* 曰:

1. It means "say", "spoken-thus", it is a verbal prefix,
2. I should be replaced by *ri4* 日, which means "sun, say".

曰 can be found twice in the received text. In 26.3, several translators (*Wilhelm, Sung, Rutt,* between others) replace it by *ri4*, although *Wang Bi* used *yue*, as well as *Kunst*, the *Harvard-Yenching* and the *Zhouyi Zezhong*.
The other place when *yue* appears is 47.6 where usually it is not replaced by any other characters, although *Rutt* takes the meaning to be "go so far as to".
According to *Lin Zhongjun*, the character 曰 might be a character left in *Zhouyi* while absorbing the divinatory remarks from *Gui Zang* (an older, lost divining text). According to this author, this character is completely superfluous since it adds no meaning to the text.

259

Rutt, citing *Gao Heng*, says that *yue* in 26.3 should be replaced by *si* 四 meaning "a team of four horses"(*si* means four). *Rutt* also adds that in old Chinese *yue* may have been a verbal prefix meaning "go so far as to". Both interpretations match well with 26.3.

月

7696

Karlgren: 306a
PinYin: yue4
Rad./Strokes: 74+0

The Moon, lunar month.
Some older versions of this character show the Moon clearly:

See **3124** 日, "the Sun".

刖

7697

Karlgren: 306h
PinYin: yue4
Rad./Strokes: 18+4

Cut off the feet as a punishment (for serious crimes).
From **7696** 月, phonetic and 刂 (刀), "knife".
See **3013** 劓, "cut off nose".

元

7707

Karlgren: 257a
PinYin: yuan2
Rad./Strokes: 10+2

Outstanding, greatest, sublime, supreme, greatest, very great, grand; source, beginning, cause, first or paramount, fundamentality; head, chief.
Used as a superlative. In the *Ten Wings* is paraphrased as *da4* **5943** 大, "great".
From **1751** 二 (older form for **5669** 上, "superior) and 儿 (**3097** 人), "person".

260

It is one of the "Four Cardinal Virtues": *yuan heng li zhen*: 元 **2099** 亨 **3867** 利 **0346** 貞.
See **9001**: *The Four Virtues*.
Karlgren believes that it could be etymologically the same word than **7725** 原.

淵

7723

Karlgren: 367a
PinYin: yuan1
Rad./Strokes: 85+8

A deep, an abyss, deep waters, a chasm with a whirlpool in its depths.
From 氵 (**5922** 水), "water"and 㳆.
Ancient representations show "whirling water at the bottom of an abyss" (*Karlgren*):

原

7725

Karlgren: 258a
PinYin: yuan2
Rad./Strokes: 27+8

Source, spring; original, beginning; repeat, again, trace to the source.
From **1674** 泉 "spring" and 厂 "hill, cliff" (obsolete meaning): "A spring that gushes out from a hill" (*Wieger*).

According to *Karlgren*, etymologically, it may be the same word that **7707** 元.

園

7731

Karlgren: 256b
PinYin: yua
Rad./Strokes: 31+10

Garden, park, enclosed garden. It only appears in 22.5:
   1213 圩園: garden in the hills, native forest, wild park.

From 囗, "surround", suggesting a garden fence and 袁, phonetic.

Karlgren: 256f
PinYin: yua
7734 **Rad./Strokes:** 162+10

Distant, far, remote; keep far from; leave. From 袁, phonetic, and 辶, "go, walk".

Karlgren: 460b
PinYin: yun
7750 **Rad./Strokes:** 173+4

Clouds.
From 云, phonetic, and **7662** 雨, "rain".

隕

Karlgren: 227g
PinYin: yun
7756 **Rad./Strokes:** 170+10

Fall, drop or throw down; fall from the sky; tumbled, tumble.
From 阝 (阜), "hill" and 員, phonetic

允

Karlgren: 468a
PinYin: yun
7759 **Rad./Strokes:** 10+2

Trust, approval, consent, confidence; sincere, true, loyal; truly, indeed; earnestly.

孕

Karlgren: 945j
PinYin: yun
7765 **Rad./Strokes:** 39+2

Pregnancy, to conceive.
From **4612** 乃, that here means the womb or a pregnant woman and **6939** 子, "child". In some versions, this character is comprised of **4937** 勹, "bundle, wrap" and **6939** 子, "child".

慍

Karlgren: 426e
PinYin: yun
7766 **Rad./Strokes:** 61+10

Angry, indignant, vexed, irritated, grieved, displeasure, hate.
From 忄 (**2735** 心), "heart" and 昷, phonetic, which in turn is composed of: 囚, "prisoner" over 皿, "dish, vessel": unsatisfied, angry with the results obtained (the food that he receives).

蹢

Karlgren: 877o
PinYin: zhi
8000 **Rad./Strokes:** 157+11

Plant feet, dig in, balk, stop walking; animal's foot, hoof. It only appears in 44.1:
蹢躅 **1388**: faltering, hesitant.
From 𧾷 (**6824** 足), "foot" and 啇, phonetic.

蔀

Karlgren: 999g'
PinYin: bu4
8001 **Rad./Strokes:** 140+11

Screen, curtain, awning, hanging mat; old unit of time (cycle of 76 years).
From 艹 (草), "grass, straw" and 部, "division, section": hanging mat used as a curtain or division.

窞

Karlgren: 672i
PinYin: dan
8002 **Rad./Strokes:** 116+8

Pit within a pit, recess or smaller pit in bottom of cave or cellar; pitfall, trap.
3245 坎窞: cave, basement, cellar or underground vault, pit.
From **2899** 穴, "cave, hole" and 臽, "pit, hole", phonetic.

Karlgren: 1039l
PinYin: gu4
Rad./Strokes: 93+7

8003

Pen, stable, enclosure; confinement; hobbled; headboard: wooden guard placed over the point of each horn to prevent beasts from causing injury. From **4737** 牛, "ox" and **3287** 告, phonetic.

Karlgren: 947m
PinYin: mei
Rad./Strokes: 130+7

8004

Back of the neck, neck, spinal flesh, meat on sides of the spine. From 月 (**3153** 肉), "flesh" and 每, phonetic

Karlgren: 182i
PinYin: pan
Rad./Strokes: 177+10

8005

Large belt, belt with pocket or pouch, rawhide belt. "Great belts were emblems of rank and authority that remained in use until the twentieth century" (*Rutt*). From 般, phonetic, "class, category" and **3314** 革, "leather".

Karlgren: 517j
PinYin: qi4
Rad./Strokes: 85+3

8006

Almost, nearly; water drying up, dried up. From 氵 (**5922** 水), "water" and 乞, phonetic

頄

Karlgren: 992e
PinYin: qiu
Rad./Strokes: 181+2

8007

Cheekbones, bones of the face, face.

262

High cheekbones indicate cruelty or a pushy character. It only appears in 43.3:

> **1453** 壯 **7592** 于頄: "mighty in his cheekbones", but it could be translated as "cruel or overbearing".

From **1198** 九, phonetic, and 頁, "head".

Karlgren: 124p
PinYin: yon
Rad./Strokes: 181+9

8008

Great, dignified, solemn, imposing; admire; a big head. From 禺, phonetic, and 頁, "head".

Karlgren: 507h
PinYin: yu4
Rad./Strokes: 120+12

8009

Rope used to draw water from a well. From 糹, "silk thread" and 矞, phonetic.

Karlgren: 148i
PinYin: zha
Rad./Strokes: 162+13

8010

Move with difficulty, difficult to proceed; turn around because one is unable to advance; quit. From 亶, phonetic, and 辶, "go, walk".

嬬

Karlgren:
PinYin: ru2
Rad./Strokes: 38+14

8011

Concubine, mistress, slave. "The received text reads **2847** 須: "to await; to require", though several early texts also read *ru* 嬬" (*Shaughnessy*).

The Eight Trigrams

Each hexagram can be divided into two trigrams, which are groups of three consecutive lines, either the lower or the upper three lines. There are only eight trigrams, which are called *ba gua*, 八卦 (*ba* means eight) because there are only eight ways to combine broken and whole lines in groups of three.

Although tradition tells us that the trigrams preceded the hexagrams, there is no proof of that. They may have been abstracted from the hexagrams something between the creation of the *ZhouYi* text (comprising The Judgment and the lines) and the composition of the Ten Wings, which mention the trigrams.

The names of the eight trigrams refer to the natural elements: *Qian* (Heaven), *Kun* (Earth), *Zhen* (Thunder), *Kan* (Water), *Gen* (Mountain), *Xun* (Wind or Wood), *Li* (Fire) and *Dui* (Lake).

It is important to understand the symbolic meanings of each trigram, and how they relate to each other to comprehend better the main idea of the hexagrams.

The image at the top of the next column shows the arrangement of the trigrams in the Inner-World (Later Heaven), arrangement, which is traditionally attributed to king *Wen*, and is the one used in the Eight Wing, the *ShuoGua*, which also provides most of the meanings for the trigrams. The South is at the top, following the traditional Chinese style. The two oracle bones characters in the middle read *ZhouYi*.

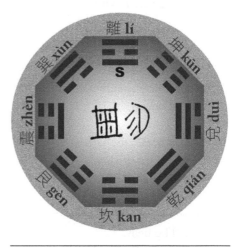

THE CREATIVE / THE HEAVEN

3233

Heaven symbolizes strength and is the beginning of all things.

Related trigram: ☷, the mother.

Action: Rules.

Pronunciation: Quian2.

Natural symbol: Heaven.

Member of the family: The father.

Body part: The head.

Animals: A good horse, an old horse, a thin horse, a wild horse, a piebald horse.

Season: Autumn.

Color: Deep red.

Cardinal points: North-West.

Other associations: A circle; a ruler, a prince; strength, hardness; strong movement, tireless work; jade; metal; cold; ice; the fruits from trees.

God strives in ☰. It means that *Yang* and *Yin* interact, stimulating each other.

THE RECEPTIVE / THE EARTH

☷坤

3684

Earth symbolizes gentleness and nourishes all beings.

Related trigram: ☰, the father.
Action: Serves, nourishes.
Pronunciation: Kun1.
Natural symbol: Earth, black soil.
Member of the family: The mother.
Body part: The belly.
Animal: Cow and calf; a heifer; a young mare.
Season: Summer.
Color: Yellow.
Cardinal points: South-West.
Other associations: Cloth, a kettle, parsimony, a turning lathe, a large wagon, variegated things, a multitude, quantity, a handle and support; frugality, thrift, passionate delivery, devotion, protection, selflessness, generosity, gentleness, ductility, the number 10.
God is served in ☷.

THE AROUSING / THE THUNDER

☳震

0315

The Thunder symbolizes movement and speed.

Related trigram: ☴, the eldest daughter, because Thunder and Wind do not hinder one another, but they excite each other.
Action: Arouses, shakes, stirs, put the things in movement.
Pronunciation: Zhen4.
Natural symbol: The thunder, wood.
Member of the family: The eldest son.
Body part: The feet, because they serve for movement.
Animal: The dragon; horses that neigh well, have white hind legs, are sprightly, or have a white star on the forehead.
Season and time: Spring, dawn.
Color: Dark yellow; violet blue and yellow; dark and pale.
Cardinal point: East.
Other associations: Development; a great highway; vehement decisions; green bamboo shoots; reeds and rushes; in respect to cultivated plants it is those that grows back to life from its disappearance (like legumes); what in the end becomes the strongest and most luxuriant.
God comes forth in ☳.

THE GENTLE / THE WIND

5550

The Wind symbolizes penetration.

Related trigram: ☳, the eldest son, because Wind and Thunder do not hinder one another, but they excite each other.
Action: Scatters (the seeds of) the things.
Pronunciation: Xun4.
Natural symbol: The wind, wood.

Member of the family: The eldest daughter.

Body part: The thighs; deficiency of hair; broad forehead; much white in the eye; crooked eyes.

Animal: The cock, fowl.

Season: Spring.

Color: White.

Cardinal points: South-East.

Other associations: Firewood; a plumb line; a carpenter's square; long; lofty; advancing and receding; unresolved; strong scents; the close pursuit of gain, those who get nearly threefold in profit; work, business; a fair; a ten days cycle; at the end point of its development it becomes *Zhen* (The Thunder).

God sets all things in order in ☴.

THE ABYSMAL / THE WATER

3245

The Water is the symbol of what is precipitous and perilous.

Related trigram: ☲ the middle daughter, because Water and Fire do not fail to complement each other.

Action: Moistens.

Pronunciation: Kan3.

Natural symbol: Water, clouds, river, Moon.

Member of the family: The middle son.

Body part: The ears.

Animals: Pig; fox; horses with beautiful backs, with high spirit, with a drooping head, with thin hooves, who shamble along.

Season: Winter.

Color: Red.

Cardinal point: North.

Other associations: Channels and ditches; lying hidden or concealed; bending and straightening; a bow, a wheel; anxiety, distress of mind; pain in the ears; blood; chariots that have many risks and damages; penetration; a thief; trees strong and sound-hearted.

God toils in ☵.

THE CLINGING / THE FIRE

3902

The Fire is the symbol of what is bright and what is catching.

Related trigram: ☵, the middle son, because Fire and Water do not fail to complement each other.

Action: Warms and dries.

Pronunciation: Li2.

Natural symbol: The Sun, fire, lightning.

Member of the family: The middle daughter.

Body part: The eyes.

Animals: Pheasant, cow, turtle, crab, clam, snail.

Season: Summer.

Cardinal points: South.

Other associations: Armor and helmet; spear and sword; men with large bellies; it is the trigram of dryness; trees that are hollow and rotten above; clarity, discernment, clear perception.

God causes creatures to perceive one another in ☲.

KEEPING STILL / THE MOUNTAIN

☶ - 艮

3327

The Mountain is the symbol of stoppage or arrest.

Related trigram: ☶, the youngest daughter, with whom it combines its force.
Action: Stops things, keep things in its place.
Pronunciation: Gen4.
Natural symbol: The Mountain.
Member of the family: The youngest son.
Body part: The hands, the fingers, the annular finger, the nose.
Animals: Dog, rodents, panther, birds with a strong beak.
Season: Winter.
Cardinal points: South-East.
Other associations: Side roads; small rocks; doorways; tree and vine fruits; gatekeeper, porter, eunuch, palace guard; strong and gnarled trees; firm rules, rest; end and beginning.
God brings things to perfection in ☶.

THE JOYOUS / THE LAKE

6560

The Lake is the symbol of pleasure and satisfaction.

Related trigram: ☳, the youngest son, with whom it combines its force
Action: Brings joy.
Pronunciation: Dui4.
Natural symbol: Lake, marsh, wetlands, pond, shallow water, calm and deep. The mirror of the lake.
Member of the family: The youngest daughter.
Body part: Mouth and tongue.
Animal: Sheep. The broken line at the top of this trigram shows the sheep horns. Sheep and goat have the same name and associations in China.
Season and time: Middle of autumn (harvest time); the evening.
Weather: Cloudy.
Cardinal point: West.
Other associations: A sorceress; decay and breaking (of plants and fruits); removal (of fruits); hard and saline soil; the concubine; smash, break; metal; defense; weapons; killing.
God brings to the creatures pleasure in ☱.

The Four Cardinal Virtues*
(The Heavenly Virtues)

One or more of the cardinal virtues appear in 50 different hexagrams, but only the hexagrams 1, 2 (with some modification), 3, 17, 19, 25 and 49 have the four virtues in its Judgment.

Since the *Han* Dynasty onwards they have become keywords of Confucian thought, four qualities or virtues applicable both to Heaven and to the noble-minded man.

	元	亨	利	貞
Pinyin	yuan2	heng1	li4	zhen1
#	7707	2099	3867	0346

元: **YUAN:** Fundamentality, primal, origin(ating), spring season, head, sublime, great, grand.

The *Yuan* sacrifice was presented in Spring, during the sowing time.

亨: **HENG:** Success, prevalence, growing, penetrating, treat, offering, sacrifice (with overtones of auspiciousness and acceptability).

The *Heng* sacrifice was presented in Summer, when the harvest was still growing.

利: **LI:** Advantageous, suitable, favorable, beneficial, suitable, lucky, favorable, beneficial, furthering, fitness.

"The word LI may have followed a semantic development like 'sharp' > 'trenchant, incisive' > 'incisive determination'> 'advantageous determination' > 'advantageous in general'." (*Kunst*).

貞: **ZHEN:** Determination, perseverance, constancy, correct and firm, divination, augury (originally it defined the divinatory act that helped to determine how to act).

---

* The dictionary entries for each character have more specific information about each virtue.

APPENDIXES

Concordance

The location of the characters is indicated by adding a point and a letter or number after the number of the hexagram.

0 indicates The Judgment;

1 a 6 indicate a Line number;

7 indicates the comment for the cases when all lines change, in hexagrams 1 and 2;

X indicates The Image.

哀
0003: appears 1 time in: 62.X.

安
0026: appears 4 times in: 2.0, 6.4, 23.X and 60.4.

占
0125: appears 1 time in: 49.5.

戰
0147: appears 1 time in: 2.6.

章
0182: appears 3 times in: 2.3, 44.5 and 55.5.

張
0195: appears 1 time in: 38.6.

丈
0200: appears 3 times in: 7.0, 17.2 and 17.3.

長
0213: appears 1 time in: 7.5.

常
0221: appears 1 time in: 29.X.

邑
0232: appears 1 time in: 51.0.

朝
0233: appears 1 time in: 6.6.

昭
0236: appears 1 time in: 35.X.

照
0238: appears 1 time in: 30.X.

巢
0253: appears 1 time in: 56.6.

折
0267: appears 5 times in: 22.X, 30.6, 50.4, 55.3 and 55.X.

宅
0275: appears 1 time in: 23.X.

澤
0277: appears 15 times in: 10.X, 17.X, 19.X, 28.X, 31.X, 38.X, 41.X, 43.X, 45.X, 47.X, 49.X, 54.X, 58.X, 60.X and 61.X.

車
0280: appears 4 times in: 14.2, 22.1, 38.6 and 47.4.

掣
0282: appears 1 time in: 38.3.

枕
0308: appears 1 time in: 29.3.

振
0313: appears 2 times in: 18.X and 32.6.

震
0315: appears 9 times in: 51.0, 51.1, 51.2, 51.3, 51.4, 51.5, 51.6, 51.X and 64.4.

臣
0327: appears 4 times in: 33.3, 39.2, 41.6 and 62.2.

貞
0346: appears 109 times in: 1.0, 2.0, 2.3, 2.7, 3.0, 3.1, 3.2, 3.5, 4.0, 5.0, 5.5, 6.3, 6.4, 7.0, 7.5, 8.0, 8.2, 8.4, 9.6, 10.2, 10.5, 11.3, 11.6, 12.0, 12.1, 13.0, 15.2, 16.2, 16.5, 17.0, 17.1, 17.3, 17.4, 18.2, 19.0, 19.1, 20.2, 21.4, 21.5, 22.3, 23.1, 23.2, 25.0, 25.4, 26.0, 26.3, 27.0, 27.3, 27.5, 30.0, 31.0, 31.4, 32.0, 32.1, 32.3, 32.5, 33.0, 33.5, 34.0, 34.2, 34.3, 34.4, 35.1, 35.2, 35.4, 35.6, 36.0, 36.3, 36.5, 37.0, 37.2, 39.0, 40.2, 40.3, 41.0, 41.2, 41.6, 42.2, 44.1, 45.0, 45.5, 46.5, 46.6, 47.0, 49.0, 49.3, 49.6, 50.5, 52.1, 53.0, 54.2, 56.0, 56.2, 56.3, 57.1, 57.5, 57.6, 58.0, 59.0, 60.0, 60.6, 61.0, 61.6, 62.0, 62.4, 63.0, 64.2, 64.4 and 64.5.

正
0351: appears 2 times in: 25.0 and 50.X.

征
0352: appears 19 times in: 9.6, 11.1, 15.6, 24.6, 27.2, 30.6, 34.1, 41.2, 46.0, 47.2, 47.6, 49.2, 49.3, 49.6, 51.6, 53.3, 54.0, 54.1 and 64.3.

政
0355: appears 1 time in: 22.X.

拯
0360: appears 3 times in: 36.2, 52.2 and 59.1.

成
0379: appears 4 times in: 2.3, 6.3, 11.X and 16.6.

城
0380: appears 1 time in: 11.6.

稱
0383: appears 1 time in: 15.X.

懲
0384: appears 1 time in: 41.X.

承
0386: appears 4 times in: 7.6, 12.2, 32.3 and 54.6.

乘
0398: appears 5 times in: 3.2, 3.4, 3.6, 13.4 and 40.3.

箕

0402: appears 1 time in: 36.5.

幾

0409: appears 4 times in: 3.3, 9.6, 54.5 and 61.4.

机

0411: appears 1 time in: 59.2.

己

0429: appears 0 vez en: **0411:** appears 1 time in: 59.2..

忌

0432: appears 1 time in: 43.X.

繼

0452: appears 1 time in: 30.X.

既

0453: appears 5 times in: 9.6, 19.3, 29.5, 63.0 and 63.X.

濟

0459: appears 5 times in: 63.0, 63.X, 64.0, 64.3 and 64.X.

躋

0461: appears 1 time in: 51.2.

齎

0464: appears 1 time in: 45.6.

祭

0465: appears 2 times in: 47.5 and 63.5.

及

0468: appears 2 times in: 43.X and 62.2.

汲

0472: appears 1 time in: 48.3.

吉

0476: appears 142 times in: 1.7, 2.0, 2.5, 3.4, 3.5, 4.2, 4.5, 5.0, 5.2, 5.5, 5.6, 6.0, 6.1, 6.3, 6.4, 6.5, 7.0, 7.2, 8.0, 8.1, 8.2, 8.4, 8.5, 9.1, 9.2, 10.2, 10.4, 10.6, 11.0, 11.1, 11.5, 12.1, 12.2, 12.5, 13.4, 14.5, 14.6, 15.1, 15.2, 15.3, 16.2, 17.1, 17.5, 18.1, 19.1, 19.2, 19.5, 19.6, 21.4, 22.3, 22.5, 24.1, 24.2, 25.1, 26.0, 26.4, 26.5, 27.0, 27.4, 27.5, 27.6, 28.4, 30.0, 30.2, 30.5, 31.0, 31.2, 31.4, 32.5, 33.3, 33.4, 33.5, 34.2, 34.4, 34.6, 35.1, 35.2, 35.5, 35.6, 36.2, 37.2, 37.3, 37.4, 37.5, 37.6, 38.0, 38.6, 39.0, 39.6, 40.0, 40.2, 40.5, 41.0, 41.5, 41.6, 42.1, 42.2, 42.5, 44.1, 45.0, 45.2, 45.4, 46.0, 46.1, 46.4, 46.5, 47.0, 47.6, 48.6, 49.2, 49.4, 49.6, 50.0, 50.2, 50.3, 50.6, 51.1, 52.6, 53.0, 53.2, 53.5, 53.6, 54.1, 54.5, 55.2, 55.4, 55.5, 56.0, 57.2, 57.5, 58.1, 58.2, 59.1, 59.4, 60.5, 61.0, 61.1, 62.0, 63.0, 64.2, 64.4 and 64.5.

擊

0481: appears 2 times in: 4.6 and 42.6.

棘

0486: appears 1 time in: 29.6.

疾

0492: appears 9 times in: 16.5, 24.0, 25.5, 33.3, 36.3, 41.4, 50.2, 55.2 and 58.4.

蒺

0494: appears 1 time in: 47.3.

卽

0495: appears 5 times in: 3.3, 6.4, 43.0, 50.2 and 56.2.

積

0500: appears 1 time in: 46.X.

岐

0522: appears 1 time in: 46.4.

其
0525: appears 90 times in: 2.6, 3.5, 6.2, 9.1, 9.5, 10.6, 11.1, 11.3, 11.4, 12.1, 12.5, 13.3, 13.4, 14.4, 15.5, 18.6, 20.6, 22.1, 22.2, 24.0, 24.6, 25.0, 26.X, 27.4, 28.2, 28.5, 30.4, 30.6, 31.1, 31.2, 31.3, 31.5, 31.6, 32.3, 32.5, 34.3, 35.2, 35.6, 36.1, 36.3, 38.3, 40.0, 41.3, 41.4, 43.4, 44.3, 44.6, 47.3, 48.0, 48.3, 50.1, 50.3, 50.4, 51.6, 52.0, 52.1, 52.2, 52.3, 52.4, 52.5, 52.X, 53.4, 53.6, 54.5, 55.1, 55.2, 55.3, 55.4, 55.6, 56.1, 56.2, 56.3, 56.4, 56.6, 57.6, 59.2, 59.3, 59.4, 59.5, 59.6, 61.2, 62.2, 63.1, 63.2, 63.5, 63.6, 64.0, 64.1, 64.2 and 64.6.

期
0526: appears 1 time in: 54.4.

祇
0538: appears 0 vez en: **0526:** appears 1 time in: 54.4..

杞
0547: appears 1 time in: 44.5.

起
0548: appears 1 time in: 44.4.

器
0549: appears 1 time in: 45.X.

棄
0550: appears 1 time in: 30.4.

妻
0555: appears 3 times in: 9.3, 28.2 and 47.3.

泣
0563: appears 2 times in: 3.6 and 61.3.

戚
0575: appears 1 time in: 30.5.

七
0579: appears 3 times in: 24.0, 51.2 and 63.2.

嘉
0592: appears 3 times in: 17.5, 30.6 and 33.5.

家
0594: appears 11 times in: 4.2, 7.6, 26.0, 37.0, 37.1, 37.3, 37.4, 37.5, 37.X, 41.6 and 55.6.

假
0599: appears 4 times in: 37.5, 45.0, 55.0 and 59.0.

甲
0610: appears 1 time in: 18.0.

頰
0614: appears 1 time in: 31.6.

皆
0620: appears 1 time in: 55.X.

階
0625: appears 1 time in: 46.5.

解
0626: appears 4 times in: 40.0, 40.4, 40.5 and 40.X.

戒
0627: appears 4 times in: 11.4, 45.X, 62.4 and 63.4.

誡
0628: appears 1 time in: 8.5.

介
0629: appears 3 times in: 16.2, 35.2 and 58.4.

疆
0643: appears 1 time in: 19.X.

講
0645: appears 1 time in: 58.X.

彊
0668: appears 1 time in: 1.X.

戕
0673: appears 1 time in: 62.3.

交
0702: appears 6 times in: 11.X, 12.X, 14.1, 14.5, 17.1 and 38.4.

校
0706: appears 2 times in: 21.1 and 21.6.

郊
0714: appears 4 times in: 5.1, 9.0, 13.6 and 62.5.

教
0719: appears 3 times in: 19.X, 20.X and 29.X.

嗟
0763: appears 4 times in: 30.3, 30.5, 45.3 and 60.3.

藉
0767: appears 1 time in: 28.1.

節
0795: appears 7 times in: 27.X, 60.0, 60.3, 60.4, 60.5, 60.6 and 60.X.

接
0800: appears 1 time in: 35.0.

且
0803: appears 5 times in: 29.3, 38.3, 40.3, 43.4 and 44.3.

妾
0814: appears 2 times in: 33.3 and 50.1.

堅
0825: appears 1 time in: 2.1.

兼
0830: appears 1 time in: 52.X.

艱
0834: appears 6 times in: 11.3, 14.1, 21.4, 26.3, 34.6 and 36.0.

蹇
0843: appears 8 times in: 39.0, 39.1, 39.2, 39.3, 39.4, 39.5, 39.6 and 39.X.

儉
0848: appears 2 times in: 12.X and 62.X.

建
0853: appears 4 times in: 3.0, 3.1, 8.X and 16.0.

健
0854: appears 1 time in: 1.X.

見
0860: appears 21 times in: 1.2, 1.5, 1.7, 4.3, 6.0, 18.4, 38.1, 38.3, 38.6, 39.0, 39.6, 42.X, 44.1, 45.0, 46.0, 47.3, 52.0, 55.2, 55.3, 55.4 and 57.0.

戔
0866: appears 1 time in: 22.5.

薦
0872: appears 2 times in: 16.X and 20.0.

漸
0878: appears 8 times in: 53.0, 53.1, 53.2, 53.3, 53.4, 53.5, 53.6 and 53.X.

洊
0880: appears 2 times in: 29.X and 51.X.

牽
0881: appears 2 times in: 9.2 and 43.4.

謙
0885: appears 7 times in: 15.0, 15.1, 15.2, 15.3, 15.4, 15.6 and 15.X.

懲
0889: appears 1 time in: 54.4.

遷
0911: appears 2 times in: 42.4 and 42.X.

潛
0918: appears 1 time in: 1.1.

前
0919: appears 3 times in: 8.5, 26.X and 43.1.

知
0932: appears 2 times in: 19.5 and 54.X.

之
0935: appears 63 times in: 2.0, 5.6, 6.6, 8.1, 8.2, 8.3, 8.4, 8.6, 11.X, 12.0, 14.6, 16.X, 17.6, 18.1, 18.2, 18.3, 18.4, 18.5, 19.3, 19.5, 20.4, 23.3, 25.3, 25.5, 26.4, 26.5, 26.6, 29.3, 30.1, 30.3, 32.3, 33.2, 34.4, 36.4, 36.5, 38.6, 39.2, 40.6, 41.0, 41.1, 41.2, 41.5, 41.6, 42.2, 42.3, 42.6, 46.6, 49.1, 49.2, 53.5, 54.2, 54.5, 55.0, 57.1, 61.2, 62.0, 62.3, 62.4, 62.6, 63.3, 63.5, 63.X and 64.5.

祉
0942: appears 2 times in: 11.5 and 12.4.

趾
0944: appears 6 times in: 21.1, 22.1, 34.1, 43.1, 50.1 and 52.1.

祇
0952: appears 2 times in: 24.1 and 29.5.

雉
0968: appears 2 times in: 50.3 and 56.5.

志
0971: appears 2 times in: 10.X and 47.X.

寘
0976: appears 1 time in: 29.6.

至
0982: appears 11 times in: 2.1, 5.3, 19.0, 19.4, 24.6, 24.X, 29.X, 40.3, 40.4, 48.0 and 55.X.

致
0984: appears 4 times in: 5.3, 40.3, 47.X and 55.X.

制
0986: appears 1 time in: 60.X.

桎
0993: appears 1 time in: 4.1.

窒
0994: appears 2 times in: 6.0 and 41.X.

執
0996: appears 3 times in: 7.5, 31.3 and 33.2.

直
1006: appears 1 time in: 2.2.

治
1021: appears 1 time in: 49.X.

遲
1024: appears 2 times in: 16.3 and 54.4.

褫
1028: appears 1 time in: 6.6.

赤
1048: appears 1 time in: 47.5.

敕
1050: appears 1 time in: 21.X.

金
1057: appears 6 times in: 4.3, 21.4, 21.5, 44.1, 47.4 and 50.5.

晉
1088: appears 6 times in: 35.0, 35.1, 35.2, 35.4, 35.6 and 35.X.

進
1091: appears 2 times in: 20.3 and 57.1.

禽
1100: appears 4 times in: 7.5, 8.5, 32.4 and 48.1.

親
1107: appears 1 time in: 8.X.

侵
1108: appears 1 time in: 15.5.

經
1123: appears 3 times in: 3.X, 27.2 and 27.5.

敬
1138: appears 2 times in: 5.6 and 30.1.

驚
1140: appears 1 time in: 51.0.

井
1143: appears 8 times in: 48.0, 48.1, 48.2, 48.3, 48.4, 48.5, 48.6 and 48.X.

傾
1161: appears 1 time in: 12.6.

慶
1167: appears 1 time in: 55.5.

角
1174: appears 3 times in: 34.3, 35.6 and 44.6.

桷
1175: appears 1 time in: 53.4.

爵
1179: appears 1 time in: 61.2.

咎
1192: appears 99 times in: 1.3, 1.4, 2.4, 5.1, 7.0, 7.2, 7.4, 7.5, 8.0, 8.1, 9.1, 9.4, 10.1, 11.3, 12.4, 13.1, 14.1, 14.2, 14.4, 16.6, 17.0, 17.4, 18.1, 18.3, 19.3, 19.4, 19.6, 20.1, 20.5, 20.6, 21.1, 21.2, 21.3, 21.5, 22.6, 23.3, 24.0, 24.3, 25.4, 27.4, 28.1, 28.5, 28.6, 29.4, 29.5, 30.1, 30.6, 32.0, 35.1, 35.6, 38.1, 38.2, 38.4, 38.5, 40.1, 41.0, 41.1, 41.4, 41.6, 42.1, 42.3, 43.1, 43.3, 43.5, 44.2, 44.3, 44.6, 45.1, 45.2, 45.3, 45.4, 45.5, 45.6, 46.2, 46.4, 47.0, 47.2, 48.4, 49.2, 50.1, 51.6, 52.0, 52.1, 52.4, 53.1, 53.4, 55.1, 55.3, 57.2, 59.5, 59.6, 60.1, 60.3, 61.4, 61.5, 62.2, 62.4, 63.1 and 64.6.

九
1198: appears 1 time in: 51.2.

舊
1205: appears 2 times in: 6.3 and 48.1.

酒
1208: appears 4 times in: 5.5, 29.4, 47.2 and 64.6.

就
1210: appears 1 time in: 49.3.

丘
1213: appears 3 times in: 22.5, 27.2 and 59.4.

求
1217: appears 5 times in: 3.4, 4.0, 17.3, 27.0 and 29.2.

窮
1247: appears 1 time in: 19.X.

酌
1257: appears 1 time in: 41.1.

畫
1302: appears 1 time in: 35.0.

毵
1305: appears 1 time in: 48.4.

疇
1322: appears 1 time in: 12.4.

愁
1325: appears 1 time in: 35.2.

醜
1327: appears 1 time in: 30.6.

仇
1332: appears 1 time in: 50.2.

主
1336: appears 5 times in: 2.0, 36.1, 38.2, 55.1 and 55.4.

朱
1346: appears 1 time in: 47.2.

株
1348: appears 1 time in: 47.1.

諸
1362: appears 1 time in: 8.X.

逐
1383: appears 5 times in: 26.3, 27.4, 38.1, 51.2 and 63.2.

躅
1388: appears 1 time in: 44.1.

初
1390: appears 5 times in: 4.0, 36.6, 38.3, 57.5 and 63.0.

除
1391: appears 1 time in: 45.X.

處
1407: appears 2 times in: 9.6 and 56.4.

出
1409: appears 17 times in: 4.X, 5.4, 7.1, 9.4, 16.X, 17.1, 24.0, 30.5, 30.6, 35.X, 36.4, 37.X, 50.1, 52.X, 59.6, 60.1 and 60.2.

畜
1412: appears 7 times in: 7.X, 9.0, 9.X, 26.0, 26.X, 30.0 and 33.3.

觸
1416: appears 2 times in: 34.3 and 34.6.

川
1439: appears 12 times in: 5.0, 6.0, 13.0, 15.1, 18.0, 26.0, 27.5, 27.6, 42.0, 59.0, 61.0 and 64.3.

遄
1444: appears 2 times in: 41.1 and 41.4.

壯
1453: appears 10 times in: 34.0, 34.1, 34.3, 34.4, 34.X, 36.2, 43.1, 43.3, 44.0 and 59.1.

牀
1459: appears 5 times in: 23.1, 23.2, 23.4, 57.2 and 57.6.

垂
1478: appears 1 time in: 36.1.

隼
1487: appears 1 time in: 40.6.

終
1500: appears 30 times in: 1.3, 2.3, 5.2, 5.6, 6.0, 6.1, 6.3, 6.6, 8.1, 10.4, 15.0, 15.3, 16.2, 18.1, 22.5, 24.6, 29.4, 37.3, 37.6, 38.3, 43.6, 45.1, 47.4, 50.3, 53.5, 54.X, 56.5, 57.5, 63.0 and 63.4.

中
1504: appears 23 times in: 3.3, 6.0, 7.2, 7.X, 11.2, 15.X, 17.X, 24.4, 24.X, 26.X, 36.X, 37.2, 42.3, 42.4, 43.5, 46.X, 49.X, 55.0, 55.2, 55.3, 55.4, 61.0 and 61.X.

衆
1517: appears 3 times in: 7.X, 35.3 and 36.X.

崇
1528: appears 1 time in: 16.X.

憧
1529: appears 1 time in: 31.4.

寵
1534: appears 1 time in: 23.5.

居
1535: appears 9 times in: 3.1, 17.3, 27.5, 31.2, 43.X, 49.6, 53.X, 59.5 and 64.X.

拘
1542: appears 1 time in: 17.6.

懼
1560: appears 2 times in: 28.X and 51.X.

據
1563: appears 1 time in: 47.3.

屨
1572: appears 1 time in: 21.1.

去
1594: appears 2 times in: 9.4 and 59.6.

驅
1602: appears 1 time in: 8.5.

衢
1611: appears 1 time in: 26.6.

取
1615: appears 5 times in: 4.3, 31.0, 44.0, 56.1 and 62.5.

闃
1627: appears 1 time in: 55.6.

勸
1662: appears 1 time in: 48.X.

泉
1674: appears 2 times in: 4.X and 48.5.

厥
1680: appears 2 times in: 14.5 and 38.5.

決
1697: appears 1 time in: 34.4.

夐
1704: appears 1 time in: 51.6.

君
1715: appears 79 times in: 1.3, 1.X, 2.0, 2.X, 3.3, 3.X, 4.X, 5.X, 6.X, 7.6, 7.X, 9.6, 9.X, 10.3, 10.X, 12.0, 12.X, 13.0, 13.X, 14.X, 15.0, 15.1, 15.3, 15.X, 17.X, 18.X, 19.5, 19.X, 20.1, 20.5, 20.6, 22.X, 23.6, 24.6, 26.X, 27.X, 28.X, 29.X, 31.X, 32.X, 33.4, 33.X, 34.3, 34.X, 35.X, 36.1, 36.X, 37.X, 38.X, 39.X, 40.5, 40.X, 41.X, 42.X, 43.3, 43.X, 45.X, 46.X, 47.X, 48.X, 49.6, 49.X, 50.X, 51.X, 52.X, 53.X, 54.5, 54.X, 55.X, 56.X, 57.X, 58.X, 60.X, 61.X, 62.2, 62.X, 63.X, 64.5 and 64.X.

浚
1729: appears 1 time in: 32.1.

羣
1737: appears 2 times in: 1.7 and 59.4.

耳
1744: appears 3 times in: 21.6, 50.3 and 50.5.

一
1751: appears 1 time in: 41.0.

貳
1752: appears 1 time in: 29.4.

爾
1754: appears 3 times in: 27.1, 31.4 and 61.2.

而
1756: appears 12 times in: 6.2, 13.5, 20.0, 22.1, 30.3, 33.X, 36.X, 37.X, 38.X, 40.4, 56.X and 63.X.

法
1762: appears 1 time in: 21.X.

伐
1765: appears 4 times in: 15.5, 35.6, 63.3 and 64.4.

發
1768: appears 2 times in: 4.1 and 55.2.

罰
1769: appears 1 time in: 21.X.

反
1781: appears 5 times in: 9.3, 24.0, 39.3, 39.X and 54.3.

蕃
1798: appears 1 time in: 35.0.

藩
1800: appears 3 times in: 34.3, 34.4 and 34.6.

方
1802: appears 12 times in: 2.2, 8.0, 20.X, 24.X, 30.X, 32.X, 44.X, 47.2, 50.3, 63.3, 64.4 and 64.X.

防
1817: appears 2 times in: 62.3 and 63.X.

非
1819: appears 1 time in: 34.X.

匪
1820: appears 13 times in: 3.2, 4.0, 8.3, 12.0, 14.1, 14.4, 22.4, 25.0, 30.6, 38.6, 39.2, 45.5 and 59.4.

腓
1830: appears 2 times in: 31.2 and 52.2.

肥
1839: appears 1 time in: 33.6.

飛
1850: appears 5 times in: 1.5, 36.1, 62.0, 62.1 and 62.6.

忿
1854: appears 1 time in: 41.X.

紛
1859: appears 1 time in: 57.2.

焚
1866: appears 3 times in: 30.4, 56.3 and 56.6.

豶
1873: appears 1 time in: 26.5.

奮
1874: appears 1 time in: 16.X.

風
1890: appears 10 times in: 9.X, 18.X, 20.X, 32.X, 37.X, 42.X, 44.X, 57.X, 59.X and 61.X.

馮
1895: appears 1 time in: 11.2.

豐
1897: appears 6 times in: 55.0, 55.2, 55.3, 55.4, 55.6 and 55.X.

否
1902: appears 8 times in: 7.1, 12.0, 12.2, 12.5, 12.6, 12.X, 33.4 and 50.1.

缶
1905: appears 3 times in: 8.1, 29.4 and 30.3.

夫
1908: appears 10 times in: 4.3, 8.0, 9.3, 17.2, 17.3, 28.2, 28.5, 32.5, 38.4 and 53.3.

鮒
1927: appears 1 time in: 48.2.

父
1933: appears 4 times in: 18.1, 18.3, 18.4 and 18.5.

斧
1934: appears 2 times in: 56.4 and 57.6.

孚
1936: appears 40 times in: 5.0, 6.0, 8.1, 9.4, 9.5, 11.3, 11.4, 14.5, 17.4, 17.5, 20.0, 29.0, 34.1, 35.1, 37.6, 38.4, 40.4, 40.5, 41.0, 42.3, 42.5, 43.0, 44.1, 45.1, 45.2, 45.5, 46.2, 48.6, 49.0, 49.3, 49.4, 49.5, 55.2, 58.2, 58.5, 61.0, 61.5, 61.X, 64.5 and 64.6.

輔
1945: appears 3 times in: 11.X, 31.6 and 52.5.

富
1952: appears 4 times in: 9.5, 11.4, 15.5 and 37.4.

負
1956: appears 2 times in: 38.6 and 40.3.

膚
1958: appears 5 times in: 21.2, 23.4, 38.5, 43.4 and 44.3.

婦
1963: appears 8 times in: 4.2, 9.6, 28.5, 32.5, 37.3, 53.3, 53.5 and 63.2.

伏
1964: appears 1 time in: 13.3.

絨
1971: appears 2 times in: 47.2 and 47.5.

福
1978: appears 4 times in: 11.3, 35.2, 48.3 and 63.5.

輻
1980: appears 1 time in: 9.3.

弗
1981: appears 10 times in: 13.4, 14.3, 34.X, 41.2, 41.5, 41.6, 42.2, 62.3, 62.4 and 62.6.

茀
1989: appears 1 time in: 63.2.

復
1992: appears 16 times in: 6.4, 9.1, 9.2, 11.3, 11.6, 24.0, 24.1, 24.2, 24.3, 24.4, 24.5, 24.6, 24.X, 38.1, 40.0 and 53.3.

覆
1993: appears 1 time in: 50.4.

腹
1994: appears 1 time in: 36.4.

鞄
1997: appears 2 times in: 26.2 and 34.4.

害
2015: appears 1 time in: 14.1.

含
2017: appears 2 times in: 2.3 and 44.5.

汗
2028: appears 1 time in: 59.5.

翰
2042: appears 2 times in: 22.4 and 61.6.

寒
2048: appears 1 time in: 48.5.

好
2062: appears 2 times in: 33.4 and 61.2.

號
2064: appears 7 times in: 13.5, 43.0, 43.2, 43.6, 45.1, 56.6 and 59.5.

亨
2099: appears 46 times in: 1.0, 2.0, 3.0, 4.0, 5.0, 9.0, 10.0, 11.0, 12.1, 12.2, 13.0, 14.0, 14.3, 15.0, 17.0, 17.6, 18.0, 19.0, 21.0, 22.0, 24.0, 25.0, 26.6, 28.0, 29.0, 30.0, 31.0, 32.0, 33.0, 45.0, 46.0, 46.4, 47.0, 49.0, 50.0, 51.0, 55.0, 56.0, 57.0, 58.0, 59.0, 60.0, 60.4, 62.0, 63.0 and 64.0.

恆
2107: appears 10 times in: 5.1, 16.5, 32.0, 32.1, 32.3, 32.5, 32.6, 32.X, 37.X and 42.6.

何
2109: appears 5 times in: 9.1, 17.4, 21.6, 26.6 and 38.5.

河
2111: appears 1 time in: 11.2.

和
2115: appears 2 times in: 58.1 and 61.2.

盍
2119: appears 1 time in: 16.4.

嗑
2120: appears 2 times in: 21.0 and 21.X.

曷
2122: appears 1 time in: 41.0.

鶴
2131: appears 1 time in: 61.2.

嚆
2134: appears 1 time in: 37.3.

侯
2135: appears 6 times in: 3.0, 3.1, 8.X, 16.0, 18.6 and 35.0.

後
2143: appears 10 times in: 2.0, 8.0, 12.6, 13.5, 18.0, 36.6, 38.6, 51.1, 56.6 and 57.5.

后
2144: appears 3 times in: 11.X, 24.X and 44.X.

厚
2147: appears 2 times in: 2.X and 23.X.

乎
2154: appears 1 time in: 62.X.

虎
2161: appears 5 times in: 10.0, 10.3, 10.4, 27.4 and 49.5.

戶
2180: appears 3 times in: 6.2, 55.6 and 60.1.

弧
2184: appears 1 time in: 38.6.

狐
2185: appears 2 times in: 40.2 and 64.0.

穫
2207: appears 1 time in: 25.2.

華
2217: appears 1 time in: 28.5.

懷
2233: appears 1 time in: 56.2.

桓
2236: appears 1 time in: 3.1.

患
2240: appears 1 time in: 63.X.

緩
2242: appears 1 time in: 61.X.

渙
2252: appears 7 times in: 59.0, 59.2, 59.3, 59.4, 59.5, 59.6 and 59.X.

荒
2271: appears 1 time in: 11.2.

隍
2295: appears 1 time in: 11.6.

黃
2297: appears 8 times in: 2.5, 2.6, 21.5, 30.2, 33.2, 40.2, 49.1 and 50.5.

悔
2336: appears 32 times in: 1.6, 13.6, 16.3, 18.3, 24.1, 24.5, 31.4, 31.5, 32.2, 34.4, 34.5, 35.3, 35.5, 37.1, 37.3, 38.1, 38.5, 43.4, 45.5, 47.6, 49.0, 49.4, 50.3, 52.5, 57.4, 57.5, 58.2, 59.2, 59.3, 60.6, 64.4 and 64.5.

晦
2337: appears 3 times in: 17.X, 36.6 and 36.X.

惠
2339: appears 1 time in: 42.5.

彙
2349: appears 2 times in: 11.1 and 12.1.

徽
2354: appears 1 time in: 29.6.

撝
2356: appears 1 time in: 15.4.

婚
2360: appears 5 times in: 3.2, 3.4, 22.4, 38.6 and 51.6.

鴻
2386: appears 6 times in: 53.1, 53.2, 53.3, 53.4, 53.5 and 53.6.

火
2395: appears 10 times in: 13.X, 14.X, 22.X, 37.X, 38.X, 49.X, 50.X, 56.X, 63.X and 64.X.

或
2402: appears 13 times in: 1.4, 2.3, 6.3, 6.6, 7.3, 25.3, 32.3, 41.5, 42.2, 42.6, 53.4, 61.3 and 62.3.

獲
2412: appears 7 times in: 17.4, 30.6, 36.4, 40.2, 40.6, 52.0 and 57.4.

係
2424: appears 5 times in: 17.2, 17.3, 17.6, 29.6 and 33.3.

喜
2434: appears 4 times in: 12.6, 25.5, 41.4 and 58.4.

嘻
2436: appears 1 time in: 37.3.

咥
2456: appears 2 times in: 10.0 and 10.3.

繫
2458: appears 3 times in: 12.5, 25.3 and 44.1.

西
2460: appears 7 times in: 2.0, 9.0, 17.6, 39.0, 40.0, 62.5 and 63.5.

虩
2480: appears 2 times in: 51.0 and 51.1.

夕
2485: appears 1 time in: 1.3.

息
2495: appears 3 times in: 1.X, 17.X and 46.6.

習

2499: appears 5 times in: 2.2, 29.0, 29.1, 29.X and 58.X.

錫

2505: appears 3 times in: 6.6, 7.2 and 35.0.

退

2517: appears 1 time in: 11.2.

下

2520: appears 15 times in: 4.X, 10.X, 18.X, 22.X, 23.X, 25.X, 27.X, 33.X, 38.X, 41.X, 43.X, 44.X, 57.2, 57.6 and 62.0.

享

2552: appears 4 times in: 41.0, 42.2, 47.2 and 59.X.

巷

2553: appears 1 time in: 38.2.

嚮

2561: appears 1 time in: 17.X.

相

2562: appears 3 times in: 11.X, 13.5 and 48.X.

祥

2577: appears 1 time in: 10.6.

小

2605: appears 35 times in: 3.5, 5.2, 6.1, 7.6, 9.0, 9.X, 11.0, 12.0, 12.2, 14.3, 17.2, 17.3, 18.3, 20.1, 21.3, 22.0, 23.6, 29.2, 33.0, 33.4, 33.X, 34.3, 38.0, 40.5, 45.3, 46.X, 49.6, 53.1, 56.0, 57.0, 62.0, 62.X, 63.0, 63.3 and 64.0.

笑

2615: appears 5 times in: 13.5, 45.1, 51.0, 51.1 and 56.6.

咸

2666: appears 9 times in: 19.1, 19.2, 31.0, 31.1, 31.2, 31.3, 31.5, 31.6 and 31.X.

賢

2671: appears 1 time in: 53.X.

閑

2679: appears 2 times in: 26.3 and 37.1.

莧

2686: appears 1 time in: 43.5.

險

2689: appears 2 times in: 29.2 and 29.3.

顯

2692: appears 1 time in: 8.5.

限

2696: appears 1 time in: 52.3.

先

2702: appears 14 times in: 2.0, 8.X, 12.6, 13.5, 16.X, 18.0, 20.X, 21.X, 24.X, 25.X, 38.6, 56.6, 57.5 and 59.X.

心

2735: appears 8 times in: 29.0, 36.4, 42.5, 42.6, 48.3, 52.2, 52.3 and 56.4.

信

2748: appears 2 times in: 43.4 and 47.0.

興

2753: appears 1 time in: 13.3.

行

2754: appears 33 times in: 1.X, 4.X, 6.X, 9.X, 11.2, 15.6, 16.0, 20.X, 24.4, 24.6, 24.X, 25.3, 25.6, 25.X, 26.X, 29.0, 29.X, 36.1, 37.X,

41.3, 42.3, 42.4, 43.3, 43.4, 43.5, 44.3, 50.3, 51.3, 52.0, 57.X, 59.X, 60.X and 62.X.

刑
2755: appears 3 times in: 4.1, 55.X and 56.X.

形
2759: appears 1 time in: 50.4.

休
2786: appears 3 times in: 12.5, 14.X and 24.2.

脩
2795: appears 2 times in: 39.X and 51.X.

羞
2797: appears 2 times in: 12.3 and 32.3.

凶
2808: appears 57 times in: 3.5, 6.0, 7.1, 7.3, 7.5, 8.0, 8.6, 9.6, 10.3, 16.1, 17.4, 19.0, 21.6, 23.1, 23.2, 23.4, 24.6, 27.1, 27.2, 27.3, 28.3, 28.6, 29.1, 29.6, 30.3, 31.2, 32.1, 32.5, 32.6, 34.1, 41.2, 42.3, 42.6, 43.3, 43.6, 44.1, 44.4, 47.2, 47.3, 48.0, 49.3, 49.6, 50.4, 51.6, 53.3, 54.0, 55.6, 56.6, 57.6, 58.3, 60.2, 60.6, 61.6, 62.1, 62.3, 62.6 and 64.3.

肝
2819: appears 1 time in: 16.3.

虛
2821: appears 2 times in: 31.X and 46.3.

徐
2841: appears 2 times in: 47.4 and 47.5.

需
2844: appears 7 times in: 5.0, 5.1, 5.2, 5.3, 5.4, 5.5 and 5.X.

繻
2845: appears 1 time in: 63.4.

須
2847: appears 1 time in: 22.2.

序
2851: appears 1 time in: 52.5.

恤
2862: appears 6 times in: 11.3, 35.5, 37.5, 43.2, 45.1 and 46.0.

玄
2881: appears 1 time in: 2.6.

鉉
2886: appears 2 times in: 50.5 and 50.6.

旋
2894: appears 1 time in: 10.6.

穴
2899: appears 3 times in: 5.4, 5.6 and 62.5.

血
2901: appears 6 times in: 2.6, 3.6, 5.4, 9.4, 54.6 and 59.6.

熏
2906: appears 1 time in: 52.3.

旬
2915: appears 1 time in: 55.1.

已
2930: appears 1 time in: 26.1.

以
2932: appears 85 times in: 1.X, 2.X, 3.X, 4.1, 4.X, 5.X, 6.X, 7.1, 7.X, 8.X, 9.5, 9.X, 10.X, 11.1, 11.4, 11.5, 11.X, 12.1, 12.X, 13.X, 14.2, 14.X, 15.5, 15.X, 16.X, 17.4, 17.X, 18.X, 19.X, 20.X, 21.X, 22.X, 23.1, 23.2, 23.4, 23.5, 23.X, 24.6, 24.X, 25.X, 26.X,

27.X, 28.X, 29.X, 30.X, 31.X, 32.X, 33.X, 34.X, 35.X, 36.X, 37.X, 38.X, 39.X, 40.X, 41.X, 42.X, 43.X, 44.5, 44.X, 45.X, 46.X, 47.X, 48.X, 49.X, 50.1, 50.X, 51.X, 52.X, 53.X, 54.1, 54.3, 54.X, 55.X, 56.5, 56.X, 57.X, 58.X, 59.X, 60.X, 61.X, 62.1, 62.X, 63.X and 64.X.

疑
2940: appears 2 times in: 16.4 and 55.2.

易
2952: appears 3 times in: 32.X, 34.5 and 56.6.

意
2960: appears 1 time in: 51.5.

頤
2969: appears 7 times in: 27.0, 27.1, 27.2, 27.3, 27.4, 27.6 and 27.X.

夷
2982: appears 9 times in: 36.0, 36.1, 36.2, 36.3, 36.4, 36.5, 36.X, 55.4 and 59.4.

洟
2986: appears 1 time in: 45.6.

衣
2989: appears 1 time in: 63.4.

依
2990: appears 1 time in: 42.4.

宜
2993: appears 4 times in: 11.X, 19.5, 55.0 and 62.0.

遺
2995: appears 2 times in: 11.2 and 62.0.

懿
2999: appears 1 time in: 9.X.

儀
3003: appears 1 time in: 53.6.

議
3006: appears 2 times in: 60.X and 61.X.

曳
3008: appears 3 times in: 38.3, 63.1 and 64.2.

異
3009: appears 1 time in: 38.X.

劓
3013: appears 2 times in: 38.3 and 47.5.

一
3016: appears 4 times in: 38.6, 41.3, 45.1 and 56.5.

乙
3017: appears 2 times in: 11.5 and 54.5.

弋
3018: appears 1 time in: 62.5.

亦
3021: appears 1 time in: 48.0.

邑
3037: appears 9 times in: 6.2, 8.5, 11.6, 15.6, 25.3, 35.6, 43.0, 46.3 and 48.0.

億
3042: appears 1 time in: 51.2.

翼
3051: appears 1 time in: 36.1.

益
3052: appears 9 times in: 15.X, 41.2, 41.5, 41.6, 42.0, 42.2, 42.3, 42.6 and 42.X.

然
3072: appears 1 time in: 30.1.

橈
3087: appears 2 times in: 28.0 and 28.3.

入
3097: appears 55 times in: 1.2, 1.5, 4.1, 5.6, 6.0, 6.2, 7.0, 7.6, 8.3, 8.5, 10.0, 10.2, 10.3, 12.0, 12.2, 12.5, 13.0, 13.1, 13.2, 13.5, 13.6, 13.X, 14.3, 20.1, 23.5, 23.6, 25.3, 30.X, 31.X, 32.5, 33.4, 33.X, 34.3, 36.1, 37.0, 37.3, 37.X, 38.1, 38.3, 39.0, 39.6, 40.5, 41.3, 45.0, 46.0, 47.0, 49.5, 49.6, 52.0, 54.2, 55.6, 56.6, 57.0, 57.1 and 63.3.

日
3124: appears 18 times in: 1.3, 16.2, 18.0, 24.0, 24.X, 30.3, 35.0, 36.1, 49.0, 49.2, 51.2, 55.0, 55.2, 55.3, 55.4, 57.5, 63.2 and 63.4.

若
3126: appears 8 times in: 1.3, 20.0, 30.5, 43.3, 45.1, 55.2, 57.2 and 60.3.

如
3137: appears 17 times in: 3.2, 3.3, 3.4, 3.6, 9.5, 14.5, 22.3, 22.4, 30.4, 35.1, 35.2, 35.4, 37.6, 45.3, 54.5, 61.5 and 63.5.

茹
3139: appears 2 times in: 11.1 and 12.1.

袽
3140: appears 1 time in: 63.4.

濡
3149: appears 7 times in: 22.3, 43.3, 63.1, 63.6, 64.0, 64.1 and 64.6.

入
3152: appears 11 times in: 3.3, 5.6, 17.X, 24.0, 29.1, 29.3, 36.4, 36.6, 36.X, 47.1 and 47.3.

肉
3153: appears 2 times in: 21.3 and 21.5.

戎
3181: appears 4 times in: 13.3, 43.0, 43.2 and 45.X.

改
3196: appears 3 times in: 42.X, 48.0 and 49.4.

開
3204: appears 1 time in: 7.6.

干
3211: appears 1 time in: 53.1.

甘
3223: appears 2 times in: 19.3 and 60.5.

敢
3229: appears 1 time in: 22.X.

乾
3233: appears 4 times in: 1.0, 1.3, 21.4 and 21.5.

幹
3235: appears 4 times in: 18.1, 18.2, 18.3 and 18.5.

坎
3245: appears 6 times in: 29.0, 29.1, 29.2, 29.3, 29.5 and 29.X.

衎
3252: appears 1 time in: 53.2.

亢
3273: appears 1 time in: 1.6.

康
3278: appears 1 time in: 35.0.

告
3287: appears 5 times in: 4.0, 11.6, 42.3, 42.4 and 43.0.

誥
3288: appears 1 time in: 44.X.

高
3290: appears 5 times in: 13.3, 18.6, 40.6, 46.X and 63.3.

膏
3296: appears 2 times in: 3.5 and 50.3.

考
3299: appears 3 times in: 10.6, 16.X and 18.1.

革
3314: appears 8 times in: 33.2, 49.0, 49.1, 49.2, 49.3, 49.6, 49.X and 50.3.

克
3320: appears 10 times in: 4.2, 6.2, 6.4, 13.4, 13.5, 14.3, 24.6, 41.5, 42.2 and 63.3.

客
3324: appears 1 time in: 5.6.

艮
3327: appears 8 times in: 52.0, 52.1, 52.2, 52.3, 52.4, 52.5, 52.6 and 52.X.

庚
3339: appears 1 time in: 57.5.

耕
3343: appears 1 time in: 25.2.

歌
3364: appears 2 times in: 30.3 and 61.3.

葛
3377: appears 1 time in: 47.6.

可
3381: appears 11 times in: 2.3, 12.X, 18.2, 25.4, 27.5, 36.3, 41.0, 48.3, 53.6, 60.0 and 62.0.

姤
3422: appears 3 times in: 44.0, 44.6 and 44.X.

媾
3426: appears 5 times in: 3.2, 3.4, 22.4, 38.6 and 51.6.

口
3434: appears 1 time in: 27.0.

寇
3444: appears 7 times in: 3.2, 4.6, 5.3, 22.4, 38.6, 40.3 and 53.3.

故
3455: appears 1 time in: 39.2.

股
3467: appears 2 times in: 31.3 and 36.2.

孤
3470: appears 2 times in: 38.4 and 38.6.

蠱
3475: appears 7 times in: 18.0, 18.1, 18.2, 18.3, 18.4, 18.5 and 18.X.

鼓
3479: appears 2 times in: 30.3 and 61.3.

谷
3483: appears 2 times in: 47.1 and 48.2.

梏
3484: appears 1 time in: 4.1.

枯
3492: appears 2 times in: 28.2 and 28.5.

苦
3493: appears 2 times in: 60.0 and 60.6.

瓜
3504: appears 1 time in: 44.5.

寡
3517: appears 1 time in: 15.X.

括
3519: appears 1 time in: 2.4.

夬
3535: appears 5 times in: 10.5, 43.0, 43.3, 43.5 and 43.X.

快
3547: appears 2 times in: 52.2 and 56.4.

官
3552: appears 1 time in: 17.1.

貫
3566: appears 1 time in: 23.5.

盥
3569: appears 1 time in: 20.0.

關
3571: appears 1 time in: 24.X.

觀
3575: appears 10 times in: 20.0, 20.1, 20.2, 20.3, 20.4, 20.5, 20.6, 20.X, 27.0 and 27.1.

光
3583: appears 3 times in: 5.0, 20.4 and 64.5.

筐
3598: appears 1 time in: 54.6.

圭
3609: appears 1 time in: 42.3.

歸
3617: appears 9 times in: 6.2, 11.5, 53.0, 54.0, 54.1, 54.3, 54.4, 54.5 and 54.X.

龜
3621: appears 3 times in: 27.1, 41.5 and 42.2.

簋
3633: appears 2 times in: 29.4 and 41.0.

鬼
3634: appears 3 times in: 38.6, 63.3 and 64.4.

刲
3642: appears 1 time in: 54.6.

闚
3649: appears 2 times in: 20.2 and 55.6.

虧
3650: appears 1 time in: 50.3.

睽
3660: appears 4 times in: 38.0, 38.4, 38.6 and 38.X.

饋
3669: appears 1 time in: 37.2.

坤
3684: appears 2 times in: 2.0 and 2.X.

困
3688: appears 9 times in: 4.4, 47.0, 47.1, 47.2, 47.3, 47.4, 47.5, 47.6 and 47.X.

功
3698: appears 1 time in: 17.1.

攻

3699: appears 1 time in: 13.4.

公

3701: appears 6 times in: 14.3, 40.6, 42.3, 42.4, 50.4 and 62.5.

躬

3704: appears 4 times in: 4.3, 39.2, 51.6 and 59.3.

宮

3705: appears 2 times in: 23.5 and 47.3.

肱

3706: appears 1 time in: 55.3.

恭

3711: appears 1 time in: 62.X.

鞏

3718: appears 1 time in: 49.1.

恐

3721: appears 1 time in: 51.X.

過

3730: appears 11 times in: 28.0, 28.6, 28.X, 40.X, 42.X, 62.0, 62.2, 62.3, 62.4, 62.6 and 62.X.

果

3732: appears 2 times in: 4.X and 23.6.

國

3738: appears 7 times in: 7.6, 8.X, 15.6, 20.4, 24.6, 42.4 and 64.4.

腊

3763: appears 1 time in: 21.3.

來

3768: appears 24 times in: 5.6, 8.0, 8.1, 11.0, 12.0, 24.0, 29.3, 30.4, 31.4, 39.1, 39.3, 39.4, 39.5, 39.6, 40.0, 47.2, 47.4, 48.0, 51.0, 51.1, 51.2, 51.5, 55.5 and 58.3.

勞

3826: appears 2 times in: 15.3 and 48.X.

老

3833: appears 2 times in: 28.2 and 28.5.

里

3857: appears 1 time in: 51.0.

利

3867: appears 99 times in: 1.0, 1.2, 1.5, 2.0, 2.2, 2.7, 3.0, 3.1, 3.4, 4.0, 4.1, 4.3, 4.6, 5.0, 5.1, 6.0, 7.5, 12.0, 13.0, 14.6, 15.4, 15.5, 15.6, 16.0, 17.0, 17.3, 18.0, 19.0, 19.2, 19.3, 20.2, 20.4, 21.0, 21.4, 22.0, 23.0, 23.5, 24.0, 25.0, 25.2, 25.6, 26.0, 26.1, 26.3, 27.3, 27.6, 28.0, 28.2, 30.0, 31.0, 32.0, 32.1, 33.0, 33.6, 34.0, 34.6, 35.5, 36.0, 36.5, 37.0, 39.0, 39.6, 40.0, 40.6, 41.0, 41.2, 41.6, 42.0, 42.1, 42.4, 43.0, 44.2, 45.0, 45.2, 45.3, 46.2, 46.6, 47.2, 47.5, 49.0, 50.1, 50.5, 50.6, 52.1, 53.0, 53.3, 54.0, 54.2, 54.6, 57.0, 57.1, 57.5, 58.0, 59.0, 61.0, 62.0, 63.0, 64.0 and 64.3.

藜

3877: appears 1 time in: 47.3.

禮

3886: appears 1 time in: 34.X.

履

3893: appears 12 times in: 2.1, 10.0, 10.1, 10.2, 10.3, 10.4, 10.5, 10.6, 10.X, 30.1, 34.X and 54.1.

離

3902: appears 6 times in: 12.4, 30.0, 30.2, 30.3, 30.X and 62.6.

厲

3906: appears 27 times in: 1.3, 6.3, 9.6,

10.5, 18.1, 21.5, 24.3, 26.1, 27.6, 33.1, 33.3, 34.3, 35.4, 35.6, 37.3, 38.4, 43.0, 44.3, 49.3, 51.2, 51.5, 52.3, 53.1, 56.3, 58.5, 62.4 and 63.6.

浬
3912: appears 1 time in: 36.X.

麗
3914: appears 1 time in: 58.X.

立
3921: appears 4 times in: 28.X, 32.X, 42.6 and 59.X.

厤
3930: appears 0 vez en: **3921:** appears 4 times in: 28.X, 32.X, 42.6 and 59.X..

歷
3931: appears 1 time in: 49.X.

良
3941: appears 2 times in: 26.3 and 54.5.

兩
3953: appears 1 time in: 30.X.

列
3984: appears 1 time in: 52.3.

洌
3987: appears 1 time in: 48.5.

連
4009: appears 1 time in: 39.4.

漣
4012: appears 1 time in: 3.6.

林
4022: appears 1 time in: 3.3.

臨
4027: appears 8 times in: 19.0, 19.1, 19.2, 19.3, 19.4, 19.5, 19.6 and 19.X.

鄰
4033: appears 5 times in: 9.5, 11.4, 15.5, 51.6 and 63.5.

吝
4040: appears 20 times in: 3.3, 4.1, 4.4, 11.6, 13.2, 18.4, 20.1, 21.3, 22.5, 28.4, 31.3, 32.3, 35.6, 37.3, 40.3, 44.6, 45.3, 47.4, 57.3 and 64.1.

陵
4067: appears 3 times in: 13.3, 51.2 and 53.5.

靈
4071: appears 1 time in: 27.1.

罍
4083: appears 1 time in: 56.X.

樂
4129: appears 2 times in: 5.X and 16.X.

漏
4152: appears 1 time in: 48.2.

廬
4158: appears 1 time in: 23.6.

陸
4191: appears 3 times in: 43.5, 53.3 and 53.6.

祿
4196: appears 2 times in: 12.X and 43.X.

鹿
4203: appears 1 time in: 3.3.

亂
4220: appears 2 times in: 45.1 and 63.0.

罱
4235: appears 1 time in: 47.6.

雷
4236: appears 15 times in: 3.X, 16.X, 17.X, 21.X, 24.X, 25.X, 27.X, 32.X, 34.X, 40.X, 42.X, 51.X, 54.X, 55.X and 62.X.

贏
4240: appears 4 times in: 34.3, 34.4, 44.1 and 48.0.

類
4244: appears 1 time in: 13.X.

綸
4252: appears 1 time in: 3.X.

輪
4254: appears 2 times in: 63.1 and 64.2.

隆
4255: appears 1 time in: 28.4.

龍
4258: appears 6 times in: 1.1, 1.2, 1.5, 1.6, 1.7 and 2.6.

旅
4286: appears 8 times in: 24.X, 56.0, 56.1, 56.2, 56.3, 56.4, 56.6 and 56.X.

律
4297: appears 1 time in: 7.1.

攣
4300: appears 2 times in: 9.5 and 61.5.

馬
4310: appears 11 times in: 2.0, 3.2, 3.4, 3.6, 22.4, 26.3, 35.0, 36.2, 38.1, 59.1 and 61.4.

莽
4354: appears 1 time in: 13.3.

茅
4364: appears 3 times in: 11.1, 12.1 and 28.1.

繼
4387: appears 1 time in: 29.6.

妹
4410: appears 7 times in: 11.5, 54.0, 54.1, 54.3, 54.4, 54.5 and 54.X.

沫
4412: appears 1 time in: 55.3.

門
4418: appears 4 times in: 13.1, 17.1, 36.4 and 60.2.

悶
4420: appears 1 time in: 28.X.

蒙
4437: appears 7 times in: 4.0, 4.1, 4.2, 4.4, 4.5, 4.6 and 4.X.

迷
4450: appears 2 times in: 2.0 and 24.6.

靡
4455: appears 1 time in: 61.2.

袂
4456: appears 1 time in: 54.5.

密
4464: appears 2 times in: 9.0 and 62.5.

廟
4473: appears 3 times in: 45.0, 59.0 and 59.X.

眇
4476: appears 2 times in: 10.3 and 54.2.

滅
4483: appears 5 times in: 21.1, 21.2, 21.6, 28.6 and 28.X.

蔑
4485: appears 2 times in: 23.1 and 23.2.

面
4497: appears 1 time in: 49.6.

民
4508: appears 7 times in: 7.X, 10.X, 11.X, 18.X, 19.X, 20.X and 48.X.

冥
4528: appears 2 times in: 16.6 and 46.6.

明
4534: appears 16 times in: 17.4, 21.X, 22.X, 30.X, 35.X, 36.0, 36.1, 36.2, 36.3, 36.4, 36.5, 36.6, 36.X, 48.3, 49.X and 56.X.

鳴
4535: appears 4 times in: 15.2, 15.6, 16.1 and 61.2.

命
4537: appears 12 times in: 6.4, 7.2, 7.6, 11.6, 12.4, 14.X, 44.X, 47.X, 49.4, 50.X, 56.5 and 57.X.

沫
4549: appears 0 vez en: **4537:** appears 12 times in: 6.4, 7.2, 7.6, 11.6, 12.4, 14.X, 44.X, 47.X, 49.4, 50.X, 56.5 and 57.X..

莫
4557: appears 4 times in: 33.2, 42.6, 43.2 and 53.5.

幕
4559: appears 1 time in: 48.6.

謀
4578: appears 1 time in: 6.X.

茂
4580: appears 1 time in: 25.X.

母
4582: appears 2 times in: 18.2 and 35.2.

拇
4584: appears 2 times in: 31.1 and 40.4.

木
4593: appears 7 times in: 28.X, 46.X, 47.1, 48.X, 50.X, 53.4 and 53.X.

目
4596: appears 1 time in: 9.3.

納
4607: appears 2 times in: 4.2 and 29.4.

乃
4612: appears 8 times in: 3.2, 17.6, 45.1, 45.2, 46.2, 47.5, 49.0 and 49.2.

南
4620: appears 5 times in: 2.0, 36.3, 39.0, 40.0 and 46.0.

難
4625: appears 1 time in: 12.X.

囊
4627: appears 1 time in: 2.4.

能
4648: appears 5 times in: 10.3, 34.6, 50.2, 54.1 and 54.2.

柅
4659: appears 1 time in: 44.1.

泥
4660: appears 3 times in: 5.3, 48.1 and 51.4.

鳥
4688: appears 4 times in: 56.6, 62.0, 62.1 and 62.6.

鵜
4700: appears 1 time in: 47.6.

年
4711: appears 5 times in: 3.2, 24.6, 27.3, 63.3 and 64.4.

寧
4725: appears 2 times in: 8.0 and 58.4.

凝
4732: appears 1 time in: 50.X.

牛
4737: appears 8 times in: 25.3, 26.4, 30.0, 33.2, 38.3, 49.1, 56.6 and 63.5.

內
4766: appears 1 time in: 8.2.

女
4776: appears 9 times in: 3.2, 4.3, 20.2, 28.2, 31.0, 37.0, 44.0, 53.0 and 54.6.

我
4778: appears 11 times in: 4.0, 9.0, 20.3, 20.5, 27.1, 42.5, 48.3, 50.2, 56.4, 61.2 and 62.5.

惡
4809: appears 3 times in: 14.X, 33.X and 38.1.

遏
4812: appears 1 time in: 14.X.

罷
4841: appears 1 time in: 61.3.

八
4845: appears 1 time in: 19.0.

拔
4848: appears 2 times in: 11.1 and 12.1.

敗
4866: appears 1 time in: 24.6.

班
4889: appears 3 times in: 3.2, 3.4 and 3.6.

磐
4904: appears 2 times in: 3.1 and 53.2.

包
4937: appears 7 times in: 4.2, 11.2, 12.2, 12.3, 44.2, 44.4 and 44.5.

苞
4941: appears 1 time in: 12.5.

保
4946: appears 1 time in: 19.X.

豹
4954: appears 1 time in: 49.6.

北
4974: appears 2 times in: 2.0 and 39.0.

白
4975: appears 3 times in: 22.4, 22.6 and 28.1.

百
4976: appears 2 times in: 6.2 and 51.0.

帛
4979: appears 1 time in: 22.5.

背
4989: appears 1 time in: 52.0.

貝
5005: appears 1 time in: 51.2.

配
5019: appears 2 times in: 16.X and 55.1.

沛
5020: appears 1 time in: 55.3.

賁
5027: appears 8 times in: 22.0, 22.1, 22.2, 22.3, 22.4, 22.5, 22.6 and 22.X.

奔
5028: appears 1 time in: 59.2.

朋
5054: appears 10 times in: 2.0, 11.2, 16.4, 24.0, 31.4, 39.5, 40.4, 41.5, 42.2 and 58.X.

彭
5060: appears 1 time in: 14.4.

匕
5076: appears 1 time in: 51.0.

比
5077: appears 8 times in: 8.0, 8.1, 8.2, 8.3, 8.4, 8.5, 8.6 and 8.X.

妣
5082: appears 1 time in: 62.2.

閉
5092: appears 1 time in: 24.X.

彼
5093: appears 1 time in: 62.5.

鼻
5100: aparec e 1 time in: 21.2.

敝
5101: appears 2 times in: 48.2 and 54.X.

必
5109: appears 1 time in: 62.4.

匹
5170: appears 1 time in: 61.4.

辟
5172: appears 1 time in: 12.X.

辨
5240: appears 4 times in: 10.X, 13.X, 23.2 and 64.X.

辯
5242: appears 0 vez en: **5240:** appears 4 times in: 10.X, 13.X, 23.2 and 64.X..

變
5245: appears 2 times in: 49.5 and 49.6.

翩
5249: appears 1 time in: 11.4.

賓
5259: appears 2 times in: 20.4 and 44.2.

頻
5275: appears 2 times in: 24.3 and 57.3.

牝
5280: appears 2 times in: 2.0 and 30.0.

品
5281: appears 1 time in: 57.4.

冰
5283: appears 1 time in: 2.1.

並
5292: appears 1 time in: 48.3.

瓶
5301: appears 1 time in: 48.0.

平
5303: appears 3 times in: 11.3, 15.X and 29.5.

跛
5317: appears 2 times in: 10.3 and 54.1.

剝
5337: appears 8 times in: 23.0, 23.1, 23.2, 23.3, 23.4, 23.6, 23.X and 58.5.

陂
5345: appears 1 time in: 11.3.

旛
5351: appears 1 time in: 22.4.

通
5373: appears 1 time in: 6.2.

不
5379: appears 96 times in: 1.X, 2.2,
3.2, 3.3, 3.4, 4.0, 4.3, 4.6, 5.6, 6.0,
6.1, 6.2, 6.4, 8.0, 8.5, 9.0, 10.0,
11.2, 11.3, 11.4, 12.0, 12.X, 13.3,
14.6, 15.4, 15.5, 16.2, 16.5, 18.2,
18.6, 19.2, 20.0, 23.0, 23.5, 23.6,
24.1, 24.6, 24.X, 25.0, 25.2, 26.0,
27.5, 28.2, 28.X, 29.5, 29.6, 30.3,
32.3, 32.X, 33.6, 33.X, 34.4, 34.6,
35.5, 36.1, 36.3, 36.6, 39.0, 40.6,
43.0, 43.1, 43.4, 44.2, 45.1, 45.X,
46.6, 47.0, 47.1, 47.3, 48.0, 48.1,
48.3, 50.2, 50.3, 50.6, 51.0, 51.6,
52.0, 52.2, 52.X, 53.3, 53.5, 54.5,
55.6, 56.4, 56.X, 57.5, 60.0, 60.1,
60.2, 60.3, 61.1, 62.0, 62.2, 62.5
and 63.5.

僕
5401: appears 2 times in: 56.2 and
56.3.

三
5415: appears 21 times in: 4.0, 5.6,
6.2, 6.6, 7.2, 8.5, 13.3, 18.0, 29.6,
35.0, 36.1, 40.2, 41.3, 47.1, 49.3,
53.5, 55.6, 57.4, 57.5, 63.3 and
64.4.

桑
5424: appears 1 time in: 12.5.

喪
5429: appears 12 times in: 2.0, 34.5,
38.1, 48.0, 51.0, 51.2, 51.5, 56.3,
56.6, 57.6, 62.X and 63.2.

塞
5446: appears 1 time in: 50.3.

索
5459: appears 1 time in: 51.6.

所
5465: appears 4 times in: 6.1, 40.0,
56.1 and 59.4.

瑣
5466: appears 1 time in: 56.1.

蘇
5488: appears 1 time in: 51.3.

素
5490: appears 1 time in: 10.1.

愬
5494: appears 1 time in: 10.4.

俗
5497: appears 1 time in: 53.X.

夙
5502: appears 1 time in: 40.0.

速
5505: appears 1 time in: 5.6.

餗
5506: appears 1 time in: 50.4.

雖
5519: appears 1 time in: 55.1.

隨
5523: appears 7 times in: 17.0, 17.3,
17.4, 17.X, 31.3, 52.2 and 57.X.

遂
5530: appears 4 times in: 34.6, 37.2,
47.X and 51.4.

歲
5538: appears 5 times in: 13.3, 29.6,
47.1, 53.5 and 55.6.

損
5548: appears 7 times in: 41.0, 41.1,
41.2, 41.3, 41.4, 41.6 and 41.X.

巽
5550: appears 5 times in: 57.0, 57.2,
57.3, 57.6 and 57.X.

訟
5558: appears 5 times in: 6.0, 6.2, 6.4, 6.5 and 6.X.

斯
5574: appears 2 times in: 40.4 and 56.1.

思
5580: appears 5 times in: 19.X, 31.4, 52.X, 59.4 and 63.X.

死
5589: appears 3 times in: 16.5, 30.4 and 61.X.

巳
5590: appears 3 times in: 41.1, 49.0 and 49.2.

祀
5592: appears 2 times in: 47.2 and 47.5.

四
5598: appears 2 times in: 30.X and 44.X.

沙
5606: appears 1 time in: 5.2.

殺
5615: appears 1 time in: 63.5.

山
5630: appears 17 times in: 4.X, 15.X, 17.6, 18.X, 22.X, 23.X, 26.X, 27.X, 31.X, 33.X, 39.X, 41.X, 46.4, 52.X, 53.X, 56.X and 62.X.

善
5657: appears 3 times in: 14.X, 42.X and 53.X.

上
5669: appears 29 times in: 5.X, 8.X, 9.X, 10.X, 14.X, 16.X, 19.X, 20.X, 23.X, 31.X, 34.X, 35.X, 38.X, 39.X, 40.6, 43.X, 45.X, 48.X, 50.X, 53.X, 54.X, 56.X, 59.X, 60.X, 61.X, 62.0, 62.X, 63.X and 64.X.

尚
5670: appears 6 times in: 9.6, 11.2, 18.6, 29.0, 55.1 and 60.5.

裳
5671: appears 1 time in: 2.5.

賞
5672: appears 1 time in: 64.4.

商
5673: appears 2 times in: 24.X and 58.4.

舍
5699: appears 3 times in: 3.3, 22.1 and 27.1.

赦
5702: appears 1 time in: 40.X.

射
5703: appears 3 times in: 40.6, 48.2 and 56.5.

舌
5705: appears 1 time in: 31.6.

涉
5707: appears 13 times in: 5.0, 6.0, 13.0, 15.1, 18.0, 26.0, 27.5, 27.6, 28.6, 42.0, 59.0, 61.0 and 64.3.

設
5711: appears 1 time in: 20.X.

申
5712: appears 1 time in: 57.X.

身
5718: appears 3 times in: 39.X, 52.0 and 52.4.

愼
5734: appears 3 times in: 27.X, 56.X and 64.X.

生
5738: appears 6 times in: 20.3, 20.5, 20.6, 28.2, 28.5 and 46.X.

牲
5739: appears 1 time in: 45.0.

眚
5741: appears 6 times in: 6.2, 24.6, 25.0, 25.6, 51.3 and 62.6.

省
5744: appears 3 times in: 20.X, 24.X and 51.X.

升
5745: appears 7 times in: 13.3, 46.0, 46.1, 46.3, 46.5, 46.6 and 46.X.

勝
5754: appears 3 times in: 33.2, 43.1 and 53.5.

尸
5756: appears 2 times in: 7.3 and 7.5.

師
5760: appears 12 times in: 7.0, 7.1, 7.2, 7.3, 7.4, 7.5, 7.X, 11.6, 13.5, 15.6, 16.0 and 24.6.

筮
5763: appears 2 times in: 4.0 and 8.0.

噬
5764: appears 7 times in: 21.0, 21.2, 21.3, 21.4, 21.5, 21.X and 38.5.

豕
5766: appears 3 times in: 26.5, 38.6 and 44.1.

施
5768: appears 3 times in: 15.X, 43.X and 44.X.

史
5769: appears 1 time in: 57.2.
298

使
5770: appears 1 time in: 41.4.

始
5772: appears 1 time in: 6.X.

士
5776: appears 2 times in: 28.5 and 54.6.

時
5780: appears 3 times in: 25.X, 49.X and 54.4.

矢
5784: appears 3 times in: 21.4, 40.2 and 56.5.

事
5787: appears 12 times in: 2.3, 6.1, 6.3, 6.X, 18.6, 29.X, 38.0, 41.1, 42.3, 51.5, 57.X and 62.0.

視
5789: appears 5 times in: 10.3, 10.6, 27.4, 51.6 and 54.2.

世
5790: appears 1 time in: 28.X.

是
5794: appears 2 times in: 62.6 and 64.6.

勢
5799: appears 1 time in: 2.X.

失
5806: appears 5 times in: 8.5, 17.2, 17.3, 35.5 and 64.6.

十
5807: appears 5 times in: 3.2, 24.6, 27.3, 41.5 and 42.2.

食
5810: appears 14 times in: 5.5, 5.X, 6.3, 11.3, 23.6, 26.0, 27.X, 36.1, 47.2, 48.1, 48.3, 48.5, 50.3 and 53.2.

石
5813: appears 2 times in: 16.2 and 47.3.

碩
5815: appears 2 times in: 23.6 and 39.6.

鼫
5816: appears 1 time in: 35.4.

實
5821: appears 4 times in: 27.0, 50.2, 54.6 and 63.5.

識
5825: appears 1 time in: 26.X.

收
5837: appears 1 time in: 48.6.

首
5839: appears 6 times in: 1.7, 8.6, 30.6, 36.3, 63.6 and 64.6.

受
5840: appears 4 times in: 31.X, 35.2, 48.3 and 63.5.

狩
5845: appears 1 time in: 36.3.

數
5865: appears 1 time in: 60.X.

鼠
5871: appears 1 time in: 35.4.

庶
5874: appears 2 times in: 22.X and 35.0.

束
5891: appears 1 time in: 22.5.

衰
5908: appears 1 time in: 15.X.

帥
5909: appears 1 time in: 7.5.

霜
5919: appears 1 time in: 2.1.

水
5922: appears 11 times in: 6.X, 7.X, 8.X, 29.X, 39.X, 47.X, 48.X, 59.X, 60.X, 63.X and 64.X.

順
5935: appears 2 times in: 14.X and 46.X.

說
5939: appears 6 times in: 4.1, 9.3, 26.2, 33.2, 38.6 and 47.5.

大
5943: appears 57 times in: 1.2, 1.5, 2.2, 3.5, 5.0, 6.0, 7.6, 10.3, 11.0, 12.0, 12.2, 12.5, 13.0, 13.5, 14.0, 14.2, 14.X, 15.1, 16.4, 18.0, 18.3, 19.5, 24.6, 26.0, 26.X, 27.5, 27.6, 28.0, 28.X, 30.3, 30.X, 34.0, 34.4, 34.X, 36.3, 37.4, 39.0, 39.5, 39.6, 42.0, 42.1, 44.3, 45.0, 45.4, 46.0, 46.1, 46.X, 47.0, 49.5, 50.6, 57.0, 59.0, 59.5, 61.0, 62.0, 64.3 and 64.4.

他
5961: appears 1 time in: 61.1.

帶
6005: appears 1 time in: 6.6.

泰
6023: appears 2 times in: 11.0 and 11.X.

眈
6028: appears 1 time in: 27.4.

坦
6057: appears 1 time in: 10.2.

道
6136: appears 5 times in: 9.1, 10.2, 11.X, 17.4 and 24.0.

咷

6152: appears 2 times in: 13.5 and 56.6.

得

6161: appears 26 times in: 2.0, 11.2, 16.4, 17.3, 21.4, 21.5, 23.6, 25.3, 28.2, 28.5, 29.2, 29.6, 35.5, 36.3, 40.2, 41.3, 41.6, 48.0, 50.1, 51.2, 53.4, 55.2, 56.2, 56.4, 61.3 and 63.2.

德

6162: appears 19 times in: 2.X, 4.X, 6.3, 9.6, 9.X, 12.X, 16.X, 18.X, 26.X, 29.X, 32.3, 32.5, 35.X, 39.X, 42.5, 43.X, 46.X, 53.X and 60.X.

登

6167: appears 2 times in: 36.6 and 61.6.

羝

6195: appears 2 times in: 34.3 and 34.6.

地

6198: appears 16 times in: 2.X, 7.X, 8.X, 11.X, 12.X, 15.X, 16.X, 19.X, 20.X, 23.X, 24.X, 35.X, 36.6, 36.X, 45.X and 46.X.

弟

6201: appears 1 time in: 7.5.

娣

6202: appears 3 times in: 54.1, 54.3 and 54.5.

帝

6204: appears 5 times in: 11.5, 16.X, 42.2, 54.5 and 59.X.

敵

6221: appears 1 time in: 61.3.

靚

6230: appears 2 times in: 47.1 and 55.6.

涕

6250: appears 2 times in: 30.5 and 45.6.

稊

6252: appears 1 time in: 28.2.

惕

6263: appears 4 times in: 1.3, 6.0, 9.4 and 43.2.

逖

6265: appears 1 time in: 59.6.

臺

6314: appears 1 time in: 30.3.

渫

6318: appears 1 time in: 48.3.

顛

6337: appears 3 times in: 27.2, 27.4 and 50.1.

電

6358: appears 2 times in: 21.X and 55.X.

天

6361: appears 23 times in: 1.5, 1.X, 5.X, 6.X, 9.X, 10.X, 11.X, 12.X, 13.X, 14.3, 14.6, 14.X, 25.X, 26.6, 26.X, 33.X, 34.X, 36.6, 38.3, 43.X, 44.5, 44.X and 61.6.

田

6362: appears 5 times in: 1.2, 7.5, 32.4, 40.2 and 57.4.

頂

6390: appears 1 time in: 28.6.

鼎

6392: appears 8 times in: 50.0, 50.1, 50.2, 50.3, 50.4, 50.5, 50.6 and 50.X.

定
6393: appears 1 time in: 10.X.

庭
6405: appears 5 times in: 36.4, 43.0, 52.0, 60.1 and 60.2.

多
6416: appears 2 times in: 15.X and 26.X.

朵
6419: appears 1 time in: 27.1.

它
6439: appears 2 times in: 8.1 and 28.4.

沱
6442: appears 1 time in: 30.5.

脫
6468: appears 0 vez en: **6442:** appears 1 time in: 30.5..

斗
6472: appears 2 times in: 55.2 and 55.4.

度
6504: appears 1 time in: 60.X.

毒
6509: appears 1 time in: 21.3.

獨
6512: appears 3 times in: 24.4, 28.X and 43.3.

瀆
6515: appears 1 time in: 4.0.

塗
6525: appears 1 time in: 38.6.

徒
6536: appears 1 time in: 22.1.

突
6540: appears 1 time in: 30.4.

兌
6560: appears 7 times in: 58.0, 58.1, 58.2, 58.3, 58.4, 58.6 and 58.X.

對
6562: appears 1 time in: 25.X.

退
6568: appears 3 times in: 20.3, 34.6 and 57.1.

敦
6571: appears 3 times in: 19.6, 24.5 and 52.6.

遯
6586: appears 8 times in: 28.X, 33.0, 33.1, 33.3, 33.4, 33.5, 33.6 and 33.X.

屯
6592: appears 4 times in: 3.0, 3.2, 3.5 and 3.X.

豚
6600: appears 1 time in: 61.0.

臀
6602: appears 3 times in: 43.4, 44.3 and 47.1.

東
6605: appears 3 times in: 2.0, 39.0 and 63.5.

棟
6607: appears 3 times in: 28.0, 28.3 and 28.4.

動
6611: appears 1 time in: 47.6.

同
6615: appears 7 times in: 13.0, 13.1, 13.2, 13.5, 13.6, 13.X and 38.X.

童
6626: appears 6 times in: 4.0, 4.5, 20.1, 26.4, 56.2 and 56.3.

災
6652: appears 4 times in: 24.6, 25.3, 56.1 and 62.6.

載
6653: appears 4 times in: 2.X, 9.6, 14.2 and 38.6.

在
6657: appears 16 times in: 1.2, 1.4, 1.5, 7.2, 14.X, 17.4, 24.X, 26.X, 34.X, 37.2, 57.2, 57.6, 61.2, 62.5, 63.X and 64.X.

再
6658: appears 1 time in: 4.0.

簪
6679: appears 1 time in: 16.4.

臧
6704: appears 1 time in: 7.1.

則
6746: appears 10 times in: 4.0, 14.1, 25.2, 30.3, 34.6, 38.6, 41.3, 42.X, 43.X and 60.3.

戻
6755: appears 1 time in: 30.3.

惻
6758: appears 1 time in: 48.3.

左
6774: appears 4 times in: 7.4, 11.X, 36.2 and 36.4.

作
6780: appears 5 times in: 6.X, 16.X, 30.X, 40.X and 42.1.

錯
6793: appears 1 time in: 30.1.

祖
6815: appears 2 times in: 16.X and 62.2.

足
6824: appears 2 times in: 23.1 and 50.4.

族
6830: appears 1 time in: 13.X.

罪
6860: appears 1 time in: 40.X.

摧
6866: appears 1 time in: 35.1.

萃
6880: appears 5 times in: 45.0, 45.1, 45.3, 45.5 and 45.X.

樽
6886: appears 1 time in: 29.4.

宗
6896: appears 3 times in: 13.2, 38.5 and 63.3.

從
6919: appears 6 times in: 2.3, 6.3, 17.6, 31.4, 42.4 and 62.3.

叢
6921: appears 1 time in: 29.6.

咨
6923: appears 1 time in: 45.6.

資
6927: appears 3 times in: 56.2, 56.4 and 57.6.

菑
6932: appears 1 time in: 25.2.

茲
6935: appears 1 time in: 35.2.

子
6939: appears 86 times in: 1.3, 1.X, 2.0, 2.X, 3.2, 3.3, 3.X, 4.2, 4.X, 5.X, 6.X, 7.5, 7.X, 9.6, 9.X, 10.X, 12.0, 12.X, 13.0, 13.X, 14.3,

14.X, 15.0, 15.1, 15.3, 15.X, 17.2, 17.3, 17.X, 18.1, 18.X, 19.X, 20.1, 20.5, 20.6, 22.X, 23.6, 26.X, 27.X, 28.X, 29.X, 31.X, 32.5, 32.X, 33.4, 33.X, 34.3, 34.X, 35.X, 36.1, 36.5, 36.X, 37.3, 37.X, 38.X, 39.X, 40.5, 40.X, 41.X, 42.X, 43.3, 43.X, 45.X, 46.X, 47.X, 48.X, 49.6, 49.X, 50.1, 50.X, 51.X, 52.X, 53.1, 53.X, 54.X, 55.X, 56.X, 57.X, 58.X, 60.X, 61.2, 61.X, 62.X, 63.X, 64.5 and 64.X.

字
6942: appears 1 time in: 3.2.

肺
6950: appears 1 time in: 21.4.

自
6960: appears 15 times in: 1.X, 5.4, 8.2, 9.0, 9.1, 11.6, 14.6, 27.0, 29.4, 35.X, 37.X, 38.1, 43.0, 44.5 and 62.5.

次
6980: appears 5 times in: 7.4, 43.4, 44.3, 56.2 and 56.3.

外
7001: appears 1 time in: 8.4.

萬
7030: appears 2 times in: 8.X and 25.X.

亡
7034: appears 23 times in: 11.2, 12.5, 31.4, 32.2, 34.4, 35.3, 35.5, 37.1, 38.1, 38.5, 43.4, 45.5, 49.0, 49.4, 52.5, 56.5, 57.4, 57.5, 58.2, 59.2, 60.6, 61.4 and 64.4.

妄
7035: appears 6 times in: 25.0, 25.1, 25.3, 25.5, 25.6 and 25.X.

王
7037: appears 26 times in: 2.3, 6.3, 7.2, 8.5, 8.X, 16.X, 17.6, 18.6, 20.4, 20.X, 21.X, 24.X, 25.X, 30.6, 35.2, 37.5, 39.2, 42.2, 43.0, 45.0, 46.4, 48.3, 55.0, 59.0, 59.5 and 59.X.

望
7043: appears 3 times in: 9.6, 54.5 and 61.4.

罔
7045: appears 2 times in: 34.3 and 35.1.

往
7050: appears 50 times in: 2.0, 3.0, 3.3, 3.4, 4.1, 10.1, 11.0, 11.3, 12.0, 14.2, 18.4, 22.0, 23.0, 24.0, 25.0, 25.1, 25.2, 26.3, 26.X, 28.0, 31.3, 31.4, 32.0, 33.1, 35.5, 36.1, 38.5, 38.6, 39.1, 39.3, 39.4, 39.6, 40.0, 41.0, 41.1, 41.6, 42.0, 43.0, 43.1, 44.1, 45.0, 45.1, 45.3, 48.0, 51.5, 55.1, 55.2, 57.0, 60.5 and 62.4.

威
7051: appears 2 times in: 14.5 and 37.6.

爲
7059: appears 8 times in: 4.6, 10.3, 42.1, 42.4, 43.1, 45.1, 48.3 and 53.6.

惟
7066: appears 1 time in: 3.3.

維
7067: appears 4 times in: 17.6, 29.0, 35.6 and 40.5.

謂
7079: appears 1 time in: 62.6.

衛
7089: appears 1 time in: 26.3.

違
7093: appears 3 times in: 6.X, 41.5 and 42.2.

尾
7109: appears 7 times in: 10.0, 10.3, 10.4, 33.1, 63.1, 64.0 and 64.1.

未
7114: appears 6 times in: 48.0, 49.5, 58.4, 64.0, 64.3 and 64.X.

位
7116: appears 3 times in: 45.5, 50.X and 52.X.

文
7129: appears 1 time in: 9.X.

問
7141: appears 1 time in: 42.5.

聞
7142: appears 1 time in: 43.4.

甕
7151: appears 1 time in: 48.2.

握
7161: appears 1 time in: 45.1.

渥
7162: appears 1 time in: 50.4.

巫
7164: appears 1 time in: 57.2.

无
7173: appears 150 times in: 1.3, 1.4, 1.7, 2.2, 2.3, 2.4, 3.3, 3.4, 4.3, 5.1, 6.2, 6.3, 7.0, 7.2, 7.4, 7.5, 8.0, 8.1, 8.6, 9.4, 10.1, 11.3, 12.4, 13.1, 13.6, 14.1, 14.2, 14.4, 14.6, 15.4, 15.5, 16.6, 17.0, 18.1, 18.3, 19.2, 19.3, 19.4, 19.6, 19.X, 20.1, 20.5, 20.6, 21.1, 21.2, 21.3, 21.5, 22.6, 22.X, 23.3, 23.5, 24.0, 24.1, 24.3, 24.5, 25.0, 25.1, 25.3, 25.4, 25.5, 25.6, 25.X, 27.3, 27.4, 28.1, 28.2, 28.5, 28.6, 28.X, 29.4, 29.5, 30.1, 30.6, 31.5, 32.0, 32.1, 32.4, 33.6, 34.5, 34.6, 35.1, 35.5, 35.6, 37.2, 38.1, 38.2, 38.3, 38.4, 40.0, 40.1, 40.6, 41.0, 41.1, 41.4, 41.6, 42.1, 42.3, 43.3, 43.4, 43.5, 43.6, 44.2, 44.3, 44.4, 44.6, 45.1, 45.2, 45.3, 45.4, 45.5, 45.6, 46.2, 46.4, 47.0, 47.2, 47.X, 48.0, 48.1, 48.4, 49.2, 50.1, 50.6, 51.3, 51.5, 51.6, 52.0, 52.1, 52.4, 53.1, 53.4, 54.0, 54.6, 55.1, 55.3, 55.6, 57.2, 57.5, 59.3, 59.5, 59.6, 60.1, 60.3, 61.4, 61.5, 62.2, 62.4, 63.1, 64.0, 64.5 and 64.6.

吾
7188: appears 1 time in: 61.2.

武
7195: appears 2 times in: 10.3 and 57.1.

勿
7208: appears 26 times in: 1.1, 3.0, 4.3, 7.6, 11.3, 11.6, 16.4, 25.5, 27.3, 29.3, 33.1, 35.5, 37.5, 38.1, 42.5, 42.6, 43.2, 44.0, 45.1, 46.0, 48.6, 51.2, 55.0, 62.4, 63.2 and 63.3.

物
7209: appears 6 times in: 2.X, 13.X, 15.X, 25.X, 37.X and 64.X.

脆
7211: appears 1 time in: 47.6.

屋
7212: appears 1 time in: 55.6.

牙
7214: appears 1 time in: 26.5.

啞
7226: appears 2 times in: 51.0 and 51.1.

羊
7247: appears 5 times in: 34.3, 34.5, 34.6, 43.4 and 54.6.

揚
7259: appears 2 times in: 14.X and 43.0.

楊
7261: appears 2 times in: 28.2 and 28.5.

野
7314: appears 2 times in: 2.6 and 13.0.

夜
7315: appears 1 time in: 43.2.

言
7334: appears 15 times in: 5.2, 6.1, 7.5, 26.X, 27.X, 36.1, 37.X, 43.4, 47.0, 49.3, 51.0, 51.1, 51.6, 52.5 and 53.1.

嚴
7347: appears 1 time in: 33.X.

宴
7364: appears 2 times in: 5.X and 17.X.

燕
7399: appears 1 time in: 61.1.

音
7418: appears 2 times in: 61.6 and 62.0.

殷
7423: appears 1 time in: 16.X.

贇
7427: appears 1 time in: 52.3.

引
7429: appears 2 times in: 45.2 and 58.6.

陰
7444: appears 1 time in: 61.2.

飲
7454: appears 4 times in: 5.X, 27.X, 53.2 and 64.6.

盈
7474: appears 2 times in: 8.1 and 29.5.

約
7493: appears 1 time in: 29.4.

禴
7498: appears 3 times in: 45.2, 46.2 and 63.5.

藥
7501: appears 1 time in: 25.5.

躍
7504: appears 1 time in: 1.4.

幽
7505: appears 3 times in: 10.2, 47.1 and 54.2.

牖
7507: appears 1 time in: 29.4.

憂
7508: appears 2 times in: 19.3 and 55.0.

由
7513: appears 2 times in: 16.4 and 27.6.

攸
7519: appears 32 times in: 2.0, 3.0, 4.3, 14.2, 19.3, 22.0, 23.0, 24.0, 25.0, 25.2, 25.6, 26.3, 27.3, 28.0, 32.0, 32.1, 33.1, 34.6, 36.1, 37.2, 40.0, 41.0, 41.6, 42.0, 43.0, 44.1, 45.0, 45.3, 54.0, 54.6, 57.0 and 64.0.

有

7533: appears 129 times in: 1.6, 2.0, 2.3, 3.0, 4.3, 5.0, 5.2, 5.6, 6.0, 6.1, 7.5, 7.6, 7.X, 8.1, 8.X, 9.4, 9.5, 11.3, 12.4, 14.0, 14.2, 14.X, 15.0, 15.3, 15.X, 16.3, 16.4, 16.6, 17.1, 17.3, 17.4, 17.X, 18.1, 18.3, 18.X, 19.0, 19.X, 20.0, 22.0, 22.X, 23.0, 24.0, 24.6, 25.0, 25.2, 25.5, 25.6, 26.1, 26.3, 27.X, 28.0, 28.4, 29.0, 29.2, 30.6, 31.X, 32.0, 33.1, 33.3, 33.X, 34.1, 36.1, 37.1, 37.5, 37.6, 37.X, 38.3, 39.X, 40.0, 40.5, 41.0, 41.4, 41.6, 41.X, 42.0, 42.3, 42.5, 42.X, 43.0, 43.2, 43.3, 43.6, 44.1, 44.2, 44.5, 44.X, 45.0, 45.1, 45.5, 47.0, 47.4, 47.5, 47.6, 48.6, 48.X, 49.3, 49.4, 49.5, 49.X, 50.2, 50.X, 51.5, 51.6, 52.5, 53.1, 53.X, 54.4, 54.X, 55.1, 55.2, 55.5, 56.X, 57.0, 57.5, 58.4, 58.5, 59.0, 59.4, 60.5, 60.X, 61.1, 61.2, 61.5, 61.X, 62.X, 63.4, 64.4, 64.5 and 64.6.

宥

7536: appears 1 time in: 40.X.

友

7540: appears 2 times in: 41.3 and 58.X.

右

7541: appears 2 times in: 11.X and 55.3.

祐

7543: appears 1 time in: 14.6.

容

7560: appears 2 times in: 7.X and 19.X.

用

7567: appears 55 times in: 1.1, 3.0, 4.1, 4.3, 5.1, 7.6, 8.5, 11.2, 11.6, 14.3, 15.1, 15.5, 15.6, 17.6, 18.5, 20.4, 21.0, 24.6, 27.3, 28.1, 29.3, 29.4, 29.6, 30.6, 33.1, 33.2, 34.3, 35.0, 35.6, 36.2, 36.X, 40.6, 41.0, 42.1, 42.2, 42.3, 42.4, 44.0, 45.0, 45.2, 46.0, 46.2, 46.4, 47.2, 47.5, 48.3, 49.1, 53.6, 56.X, 57.2, 59.1, 62.4, 62.X, 63.3 and 64.4.

墉

7578: appears 2 times in: 13.4 and 40.6.

榮

7582: appears 1 time in: 12.X.

永

7589: appears 9 times in: 2.7, 6.1, 8.0, 22.3, 42.2, 45.5, 52.1, 54.X and 62.4.

于

7592: appears 71 times in: 2.6, 3.3, 5.1, 5.2, 5.3, 5.4, 5.5, 5.6, 10.3, 11.2, 11.3, 11.6, 12.5, 13.0, 13.1, 13.2, 13.3, 13.6, 14.3, 16.2, 17.5, 17.6, 19.0, 20.4, 22.5, 24.6, 27.2, 29.1, 29.3, 29.6, 30.X, 34.1, 34.4, 34.5, 35.2, 36.1, 36.2, 36.3, 36.4, 36.6, 38.2, 40.5, 40.6, 42.2, 43.0, 43.1, 43.3, 44.1, 46.4, 46.6, 47.1, 47.2, 47.3, 47.4, 47.5, 47.6, 51.2, 51.6, 53.1, 53.2, 53.3, 53.4, 53.5, 53.6, 56.4, 56.6, 58.5, 59.X, 61.6, 64.4 and 64.6.

豫

7603: appears 7 times in: 16.0, 16.1, 16.3, 16.4, 16.6, 16.X and 63.X.

畣

7606: appears 1 time in: 25.2.

與

7615: appears 4 times in: 6.X, 13.X, 25.X and 61.2.

譽
7617: appears 6 times in: 2.4, 18.5, 28.5, 39.1, 55.5 and 56.5.

輿
7618: appears 8 times in: 7.3, 7.5, 9.3, 23.6, 26.2, 26.3, 34.4 and 38.3.

遇
7625: appears 11 times in: 13.5, 21.3, 38.2, 38.4, 38.6, 43.3, 55.1, 55.4, 62.2, 62.4 and 62.6.

渝
7635: appears 3 times in: 6.4, 16.6 and 17.1.

於
7643: appears 4 times in: 5.X, 23.X, 43.X and 45.X.

虞
7648: appears 3 times in: 3.3, 45.X and 61.1.

語
7651: appears 1 time in: 27.X.

羽
7658: appears 1 time in: 53.6.

雨
7662: appears 7 times in: 9.0, 9.6, 38.6, 40.X, 43.3, 50.3 and 62.5.

禦
7665: appears 2 times in: 4.6 and 53.3.

玉
7666: appears 1 time in: 50.6.

裕
7667: appears 2 times in: 18.4 and 35.1.

魚
7668: appears 4 times in: 23.5, 44.2, 44.4 and 61.0.

欲
7671: appears 2 times in: 27.4 and 41.X.

獄
7685: appears 5 times in: 21.0, 22.X, 55.X, 56.X and 61.X.

育
7687: appears 4 times in: 4.X, 18.X, 25.X and 53.3.

曰
7694: appears 2 times in: 26.3 and 47.6.

月
7696: appears 4 times in: 9.6, 19.0, 54.5 and 61.4.

刖
7697: appears 1 time in: 47.5.

元
7707: appears 27 times in: 1.0, 2.0, 2.5, 3.0, 6.5, 8.0, 10.6, 11.5, 14.0, 17.0, 18.0, 19.0, 24.1, 25.0, 26.4, 30.2, 38.4, 41.0, 41.5, 42.1, 42.5, 45.5, 46.0, 48.6, 49.0, 50.0 and 59.4.

淵
7723: appears 1 time in: 1.4.

原
7725: appears 1 time in: 8.0.

園
7731: appears 1 time in: 22.5.

遠
7734: appears 2 times in: 24.1 and 33.X.

雲
7750: appears 4 times in: 3.X, 5.X, 9.0 and 62.5.

隕
7756: appears 1 time in: 44.5.

允
7759: appears 2 times in: 35.3 and 46.1.

孕
7765: appears 2 times in: 53.3 and 53.5.

慍
7766: appears 1 time in: 43.3.

蹢
8000: appears 1 time in: 44.1.

蔀
8001: appears 3 times in: 55.2, 55.4 and 55.6.

窗
8002: appears 2 times in: 29.1 and 29.3.

牿
8003: appears 1 time in: 26.4.

脢
8004: appears 1 time in: 31.5.

鞏
8005: appears 1 time in: 6.6.

汔
8006: appears 2 times in: 48.0 and 64.0.

頄
8007: appears 1 time in: 43.3.

顒
8008: appears 1 time in: 20.0.

繘
8009: appears 1 time in: 48.0.

遄
8010: appears 1 time in: 3.2.

嬬
8011: appears 1 time in: 54.3.

Bibliography

Balkin, Jack M. *The Laws of Change*. Shocken Books, 2002. ISBN 0-8052-4199-X.

Blofeld, John. *I Ching, The Book of Change*, George Allen & Unwin Ltd., 1965.

Bradford Hatcher, *The Book of Changes*. Bradford Hatcher, 2009. ISBN 978-0-9824191-3 and 978-0-9824191-2-0.

Chu, W.K. and Sherrill, W.A. *The Astrology of I Ching*. London: Arkana, 1976.

Cleary, Thomas. *The Taoist I Ching*. Boston: Shambhala, 1986.

I *Ching: The Tao of Organization*. Boston: Shambhala, 1988.

Huang, Alfred. *The Complete I Ching*. Rochester, VT: Inner Traditions, 1998.

Kunst, Richard Alan. *"The Original Yijing: A Text, Phonetic Transcription, Translation and Indexes, with Sample Glosses."* Ph.D. dissertation in Oriental Languages: University of California at Berkeley, 1985.

Legge, James, *The I Ching*. NY: Dover, 1963.

Li Guangdi, et al, ed's. (Yuzuan) 周易折中 *Zhouyi Zhezhong*. 1715; Reprint, Taibei: Chengwen, 1975. ISBN 957785313 or 669244007.

Lynn, Richard John. *The Classic of Changes*. NY: Columbia University Press, 1994.

Marshall, S.J. *The Mandate of Heaven: Hidden History in the I Ching*. NY: Columbia University Press, 2001.

Richard Smith. *Fathoming the Cosmos and Ordering the World: The Yijing (I Ching, or Classic of Changes) and Its Evolution in China* (Richard Lectures)

Ritsema, Rudolf and Stephen Karcher. *I Ching, The Classic Chinese Oracle of Change*. Rockport, MA: Element, 1994.

Rutt, Richard. *The Book of Changes (Zhouyi) A Bronze Age Document*. Surrey, GB: Curzon Press, 1996.

Shaughnessy, Edward Louis. *I Ching: The Classic of Changes*. NY: Ballantine Books, 1996. Mawangdui version translation.

Sung, Z.D. *The Text of the Yi King (And its Appendices) Chinese original with English translation*. NY: Paragon Book Reprint Corp., 1969.

Whincup, Greg. *Rediscovering the I Ching*. Garden City, NY: Doubleday, 1986.

Wilhelm, Richard. *The I Ching or Book of Changes*. Princeton University Press, 1967.

Dictionaries

John DeFrancis, *ABC Chinese-English Dictionary*, University of Hawai'i, 1996-2011. Text used for Wenlin Software for Learning Chinese, Version 4.02.

Karlgren, Bernhard. *Analytic Dictionary of Chinese and Sino-Japanese*. Chéng-Wen Publishing Company, Taipei, 1966. Originally published in 1923.

Karlgren, Bernhard. *Grammata Serica Recensa*. Museum of Far Eastern Antiquities, Stockholm, 1964.

Liang Shih-Chiu, *Far East Chinese-English Dictionary*. The Far East Book Co., 1992.

Luo Zhufeng et al. 1986-1993. *Hanyu da cidian* ("Comprehensive Chinese Dictionary"). CD-ROM. Commercial Press, 2007. ISBN 13: 9789620702778.

Mathews, R H. *Mathews' Chinese-English Dictionary*. Harvard University Press, 1993. ISBN 0-674-12350-6.

Schuessler, Axel, *ABC Etymological Dictionary of Old Chinese*. University of Hawai'I Press, 2007.

Wieger, Dr. L., *Chinese Characters*. Paragon Book Reprint Corp. and Dover Publications Inc., 1965.

PinYin Pronunciation

Pinyin	English	Explanation
b	spit	unaspirated p, as in spit
p	pay	strongly aspirated p, as in pit
m	may	as in English mummy
f	fair	as in English fun
d	stop	unaspirated t, as in stop
t	take	strongly aspirated t, as in top
n	nay	as in English nit
l	lay	as in English love
g	skill	unaspirated k, as in skill
k	kay	strongly aspirated k, as in kill
h	hay	like the English h if followed by "a". It is pronounced roughly like the Scots ch and Russian x (Cyrillic "kha").
j	hatch	No equivalent in English. Like q, but unaspirated. Not the s in Asia, despite the common English pronunciation of "Beijing".
Pinyin	English	Explanation
q	cheek	No equivalent in English. Like cheek, with the lips spread wide with ee. Curl the tip of the tongue downwards to stick it at the back of the teeth and strongly aspirate.

x	she	No equivalent in English. Like she, with the lips spread and the tip of your tongue curled downwards and stuck to the back of teeth when you say ee.
zh	junk	Rather like ch (a sound between choke, joke, true, and drew, tongue tip curled more upwards). Voiced in a toneless syllable.
ch	church	as in chin, but with the tongue curled upwards; very similar to nurture in American English, but strongly aspirated.
sh	shirt	as in shoe, but with the tongue curled upwards; very similar to marsh in American English
r	ray	Similar to the English z in azure and r in reduce, but with the tongue curled upwards, like a cross between English "r" and French "j".
z	reads	unaspirated c, similar to something between suds and cats; as in suds in a toneless syllable
c	hats	like the English ts in cats, but strongly aspirated, very similar to the Polish c.
s	say	as in sun
w	way	as in water.
y	yea	as in yes. Before a u, pronounce it with rounded lips.

Chart of the Trigrams and Hexagrams

Upper ▶ Lower ▼	Quian ☰	Zhen ☳	Kan ☵	Gen ☶	Kun ☷	Xun ☴	Li ☲	Dui ☱
Quian ☰	1	34	5	26	11	9	14	43
Zhen ☳	25	51	3	27	24	42	21	17
Kan ☵	6	40	29	4	7	59	64	47
Gen ☶	33	62	39	52	15	53	56	31
Kun ☷	12	16	8	23	2	20	35	45
Xun ☴	44	32	48	18	46	57	50	28
Li ☲	13	55	63	22	36	37	30	49
Dui ☱	10	54	60	41	19	61	38	58

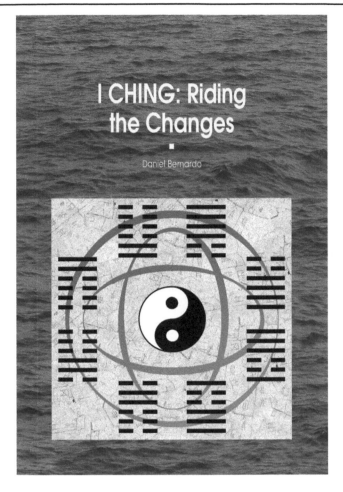

Riding the changes means to take the best course between the rough waves of life. Changes are the natural waves that traverse time. The I Ching can help us to understand better the relation between external reality and our will; such insight will allow us to chart the best possible course of action and will enhance the quality of our lives.

This I Ching translation is concise and oriented towards divinatory usage. To help readers understand better the true meaning of the text, notes with historical and cultural information have been added, as well as cross-references between hexagrams.

Line by line interpretations are both general and oriented toward different aspects of life like Career, Private life and Health, Feelings and Social life.

380 pages
Dimensions: 6 x 9 x 1 inches

Available at **Amazon.com** and **Amazon.co.uk**

An abridged version can be downloaded freely at http://yijingdao.org

Lightning Source UK Ltd.
Milton Keynes UK
UKHW02n0204090818
326968UK00010B/77/P